INTERNATIONAL STUDIES

The Defence of Malaysia and Singapore

INTERNATIONAL STUDIES

PUBLISHED FOR THE CENTRE FOR
INTERNATIONAL STUDIES, LONDON SCHOOL OF
ECONOMICS AND POLITICAL SCIENCE

Editorial Board

Dr I. Nish
Professor G. L. Goodwin
Professor J. B. Joll
Professor P. J. Wiles
Professor L. B. Schapiro

Mr J. N. B. Mayall
Professor D. C. Watt
Mr P. Windsor
Dr M. Leifer

The Centre for International Studies at the London School of Economics and Political Science was established in 1967 with the aid of a grant from the Ford Foundation. Its aim is to promote research and advanced training on a multi-disciplinary basis in the general field of international studies.

To this end the Centre sponsors research projects and seminars and endeavours to secure the publication of manuscripts arising out of them.

Whilst the Editorial Board accepts responsibility for recommending the inclusion of a volume in the series, the author is alone responsible for the views and opinions expressed.

ALSO IN THIS SERIES

The Origins of Polish Socialism – Lucjan Blit
The Slovak Dilemma – Eugen Steiner
China's Policy in Africa, 1958–1971 – Alaba Ogunsanwo
Hitler's Strategy 1940–41: The Balkan Clue – Martin van Creveld
The Totalitarian Party: Party and People in Nazi Germany and Soviet Russia – Aryeh L. Unger
Britain and East Asia, 1933–1937 – Ann Trotter
The Pattern of Sino-American Crisis: Political Military Interactions in the 1950s – J. H. Kalicki
Britain and the Origins of the New Europe, 1914–1918 – Kenneth J. Calder
The Marxist Conception of Ideology: A Critical Essay – Martin Seliger
The Middle East in China's Foreign Policy, 1949–1977 – Yitzhak Shichor
The Politics of the Soviet Cinema, 1917–1929 – Richard Taylor
The End of the Post-war Era: Documents on Great Power Relations, 1968–1975 – edited by James Mayall and Cornelia Navari
Anglo-Japanese Alienation 1919–1952: Papers of the Anglo-Japanese Conference on the History of the Second World War – edited by Ian Nish
Occupation Diplomacy: Britain, the United States and Japan 1945–1952 – Roger Buckley

THE DEFENCE OF MALAYSIA AND SINGAPORE

The transformation of a security system 1957–1971

CHIN KIN WAH

CAMBRIDGE UNIVERSITY PRESS
Cambridge
London   New York   New Rochelle
Melbourne   Sydney

Published by the Press Syndicate of the University of Cambridge
The Pitt Building, Trumpington Street, Cambridge CB2 1RP
32 East 57th Street, New York, NY 10022, USA
296 Beaconsfield Parade, Middle Park, Melbourne 3206, Australia

© Cambridge University Press 1983

First published 1983

Printed in Great Britain at
the University Press, Cambridge

Library of Congress catalogue card number: 82–4330

British Library Cataloguing in Publication Data

Chin, Kin Wah
The defence of Malaysia and Singapore.
—(International studies)
1. Anglo-Malaysian Defence Agreement
2. Malaya—History
I. Title II. Series
341.7′2′0265 DS596

ISBN 0 521 24325 4

CONTENTS

		page
	Preface	vii
	Acknowledgements	viii
	List of abbreviations	x
	Note on currency units	xii
1	Introduction	1
2	Pre-treaty defence relations	8
3	Decolonisation and the institution of the defence agreement	23
4	The extension of AMDA	37
5	The external testing of AMDA	58
6	Towards a closing of ranks	82
7	The fractured axis	102
8	Britain weighs anchor	125
9	From AMDA to the five-power defence system	144
10	Conclusions	179
	Postscript on five-power arrangements	192
	Notes	195
	Bibliography	212
	Index	215

PREFACE

This book examines the hitherto under-explored subject of Commonwealth defence relations with Malaysia and Singapore. It is a case study of intra-alliance politics spanning that period when the Anglo-Malaysian Defence Agreement (AMDA) constituted the formal context for the provision of external security. This unique military alliance embracing an anchor power (Britain), two associates (Australia and New Zealand), and two recipients of alliance security (Malaysia and Singapore) was built on a British guarantee to defend the Malaysia–Singapore region. The process by which that defence guarantee was transformed into a loose five-power arrangement which limited the liability of the external powers took nearly fourteen years to run its course. I have not attempted any 'grand theorising' in this book. It is hoped however that some understanding of the process of transformation of an alliance system from birth, through consolidation, extension and decline, to demise will be conveyed.

The purpose of this study is to follow the thread of policies of the five AMDA allies to explain the unfolding interaction of national interests and consequential diplomatic manoeuvrings. While resisting the temptation to digress from the central enquiry into the life cycle of a little-known alliance, I have tried to avoid an extended discussion of the changes in the wider regional environment, such as the vicissitudes of the Vietnam war or the redefinition of policies of the other major powers towards the region. Significant as these events were in the international relations of Southeast Asia, they did not exercise a dominant influence on the major turning points in the transformation of AMDA.

Although reference is made to the Anglo-Malaysian Defence Agreement throughout this book, the reader should note that for the period prior to the formation of Malaysia, the acronym AMDA refers to the Anglo-Malayan Defence Agreement.

ACKNOWLEDGEMENTS

This book is a revised version of a doctoral dissertation submitted to the University of London in 1977. It owes much to the encouragement, advice and helpful criticisms of friends, well-wishers and colleagues. Limitation of space prevents me from thanking them all individually here. It is, however, a duty as much as it is a pleasure to acknowledge the contributions of those institutions and individuals without whom this work would have been much impoverished.

In London, where a major part of the initial research was conducted, I drew heavily on the facilities of the Royal Institute of International Affairs (Chatham House), the International Institute for Strategic Studies, the Institute of Commonwealth Studies and the British Library of Political and Economic Science. I am grateful to their librarians and staffs for their ready assistance and co-operation.

To the University of London, I am deeply indebted for the award of a postgraduate travelling studentship which enabled me to carry out research in Australia, New Zealand and the Malaysia–Singapore region. My visit to New Zealand was further assisted by a supplementary grant from the London Committee of the London–Cornell Project.

While in Australia, I enjoyed the hospitality and amenities of the Australian National University, particularly the Department of International Relations. Dr T. B. Millar most kindly read and commented upon an early chapter of the work and provided me with useful contacts in Canberra. I am also grateful to Dr R. J. O'Neill, Director of the Strategic and Defence Studies Centre, Australian National University, who made available to me research materials at the Centre.

During my brief visit to Wellington, I met with much kindness and received helpful advice and assistance from the late Dr Alan Robinson of the Victoria University of Wellington.

Further research in the Malaysia–Singapore area was facilitated by the award of a Research Fellowship from the Institute of Southeast Asian Studies, Singapore. I am grateful to Professor Kernial S. Sandhu, Director of the Institute, for his concern and hospitality and to the Librarian, Mrs Patricia Lim, for excellent library services.

Thanks are due to the Department of Political Science, National University of Singapore, for financial support in the preparation of the typescript.

I also wish to thank all my interviewees who so kindly took time off from busy schedules to meet me and answer my numerous queries, test my propositions and offer their valuable comments. To preserve the confidentiality of my discussions with them I have chosen not to name my interview sources.

Above all, I am indebted to my supervisors, Dr Michael Leifer and Mr Philip Windsor. They gave me, the inspiration to pursue the important, the courage to ignore the unimportant and the enlightenment to discern the difference.

Finally, I wish to express my thanks and deep gratitude to my parents for their personal sacrifices, sustained moral support and forbearance. To them this book is dedicated.

ABBREVIATIONS

AFR	*Australian Financial Review*
AIIA	Australian Institute of International Affairs
AIPS	Australian Institute of Political Science
AJPH	*Australian Journal of Politics and History*
ALP	Australian Labor Party
AMDA	Anglo-Malaysian Defence Agreement
ANZAM	Australian, New Zealand and Malayan Area
ANZUK	Australian, New Zealand and United Kingdom (Force)
ANZUS	Australian, New Zealand and United States Treaty
ASA	Association of Southeast Asia
ASEAN	Association of Southeast Asian Nations
CCO	Clandestine Communist Organisation
CDC	Combined Defence Council
CIGS	Chief of Imperial General Staff
CN	*Current notes on International Affairs*
CPD (H/R)	*Commonwealth Parliamentary Debates (House of Representatives)*
CRO	Commonwealth Relations Office
CSM	*Christian Science Monitor*
CSR	Commonwealth Strategic Reserve
CT	*Canberra Times*
DT	*Daily Telegraph*
EAR	*External Affairs Review (New Zealand)*
ECAFE	Economic Commission for Asia and the Far East
EOC	Emergency Operations Council
FARELF	Far East Land Forces (British)
FEAF	Far East Air Forces (British)
FEER	*Far Eastern Economic Review*
FT	*Financial Times*
GOC	General Officer Commanding
HCD	*House of Commons Debates*
HLD	*House of Lords Debates*
IADS	Integrated Air Defence System
ISC	Internal Security Council
JDC	Joint Defence Council
JSEAH	*Journal of Southeast Asian History*
JSEAS	*Journal of Southeast Asian Studies*

Abbreviations xi

JWS	Jungle Warfare School
MAPHILINDO	Malaya–Philippines–Indonesia (Confederation)
MCA	Malayan Chinese Association
MCP	Malayan Communist Party
MLCD	*Malayan Legislative Council Debates*
NDC	National Defence Council (Malaysia)
NYHT	*New York Herald Tribune*
NYT	*New York Times*
NZAJHR	*New Zealand Annual Journal of the House of Representatives*
NZGNB	*New Zealand Government News Bulletin*
NZH	*New Zealand Herald*
NZIIA	New Zealand Institute of International Affairs
NZPD	*New Zealand Parliamentary Debates*
OFNS	*Observer Foreign News Service*
PAP	People's Action Party
PKI	Partai Komunis Indonesia (Indonesian Communist Party)
PLP	Parliamentary Labour Party
PMIP	Pan-Malayan Islamic Party
RAAF	Royal Australian Air Force
RAF	Royal Air Force
RAN	Royal Australian Navy
RIIA	Royal Institute of International Affairs
RMAF	Royal Malaysian Air Force
RMN	Royal Malaysian Navy
RN	Royal Navy
RNFE	Royal Navy, Far East Station
RNZAF	Royal New Zealand Air Force
RUSIJ	*Royal United Service Institution, Journal*
SAF	Singapore Armed Forces
SAS	Special Air Service
SEATO	Southeast Asia Treaty Organisation
SIR	Singapore Infantry Regiment
SLAD	*Singapore Legislative Assembly Debates*
SMH	*Sydney Morning Herald*
SPD	*Singapore Parliamentary Debates*
ST	*Straits Times*
Sun.T	*Sunday Times*
Sun.T (M)	*Sunday Times (Malaysian Edition)*
Sun.T (S)	*Sunday Times (Singapore Edition)*
TNKU	Tentera National Kalimantan Utara (North Borneo National Army)
UMNO	United Malays National Organisation
UN	United Nations

NOTE ON CURRENCY UNITS

Defence expenditures are quoted in the national currency of each country. Unless otherwise stated, '£' refers to pound sterling. In February 1966 Australia introduced a new currency unit, the Australian dollar, valued at half the former Australian pound. In July 1967 New Zealand introduced the New Zealand dollar, valued at approximately half the former New Zealand pound.

	Exchange rates US dollars per currency unit (approximate value)			
	1965	1966	1967	June 1972
UK	2.8	2.8	2.4 (Nov.)	exchange rate floated
Australia	2.2	1.1 (Feb.)	1.1	1.2
New Zealand	2.8	2.8	1.1 (June)	1.4
Malaysian dollar (per US$)	3.1	3.1	3.1	2.8

Following the floating of the pound sterling, Malaysia repegged from sterling to the US dollar.

1. INTRODUCTION

During the fourteen years that followed Malayan independence in 1957 the formal context for the defence of Malaya (subsequently Malaysia) and Singapore was set by the Anglo-Malaysian Defence Agreement or AMDA. This 'unequal burden treaty', embodying a 'blank cheque' from Britain, had had no parallel elsewhere in Southeast Asia. The unique structure of this alliance was characterised by a hierarchy of powers embracing a hierarchy of roles. The AMDA system contained one anchor power (Britain), two principal consumers of alliance security (Malaysia and Singapore), and two associate powers (Australia and New Zealand) which were both providers and consumers of alliance security.

AMDA emerged against the background of an increasingly bipolar world in which alliances tended to be the most overt expression of either Western or Soviet spheres of interest. However, AMDA's essential function was to facilitate an orderly process of colonial disengagement from Malaya rather than to add to a growing 'cold war front' in Southeast Asia. In that sense AMDA contained an inherent paradox, i.e. that an effective functioning of the alliance in the face of external threat depended on a military reinvolvement by the ex-colonial anchor power. AMDA facilitated colonial disengagement, but for AMDA to work re-engagement of a different kind might be necessary.

This assumption of post-colonial responsibility was never seriously questioned in Britain at the time of AMDA's formation. And when AMDA's protective mantle was extended, during the next phase of colonial disengagement from Singapore, Sabah and Sarawak, the serious external challenge – in the form of Indonesian Confrontation – triggered by the formation of Malaysia, reinforced Britain's interest in a policing role East of Suez. But increasing domestic economic strains in the mid-sixties forced a fundamental reconsideration of the ends of policy. The ending of Confrontation removed any constraints from a re-evaluation of Britain's anchor role within AMDA. In this respect the anchor power itself provided the greatest impetus for a redefinition of the framework for the defence of Malaysia and Singapore.

Until the mid-sixties, and despite a persisting economic weakness since the end of the Second World War, British policy was guided by a general attitude of post-colonial obligation with which were mixed wider and vaguer strategic concerns stemming from Britain's view of itself as a 'great power'. These 'generalised conceptions', observed Darby, 'sit uneasily alongside changing perspectives of the true nature of the relationship between the metropoles and the periphery'.[1] To the extent that AMDA institutionalised Malayan dependence on external protection, delayed the process of psychological decolonisation and facilitated Sukarno's distortion of Malaysia's international identity, AMDA clouded the true nature of the relationship between the 'providers' and the 'consumers' of security. Yet AMDA sought to provide a stable external environment for a Malaya which had now acquired competence in foreign policy formation. This, coupled with an undercurrent of national self-assertion, was to lead to the emergence of a Malayan foreign policy which did not completely coincide with the defence interests of the external allies.

Specifically, the defence guarantee in AMDA made it unnecessary for Malaysia to consider other forms of alliance relationship. This had greater strategic repercussions on the AMDA associates than on Britain which, despite an awareness of a wider regional threat, was more inclined to view its Southeast Asian commitments in terms of efforts, first, to counter the Malayan communist insurgency and, second, to provide for the external defence of Malaya, Singapore and other British territories in the area. Like Britain, Australia and New Zealand had acquired an interest in the defence of the Malayan area long before AMDA's formation. In Australia, a minority of military officials had shown interest in a proposed naval base in Singapore as early as 1923. Later, the Japanese invasion of 1941–2 caused widespread Australian concern for the defence of Malaya and Singapore. In December 1940 the New Zealand Chiefs of Staff recommended the dispatch of an infantry battalion to Malaya on the assumption that it was vital to New Zealand's defence. The strategic assumption behind this recommendation was not translated into policy until fifteen years later.[2]

After the Second World War, defence planning in the Malayan area among Britain, Australia and New Zealand was placed on a regular basis by the informal ANZAM understanding. It was within this loose consultative framework that Australian–New Zealand defence contributions in a material, though not substantive, form were made to British Malaya in 1950.

The image of a regional threat, implanted by the Japanese advance, influenced particularly Australia's post-war perception of its security and was reinforced by communist activities in Southeast Asia. This perception assumed form in the 'domino theory' which was to provide the guidelines for Australia's external defence strategy. Its contribution to Malayan defence had a correspondingly strong regional bias. New Zealand, on the other hand, more detached both physically and psychologically from Southeast Asia, and hence with a less pronounced regional orientation, was inclined to be guided by Britain-centred attitudes. Its initial contribution to Malayan defence suggested that Malaya was almost incidental to a decision which was made in the spirit of helping to 'draw the line' in a British country.

The separate but nevertheless overlapping interests of the three external powers acquired more substantive form in 1955 with the establishment of the Commonwealth Strategic Reserve (CSR) in Malaya. However, the strategic purpose of the reserve (seen as a readily available force for brush-fire wars in Southeast Asia) was not wholly fulfilled when independent Malaya chose not to join the Southeast Asia Treaty Organisation (SEATO). Hopes of using Australia's contribution to the CSR to extract more substantive American involvement in SEATO defence (such as the creation of a SEATO land force) were also unfulfilled. The consequence, as with the earlier Australian failure to involve Britain and the US in a NATO-type pact in the Pacific and the later 'exclusion' of Britain from the American-centred ANZUS treaty (in which Australia and New Zealand were also allies), was the superimposition of a system of overlapping alliances upon 'a shatter-belt' of Southeast Asian instability.[3] The US was wary of underwriting militarily what it saw as British colonialism in Malaya, while Britain tended in real terms to regard its Southeast Asian defence commitments as essentially confined to the defence of Malaya. Hence Southeast Asia had two distinct poles of attraction – one British and the other American. The absence of a cohesive region for alliance purposes was reflected by the degree of overlap between SEATO, AMDA and ANZUS.

Against this background of overlapping alliances, Australia had to sustain the respective pulls – not always in the same direction – of its two 'great and powerful friends'. This had two important consequences. First, Australia's (and to a lesser degree, New Zealand's) contribution to Malayan defence was marked by a constant looking-over-the-shoulder for an American underwriting in case, as in the Second World War, British power alone proved inadequate to guarantee Malayan security. This imparted to the Australian (and New Zealand) posture the characteristic of being both a supplier and a consumer of alliance security. Second, the not wholly congruent policies of the 'great and powerful friends' resulted in deliberate ambiguity over the role, or rather roles, of the CSR. The ambiguity was made doubly necessary by Malayan antipathy towards the SEATO connection.

Two years after Malaya's independence, Australia and New Zealand formally associated themselves by an Exchange of Letters with those articles in AMDA which provided for the continued stationing of Commonwealth forces in the country. Underlying their associate status was the assumption that their 'commitments' depended on British willingness to uphold the defence system in the first place – that their secondary roles were fundamentally different from that of the guarantor power. However, the fact that their 'commitments' could only be perceived with reference to AMDA made it easy for the client state to confuse (deliberately or inadvertently) these different roles when the alliance came under external challenge. In this sense AMDA distorted the reality of Malaysia's relations with the associate powers.

AMDA's assumption of the indivisibility of Malaya–Singapore defence, extended by the creation of Malaysia in 1963 and delicately preserved by the agreement which formalised Singapore's ejection from the Federation two years later, also distorted the reality of relations between the two local states. That reality was characterised not only by co-operation but also by intense political competition leading up to, and following, Singapore's separation from Malaysia. Their changing relations in turn sharpened the perspectives of the external powers *vis-à-vis* their local defence clients.

That AMDA was founded upon overlapping rather than convergent interests can be perceived in its political genesis as well as in the circumstances of its formal establishment. In a three-dimensional perspective, AMDA may be seen as a cone (representing the hierarchy of powers) resting on a base composed of overlapping circles of interests, the separate focuses of which shifted over time until the cone itself, increasingly destabilised by its moving foundations, eventually collapsed and had to be replaced by new and much looser arrangements.

The manner in which the alliance was transformed, making AMDA progressively less than the sum of its parts, is the central concern of this book. The transformation of intra-alliance relationships should not be confused, however, with the transformation of AMDA since, strictly speaking, AMDA was not transformed. Rather it was terminated by the Exchange of Letters which brought the succeeding Five-Power Defence Arrangements into being in November 1971. But in spite of AMDA's demise, the formal allies have remained the same and, although the means have changed, the 'technical' objective of the external defence of the Malaysia–Singapore area has been sustained. Technically, the two widely accepted distinguishing features of an alliance, namely 'the formality of the relationship . . . and the military focus of the mutual effort',[4] have survived the termination òf AMDA. 'Transformation' is thus used to convey elements of both continuity and change within the alliance – the term 'alliance' (as contrasted with the treaty) being used in a political (i.e. dynamic) rather than in an institutional (i.e. static) sense.

The foregoing distinction leads us to consider two interacting streams of developments – that of the formal treaty, including *de facto* amendments made to it, and that of the political relationships among the allies within the treaty framework. As Osgood points out, the treaty 'is simply an attempt to make more precise and binding a particular obligation or relationship between states, which is part of a continually changing network of interests and sentiments'.[5] Hence successful functioning of the treaty is reflected in an ability to accommodate the vicissitudes of intra-alliance relations resulting from the redefinition of interests in the light of changing domestic and international circumstances. The demise of AMDA represented the culmination of increasing difficulty in accommodating divergent interests. Political relations overtook the treaty framework (which, as long as AMDA existed, sustained certain expectations and distorted the changing realities of intra-alliance relations) until it could be sustained no longer in its existing form.

6   *The defence of Malaysia and Singapore*

The demise of AMDA marked the end of one cycle of alliance relations. That cycle was marked by the political genesis and birth of the formal treaty; the extension and consolidation of AMDA; the period of stress arising from external and internal challenges; the *de facto* amendment of AMDA following the fracture of its local axis; its period of decline, diminishing political will and growing problems of cohesion; and, finally, its dissolution and demise.

AMDA's successor system continues to endure despite changes in the deployment of external forces in the Malaysia–Singapore area; its loose consultative framework has enabled it to accommodate, without much internal strain, the different interests of its defence members. The present Five-Power Defence Arrangements are based on a qualitative change in intra-alliance relations. There has been a reversal of the hierarchy of power and the hierarchy of roles with Malaysia and Singapore now assuming primary responsibility for their external defence. While the vestigial external military presence certainly facilitates joint military exercises, the 'commitments' of the external powers to the area are essentially symbolic and consultative in nature. Among the external powers there has been a levelling up of the Australian–New Zealand roles corresponding to the levelling down of British responsibilities in the area and the decline of the 'special relationship' with the two local powers.

For Malaysia and Singapore, it has meant growing national assertiveness as they came increasingly into their own as distinct and separate local centres within the loose defence arrangements. In this context of separate yet complementary interests, the existing loose arrangements allow Malaysia to reserve its military options while making public a long-term commitment to a Zone of Peace, Freedom and Neutrality in the region. They also fit into Singapore's conception of regional security as deriving from a balance of countervailing forces and, for the external powers, institutionalise an area of continuing Commonwealth interest at a time of renewed concern (especially in Australia) over regional insecurity following the Vietnamese invasion of Kampuchea.

The record of past intra-alliance relations provides an appreciation of the existing constraints upon, and limited efficacy of, five-power defence (which remains less than multilateral in a number of respects) notwithstanding the initiatives of the Australian Prime Minister, Malcolm Fraser, during 1980 to revitalise five-power military exercises. The history of relations within the alliance, as well as between the alliance and its immediate environment, also helps to illuminate existing difficulties in coming to terms over certain aspects of military collaboration between the two local powers and also between Malaysia and the Philippines, despite the political success of the Association of Southeast Asian Nations (ASEAN) of which they are members. Singapore has not been given access to military training facilities in Malaysia, while a border agreement and anti-smuggling pact are still lacking between Malaysia and the Philippines. One task of this book is to provide some understanding of the legacy bequeathed by AMDA as a framework for defence collaboration in the Malaysia–Singapore area.

2. PRE-TREATY DEFENCE RELATIONS

Collaboration among the partners involved in the defence of the Malaya–Singapore area did not begin with AMDA. Nor did it end with the treaty's demise. Among the external powers, pre-AMDA defence relations were regularised under a loose consultative arrangement known as ANZAM, which was later subsumed under AMDA, which in turn was replaced by the five-power defence arrangements. Although the fortunes of AMDA were influenced more by changes from within the alliance than from its international environment, the pre-treaty phase of intra-alliance relations (when Malaya itself was still largely a *de jure* 'object' of international relations) did bear the imprint of systemic influences. Australia's commitment of ground forces to Malaya was founded on wider considerations than the immediate problem of Malayan security. Events in Indochina in 1954 had an important bearing on the decision, taken within the ANZAM framework of consultation (established since 1948), to form the CSR which had to be accommodated within a formal Anglo-Malayan treaty when Malaya attained independence. The legacy of the pre-treaty relationships was reflected in the structure of AMDA.

The convergence of British, Australian, New Zealand and Malayan interests which resulted in the making of AMDA with its singular structure represented a culmination rather than a beginning. Indeed post-war Commonwealth co-operation in Malayan defence antedated AMDA by several years. The vague outline of such co-operation emerged in the late forties. According to Mr (later Sir) Robert Menzies, the Prime Minister of Australia, the decision to authorise strategic planning with Britain and New Zealand for the defence of the south-west Pacific area, including Malaya, was taken in May 1948.[1] This followed an initial British proposal, at the 1946 Commonwealth Prime Ministers' Conference in London, that liaison officers from Britain and the Dominions be established in one another's capitals to study regional security problems. In April 1946

Australia had announced preliminary arrangements for consultations with the British and New Zealand High Commissioners and among their service representatives.[2]

The May 1948 decision marked the 'formal beginning' of ANZAM.[3] The acronym 'ANZAM' refers to Australia, New Zealand and the Malayan area. An RIIA report included within the 'Malayan area' 'the British territories in Malaya and Borneo together with the adjacent sea areas'. It also indicated that service-level planning was at first limited to the defence of sea and air communications. Only later (possibly around 1954–5) was ANZAM extended to cover 'planning responsibility for the defence of Malaya'.[4] Initially, no firm commitments were given by the governments concerned. That ANZAM was not a written agreement was confirmed by General Sir Richard Hull (CIGS) during a visit to Australia in 1963.[5] (The obscurity of the arrangement was due to the fact that 'ANZAM' was once almost a classified term. Millar reckons that ANZAM came into popular usage around 1953.) The co-ordinating arm of ANZAM was the ANZAM Defence Committee and the Chiefs of Staff Committee of Britain, Australia and New Zealand. Meetings were rotated around London, Singapore and Canberra (initially Melbourne), although the Canberra group came to be known as the ANZAM Defence Committee.[6]

The inception of ANZAM overlapped with increasing communist terrorist activities in Malaya – the Malayan Communist Party having moved progressively towards a policy of armed struggle since March 1948. On 18 June the Emergency Regulations brought into effect two days before in Perak and Johore were extended to the whole of Malaya. In Australia considerable speculation was aroused that arms, equipment, perhaps even troops, might be dispatched to Malaya. But official Government policy was restrained. The Australian Prime Minister, Ben Chifley, saw the Malayan turmoil as an expression of nationalism and economic discontent.[7]

The Malayan problem did, however, confront the loose ANZAM arrangement with a concrete situation, making it difficult for Chifley's Government to prevaricate. Finally it decided in July 1948 to send arms to Malaya 'if requested by the British'. There was no mention of troops.[8] In meeting the subsequent British request, the Government even stopped a threatened boycott by the Australian Seaman's Union of the loading of arms for Malaya. But as Arthur Calwell (then Minister of Immigration) urged: 'The Government

... should do no more. It is not the policy of this Government to fish in the troubled waters of Malaya.'[9]

If, as Millar suggests, the Australian Labour Government did not see ANZAM as an instrument of Australian security in the years immediately following its initiation (although close liaison had been established),[10] neither did it consider Malayan developments (towards which a greater ANZAM effort could have been directed) as being directly linked to it. But ANZAM did provide a co-ordinating framework for the New Zealand decision in 1949 to dispatch transport aircraft to Malaya. This followed a meeting of ANZAM liaison staff and service chiefs at Melbourne in August 1949. Australia however was reluctant to expand existing commitments.

The original New Zealand 'commitment' was limited and informal, and Malaya itself was almost incidental to the arrangement. The deployment of No. 41 Transport Squadron RNZAF to Singapore was seen primarily as New Zealand's fulfilment of its promise to Britain to provide a Dakota flight to assist in relieving the RAF in Hong Kong, its supply-dropping role in Malaya being secondary.[11] Since the squadron was placed at the disposal of the Air-Officer Commanding, Malaya, it was progressively called upon to aid the RAF in supply-dropping in the Malayan jungle as the situation deteriorated.

By the end of 1949 a combination of internal and external changes led Australia to upgrade its contribution to Malayan defence. In December the Liberal–Country Coalition (hereafter referred to as the Liberal Party) was voted into office under Robert Menzies. Menzies' pro-British biases were doubtless reinforced by the advent of the cold war. Events in Europe – the launching of the Cominform in September 1947, Stalin's blockade of Berlin, the signing of the North Atlantic Treaty – overlapped with the outbreak of communist insurrections in Malaya, the Philippines, Burma, Indonesia and India (the Telengana area) and followed the militant Calcutta (Communist) Youth Conference in February 1948 and the second Congress of the Communist Party of India which took place immediately after. Malcolm MacDonald, the British Commissioner-General for Southeast Asia, saw these developments as interrelated and Moscow-centred.[12] In Australia, the new Minister for External Affairs, Mr (later Sir) Percy Spender, similarly voiced his Government's concern.[13] China was then beginning to replace Japan as a perceived threat to Australian security.

The Commonwealth Foreign Ministers' Conference which met in Colombo in January 1950 (the first held outside Britain) reflected the sharpening focus on Asia. By then New Zealand too had changed its government, Mr (later Sir) Sidney Holland's National Party having defeated Labour in the general elections. On his departure for Colombo, the New Zealand External Affairs Minister, Mr (later Sir) Frederick Doidge, called for active co-operation between Australia and New Zealand in defining their attitudes towards Pacific and Far Eastern problems, with greater emphasis on the Commonwealth.[14] His Australian counterpart saw emerging communism in the Far East as a threat to Australia and hoped that the conference would produce a positive contribution by Commonwealth countries.

Spender's view was that political stability in Southeast Asia could only be achieved by both economic and military measures, but his idea of a Pacific Pact to link Britain and the United States in Asian defence was cold-shouldered by the British Foreign Secretary, Ernest Bevin, and the Indian Prime Minister, Jawaharlal Nehru.[15] Britain saw its primary Far Eastern obligation as the completion of operations to restore order in Malaya. Australia and New Zealand accepted the long-term economic approach (the Colombo Plan) to counter communist expansion. The short-term security approach of 'holding the ring' would have to be developed within ANZAM. Yet a British lead (expected by Australia and New Zealand) towards this end was lacking at Colombo, although the final communiqué mentioned the particular attention given 'to the situation in Indochina, Burma and Malaya'.

That Britain was hard pressed in Malaya was evinced by the fact that by March 1950 there were nearly 100,000 troops and police (both British and local) who were having only limited success in checking the 3,000 or so guerrillas. The Colonial Secretary, James Griffiths, admitted as much in Parliament when he neither denied nor refuted suggestions of inadequate military strength and equipment in Malaya.[16] In Australia, continuous press speculations on the dispatch of troops to Malaya produced a denial from the Army Minister, Josiah Francis. However, on 17 April, Menzies publicly hinted that Australia was contemplating some form of new military aid (apart from economic help) but that it depended on what proposals Britain had to make.[17] A similar willingness to offer further assistance was signalled by Sidney Holland the following day.

Menzies' statement was 'noted with the greatest interest' by the British Secretary for Commonwealth Relations, Mr Patrick (later Lord) Gordon-Walker, in the Commons. But when asked whether this meant that Britain had not previously requested Australian aid, he replied that 'requests of that sort were not made between one country and another in the Commonwealth ... [and that there were] always elaborate consultations on those matters'.[18] Menzies himself confirmed that no requests had been made.[19]

In Britain *The Daily Telegraph* demanded an explanation 'why a Dominion has been left in doubt about [British] readiness ... to give a hand in matters of such vital common interest'.[20] It wondered why such doubt should persist if indeed there had been communications. The truth of the matter was that the definite arrangements for 'elaborate consultations' were built upon indefinite commitments. In practice, therefore, the 'ANZAM understanding' had to be amended 'from time to time as the situation changes'.[21] After all, the principle that the Dominions should shoulder a greater share of Empire defence had been established by Britain itself at the 1948 Commonwealth Prime Ministers' meeting. The 'signalling' was a public confirmation that a redefinition of the commitments was in progress.

Discussions between the two Governments began formally when Malcolm MacDonald (who was also Chairman of the Far East Defence Co-ordinating Committee) arrived two days ahead of the Commonwealth Conference on Aid to Southeast Asia (opening in Sydney on 15 May 1950) which he was attending. His meeting with Menzies was attended by the Air Officer Commanding, Malaya, Air Vice-Marshal Mellersh. On 31 May Menzies announced that, in response to a British request, Australia had agreed to provide transport aircraft and crews to assist in operations in Malaya and in servicing certain RAF aircraft in Australia.[22] Menzies also said that no request for other forms of military assistance had been made, but, according to Mellersh later, the British had asked for a heavy bomber squadron to be sent too.[23] Australia decided to send the Lincoln bombers only after the Korean war erupted in June. Menzies himself acknowledged on 27 June that the decision to send the bombers to Malaya was linked to events in Korea.

The Australian announcement of 31 May was more significant in its effect than in its substance. Having elicited a British request for assistance, Australia appeared to be wary lest it give too much.

While it is easy to assume that Australian caution reflected the careful moves of a Government newly returned to office and facing Labour Party opposition to Malayan aid, Menzies' limited offer may also be seen as a calculated 'investment' for firmer British assurance in Commonwealth defence. An offer of Australian and New Zealand land forces was not forthcoming for another five years. Korea, where their forces were committed as part of a Commonwealth brigade, was then much higher in their priorities. On a practical level, limited manpower and economic resources defined for the antipodean partners a symbolic role of 'pulling our weight in the British boat', as the New Zealand Prime Minister put it in 1955.[24]

Concurrently, the reality of their dependence on the United States for protection in the western Pacific emerged and materialised in the ANZUS treaty which came into operation on 29 April 1952. The non-membership of Britain in ANZUS, while regretted by Australia and New Zealand, was preferred to no American alliance at all, although they were anxious lest their dependence on the United States affect their Commonwealth links with Britain. For Australia in particular, attempts to demonstrate an increasing association with British defence in Malaya had to be matched by a constant eyeing for a substantive American surety. ANZUS itself, which originally began as a US quid pro quo for Australian and New Zealand acceptance of the Japanese peace treaty, was 'increasingly dilated' by them into 'the guarantee against communism'.[25] Yet, ironically, one of the reasons for British 'exclusion' from ANZUS was precisely the US fear of entanglement with Britain's colonial responsibilities, which included Malaya and Singapore.

The month following the signing of ANZUS in September 1951 saw the nadir of the Malayan Emergency with the assassination of the British High Commissioner, Sir Henry Gurney. Britain was forced to draw upon reinforcements from Fiji and East Africa in January 1952. But Australia and New Zealand cautiously maintained only token roles in Malayan defence. The Fijian battalion, dispatched in January, was accompanied by about twenty New Zealand officers and NCOs, while Australia merely committed some Australian officers to training in jungle warfare in Malaya. Sir Gerald Templer, the new High Commissioner and Director of Operations in Malaya, had asked for Australian ex-officers with jungle warfare experience to be enlisted as officers in the Malayan Home Guard.[26] Australia's token role was extended in July with the appointment of an Australian to the post of Air-Officer Commanding, Malaya.

It is worthy of note at this juncture that elements critical of the presence of foreign troops in Malaya were evident within the United Malays National Organisation (UMNO). In August it was reported that the UMNO General Assembly meeting the following month would be asked to pass a resolution calling upon the Government to cease bringing foreign troops into the country.[27] This issue was to resurface at a later stage.

Although Boyce records that the impending arrival of Australian troops was first rumoured in the Malayan press in August 1954,[28] Millar suggests that an agreement in principle within ANZAM to the deployment of a combined land force in Malaya could have been made in October 1953 following the meeting in Melbourne of Field Marshal Sir John Harding (CIGS) with Menzies and other ministers, the High Commissioners of Britain and New Zealand and the Chiefs of Staff of Australia and New Zealand.[29] Broadly, the second session of the Commonwealth Prime Ministers' Conference held in June 1953 under Mr (later Sir) Winston Churchill's chairmanship (the Conservatives having been voted in at the end of 1951) was devoted to the Far East and Southeast Asia. Malaya was specifically discussed five days later when the ANZAM partners and the UK Chiefs of Staff convened at 10 Downing Street. It was this meeting which decided on the Harding visit.[30] The Harding mission of October resulted in an ANZAM feasibility survey which recommended the creation of a strategic reserve.[31] Harding's visit was followed later in the month by a meeting in Kuala Lumpur between Templer and Richard Casey, the Australian External Affairs Minister. During a broadcast from Kuala Lumpur, Mr Richard (later Lord) Casey, reflecting Australia's strategic interest, spoke of 'the geographical facts [which] had placed Malaya and Australia together'.

The final decision to commit Australian (and New Zealand) ground forces to Malaya was not taken until after the ANZAM partners met during the 1955 Commonwealth Conference. Menzies himself was initially reluctant to commit ground forces to Malaya and showed readiness for such an involvement only after the Harding misssion had demonstrated Britain's acceptance of involvement in the strategic reserve.[32] Australia's reluctance to undertake specific troop commitments was confirmed by the fact that between 1952 and 1954 it had increasingly underspent its defence allocations

– the consequence of full employment, shortages of basic materials and a National Service Act which precluded overseas service for conscripts.[33]

In August 1954 McBride announced an increase in the defence budget. This came shortly after Menzies had repudiated 'the tradition of the Australian Government that commitments are not accepted in advance'.[34] The context of his statement was not specifically Malaya but rather the perceived deterioration in the general Southeast Asian situation which the communist victory over the French in Indochina had indicated. Indochinese events had revitalised the idea of collective defence in Southeast Asia, as was evident in Dulles' call for united action on 29 March 1954. By the time Menzies made his declaration in Parliament, the ceasefire in Indochina had been signed and the Southeast Asia Treaty Organisation (SEATO), as a limited response to Indochinese developments, was in the process of formulation. Thus, the declaration of Australian willingness to accept military commitments was made within the context of a 'great defensive organisation of the kind envisaged' – namely SEATO. Australian policy sought to put 'flesh and blood on the military skeleton'[35] of SEATO, to provide an effective defence in depth against perceived southward communist expansion.

On account of Australia's 'domino complex',[36] Malaya acquired a derivative strategic significance which Menzies again articulated around this time. He told a Liberal–Country Party Conference that Malaya must be regarded as Australia's 'boundary in the north'.[37] Preparations too were begun in anticipation of possible action in Southeast Asia. Already in September the Director of Australia's Army Military Training had visited Malaya to study jungle training as a prelude to the reopening of the jungle warfare school in Canungra, Queensland. But privately, Casey was still arguing in early January 1955 against '*any* [his emphasis] irrevocable commitment of Australian forces to Malaya'. Rather, Australia should have plans available (indicating readiness for such commitment) with which to press for firmer American plans for the defence of the area. Casey was unhappy with the absence of Anglo-American discussions on the defence of the area – or even of Malaya.[38] Australia was attempting to involve the US in specific force commitments not only in Thailand and Indochina but also in Malaya.

The flurry of the ANZAM conversations between November 1954

and February 1955 may thus be seen as well-timed Australian attempts to demonstrate good faith to the United States[39] and thus 'encourage Washington to consent to a standing SEATO force during the ... meetings at Bangkok' (scheduled for 23–25 February).[40] On the other hand, it may be argued that the British must also have seen this conjunction of events as an opportune moment to press Australia and New Zealand for a more definite commitment of ground forces – to which an agreement had, in principle, already been made. If it was London which initiated the ANZAM discussions in late 1954, the move was equally well timed in its coincidence with Australia's own push to secure parliamentary ratification of the Manila Pact.

In November 1954 Malcolm MacDonald led one of the most important military missions ever to Australia, all the three British Far East Commanders-in-Chief representing the three services being present. MacDonald's mission conferred with Menzies, Casey, McBride and other military leaders during the same week as the Australian and New Zealand Chiefs of Staff were meeting their British counterparts in Singapore.

The committal of Australian and New Zealand forces to Malaya moved closer to realisation when the ANZAM partners met to consider regional defence problems during the Commonwealth Prime Ministers' Conference in early February 1955. Menzies had indicated to the London conference that specific commitments depended on decisions at home and on American assurances of support in certain eventualities,[41] but he had also pointed to the likely direction of Australian policy with regard to the dispatch of forces to Malaya. Indeed the policy outline agreed to at the conference raised expectations of an impending Australian commitment of forces, although Canberra publicly indicated that no decision would be reached until Menzies had returned from Washington, where he had gone after the London talks. Menzies did not announce the decision to send forces to Malaya until 1 April 1955, and another twenty days passed before he first elaborated on the role of these forces.

The New Zealand Prime Minister, on the other hand, was less hesitant. At the end of the London conference, Holland revealed that he (with the agreement of Churchill and Menzies) was sending, for Malayan defence, a fighter-bomber squadron and half a transport squadron. The following week he added in Ipoh (Malaya) that recommendations would be made for New Zealand army units to be sent to Malaya to help fight the communists.[42] Meanwhile, his External Affairs and Defence Minister, T. L. MacDonald, was saying in Bangkok that the proposal to send New Zealand ground forces to Malaya was a step towards implementing the ANZAM understandings.[43] Details of the New Zealand plans were released in Parliament on 24 March – one week before Menzies announced the Australian contributions.[44] Holland said that New Zealand had been invited to perform a 'special duty on the cold war front in Malaya'. After parliamentary discussions (marked by an absence of Labour opposition), Holland said that the troops would only be used for fighting communists and not for 'settling strikes in other countries'.[45]

The straightforward manner in which New Zealand announced its commitment to Malayan defence indicated its 'British centricity', although one may well ask whether New Zealand would have so confidently shifted its strategic posture (from the Middle East to Southeast Asia) independently of any indication of Australian policy in this respect, given their close strategic interests. Australian guardedness reflected not so much Cabinet indecision, to which Boyce partly alluded, but Menzies' attempts, first (before the SEATO meeting at Bangkok, held after the London conference, dispelled Australian hopes for a combined SEATO army), to give a regional definition to a tentative Malayan commitment and, second, to obtain a US underwriting of this commitment, should it materialise, while keeping options open for any future association with SEATO. But the fact that the Australian contributions were publicised belatedly, and only after Menzies' Washington discussions, did not mean that Washington was instrumental in influencing the decision. Although Menzies played up the agreed statement brought back from Washington as indicating effective American cooperation in the ANZAM venture, the statement in fact indicated no more than an affirmation that 'the United States considered the defence of Southeast Asia, of which Malaya is an integral part, to be of very great importance'.[46] Strategically, Dulles had 'firmly resisted Australian pressure to budge from his opposition to the chopping up and segregating of its [American] forces by allocation to Southeast Asia'. Politically, the United States was sensitive lest SEATO appear to be a colonial prop to British Malaya.[47] What was demonstrated was the 'ambivalent position of Australian policy torn between the ... pulls to London and to Washington'.

This ambivalence, coupled with the early unsettled state of SEATO itself, caused confusion over the expected role of the Australian troops, especially since 'the decision to send them was made before they were publicly given a specific role'.[48] It follows that the actual role or roles were not necessarily related to the original public justifications of the commitment. One way of assessing the ensuing conflicting definitions of the Australian role is to consider them as attempts to identify the commitment in terms of the respective interests of the claimants and of the prevailing circumstances. SEATO, however, was the principal consideration behind Menzies' initial announcement on 1 April. Australian forces going to Malaya were to be 'a contribution to the defence of the [Manila] Treaty area'.[49]

Menzies' regional definition of a British-centred commitment was clearer in his parliamentary statement on 20 April. He said, 'we have ... pursued our Malayan plans while at the same time seizing every opportunity to have them integrated into the overall defence of Southeast Asia'.[50] In actuality this regional definition did not seem at the time to go beyond committing Australian troops 'to draw the line' in north Malaya.[51] Indeed, Menzies' Chief of Staff distinguished this role from the British one by saying Australia was 'training troops for war in Malaya and not for chasing terrorists'.[52] Such a role was consistent with the Australian Army Minister's statement on 7 September that 'the primary purpose ... is to contribute our share to the British Commonwealth Strategic Reserve'. Official pronouncement that the forces would be available for use against local terrorists, though not against civil disturbances, nor in Malayan–Singaporean internal affairs, was not made until 15 June.[53]

The British military, for their part, were inclined towards a broader definition of Australia's regional posture once the Australian troops were forthcoming, given the fact that the idea of a mobile strategic reserve to fight brush-fire wars in SEATO areas was then being canvassed. Moreover, the worst of the Emergency was already over and if longer-term strategic considerations were to be taken into account these would go beyond the Malayan context. As Major-General Churchill, head of British Administration of Land Forces in Singapore (then leading a British mission to Melbourne), injudiciously remarked, Australian troops would be 'used anywhere in Southeast Asia and not just against Malayan terrorists'[54] – a comment interpreted by Dr H. V. Evatt as indicating that the troops would be used as a task force in any Southeast Asian area at British discretion. McBride firmly denied this and reiterated the external defence and anti-terrorist roles of the troops as defined by Menzies.[55] Nevertheless the fact remained that while the distinction between 'external defence' and 'strategic reserve' roles was politically desirable, it made little strategic sense to those involved in planning within a wider SEATO framework. The statement issued by FARELF HQ in Singapore to coincide with the arrival of the Australian troops in Penang, while avoiding the acronym 'SEATO', did state that 'Commonwealth policy in the Far East is aligned with that of the South-East Asia Collective Defence Treaty Organisation. S.E.A.C.D.T. policy seeks ... to prevent aggression and expansion whether by overt attack, subversion or a combination of both. Security demands strength which in turn means having armed forces readily available.'[56]

Important as were the strategic implications of Australia's unprecedented decision to station troops abroad in peacetime, there was little questioning of the assumptions of that strategic posture during the lengthy and heated debate in the Australian Parliament. Instead, the debate centred on the political implications of that posture, with the ALP accusing the Government of 'colonialism' or 'imperialism'. It was left to a New Zealand MP to ask his Government what it would do if the cold war front were to be maintained in Malaya, while Indonesia (closer to Australia than Malaya) were to turn communist.[57] Concern about the rear area was not missed by Menzies, but was never explicitly spelled out at the time. He had referred to those 'vulnerable respects' in which Australian troops involved in forward defence in Malaya could be bypassed and taken in the rear by an enemy. In precisely those respects American support was desirable.[58] Certainly Menzies saw the commitment in Malaya as dependent on British readiness to guarantee Malayan security in the first place. But there was also the assumption that should the cold war front in Malaya hot up it would require more than British power to redress the situation. These Australian concerns resurfaced in Menzies' Washington trip and his 20 April statement.

Public statements in New Zealand displayed the same confusion over the role of the New Zealand troops in Malaya. There was an echo of the underlying Australian fear of the Chinese threat but, unlike Australia, a more forthright approach in expressing commitments showed a more British-centred and less developed regional concern. To Sidney Holland, the support of the US should also be earned, but the New Zealand contribution was basically an assumption of responsibility in a characteristic 'British' manner. Yet New Zealand's economic circumstances (27,000 vacant jobs, a meagre population of two million and a balance of payments deficit of £38.5 million, the highest in five years) dictated a different kind of caution. Holland thus worked for a provision to review his commitments within two years.[59]

For Singapore and Malaya, the rounds of Commonwealth decision making reflected the extent to which they were still held as 'objects' of the strategic relations between Britain, Australia and New Zealand. Little attempt was made to co-ordinate the co-operative processes among the Commonwealth partners with internal political developments in Singapore and Malaya, so that the Australian handling of the issue looked more like a series of *ad hoc* and often mistimed reactions to local events. This might have been due, in part, to the possessiveness with which the British colonial administration regarded the internal developments of Malaya and Singapore.[60]

Menzies' announcement on 1 April coincided with the first elections held under the Rendel constitution, which provided for limited self-government in Singapore. Although external defence and internal security were constitutionally British responsibilities, the issue of foreign troops was exploited for electoral advantage among a predominantly Chinese population. The Australian Commissioner in Singapore, Sir Alan Watt, had privately conferred with David Marshall, the Singapore Chief Minister, over the dispatch of Australian troops.[61] To Marshall, the British military presence was a continuing necessity, but stationing Australian troops in Singapore at that political juncture (when the local government was faced with a wave of strikes, organised sabotage and political violence) might be 'misunderstood'.[62] Against this unsettled background Australia announced on 15 June that its troops would disembark at Penang and that they would not be used in any internal civil disturbances.

By mid-June preparations had also begun in Malaya for the first national elections to a Legislative Assembly with an elected majority. On balance the weight of political opinion favoured the presence of Australian troops. The UMNO–MCA Alliance (the major political party) was not averse to mobilising all resources, including foreign assistance, to intensify the fight against the terrorists should a general amnesty prove ineffective.[63] The Australian announcement in June was generally welcomed in Malaya by the Alliance, Party Negara and the business sector, but Tunku Abdul Rahman (the Alliance's leader) had to confront criticisms from the Labour Party as well as from right-wing nationalist elements within his own UMNO.[64] Casey was anxious to minimise difficulties for the Tunku. Since the strategic reserve role proved controversial, he sought the Tunku's opinion (during their Kuala Lumpur meeting in October) on his (Casey's) referring to the two roles of the Australian forces as 'the internal and external defence of Malaya', or, alternatively, as 'the defence of Malaya'. The Tunku 'did not demur at either of these forms of words, *although he did not enthuse*' (emphasis mine). However, the Tunku's attitude towards the anti-terrorist role of Australian forces was more clearly put: like other foreign troops similarly engaged, Australian troops would not be objected to.[65]

In the July elections the Alliance won 51 of the 52 contested seats. Shortly after taking office the Alliance announced an amnesty for all persons who had committed any offence connected with the Emergency. The Australian Government, which did not participate in the preliminaries of the amnesty, was caught in an embarrassing situation when the vanguard of the Australian forces landed in Penang just three days after the proclamation. Although the Tunku welcomed the Australians and admonished the local press for publishing statements that the Australians were there to fight the communists, the Secretary-General of UMNO described the action as a 'psychological blunder' – Alliance opinion being that nothing should be done or said at that stage to make the terrorists question the amnesty offer.[66] But if it was a 'psychological blunder', then it was surely not mitigated by Menzies' announcement on 19 December that the Australian battalion would go into action (with British and New Zealand forces) against the terrorists by the end of December. Although disappointing in results, the amnesty was still operative. Moreover, arrangements were then being made by the Alliance Government to hold 'peace talks' with Communist leaders.[67] On the other hand, the New Zealand forces which arrived in transit in Singapore on 10 November received little public attention. By then the heat of local electioneering had passed; moreover, the small size of the force (130 men compared to Australia's 1,400) made them physically and psychologically less conspicuous.

Given the bitter dissensions between Government and Opposition and the need to reconcile the pulls between Britain and the United States, Australia tended to stress the wider regional issues by portraying its Malayan commitment as a defence of Australian interests against a regional threat. Levi has argued that the ambiguity of the Australian role could have been deliberate since any regional definition of the Australian commitment was likely to be more palatable to the Australian public due to their generally favourable attitude towards SEATO.[68] But ambiguity worked both ways. The more Australia emphasised its regional preoccupations, the easier it was for critics in the host countries to attack them as an Australian attempt to turn Malaya and Singapore into 'the front line of a country 2,000 miles away'.[69] Although the Alliance Government was well disposed towards receiving Australian aid in the local war, it saw the linkage with SEATO in an entirely different light.

By the end of 1955 the overlapping Commonwealth interests in Malaya had been consolidated by the formation of the Commonwealth Strategic Reserve (CSR) operating under a British command structure within the ANZAM consultative framework. British forces constituted the bulk of the CSR. Divisional HQ was at Penang and although most of the Australian ground detachment operated in the north Malayan sector against the terrorists, some were also sent to Taiping and Kuala Lumpur with British ancillary units. But the persisting ambiguity over the role of the CSR reflected a situation of overlapping circles of interests rather than a single circle containing convergent interests among the ANZAM partners. If the overlapping circles were caused by the difference in circumstances of each of the partners, then continuing internal developments in Malaya were to present yet another set of political circumstances.

3. DECOLONISATION AND THE INSTITUTION OF THE DEFENCE AGREEMENT

The Malayan elections of July 1955, in which the Tunku's Alliance Party won 51 out of 52 elective seats, marked an acceleration in the process towards full independence. Constitutional progress had, after the 1955 elections, reached the stage where a diarchy of elected politicians and British officials held important ministries with the Tunku as Chief Minister, although Britain still controlled important areas like defence, finance and the civil service. Following the visit of the Colonial Secretary, Mr Alan Lennox-Boyd (later Lord Boyd), to Kuala Lumpur at the end of August, constitutional talks on the question of self-government were scheduled for early 1956.

Even while the CSR was being made operational, the imminence of Malayan independence reopened the issue of foreign involvement in Malayan defence, this time not only to public debate but also to quiet negotiation. By the beginning of 1956, when the Malayan delegation arrived in London for the scheduled conference on independence, an admixture of circumstances influenced the Tunku's attitude towards the problem of an eventual transfer of responsibility for defence, which, together with the issues of finance and the public services, constituted the core of discussion.[1]

The Tunku's delegation left for London shortly after the abortive Baling talks with the MCP leaders (held on 28 and 29 December 1955) following 'peace soundings' by the MCP in response to the declared amnesty. These talks failed when it became clear that the amnesty terms, over which the Tunku refused to compromise, were unacceptable to the communists. The talks convinced the Tunku of the MCP's tenaciously held aim of a communist Malaya, and underlined the imperative of demonstrating Malayan control over the anti-guerrilla operations – if only to call the communists' bluff that hostilities would cease as soon as the elected government obtained control over internal security.

However, the practical realities of assuming effective operational responsibilities over internal security were apparent to the Tunku. The Federation's own armed forces amounted to barely six battalions, with neither navy nor air force. In addition, the arguments and justification for the formation of the CSR had continuing relevance to the Malayan situation. With diminishing hopes that the offer of an amnesty would successfully persuade the communist terrorists to surrender, Commonwealth forces would be needed all the more to sustain the momentum of the anti-guerrilla war. Moreover, the Alliance Party would rather avoid further military expenditure. It had declared that M$50 million per annum for the Federation would be a fair share of the total cost of the Emergency – the rest would be met 'by all other nations interested in fighting world communism'.[2] Furthermore, the Malayans were unready for any immediate transfer of full control over defence. The problem at the London conference, therefore, was how 'to reconcile the factors of continuity and efficiency ... with recognition of the evolving political facts of the situation'.

The British, while recognising the inevitability of decolonisation, were nevertheless concerned lest their stabilising influence in the Malayan area be undermined by any hasty withdrawal from Malayan bases. The Tunku, however, quickly declared his negotiating position. He forthrightly expressed his sentiments and outlined the main demands at the very opening of the conference on 18 January. Even before the closed sessions, it was known that he would ask for independence in 1957. The Federation should meanwhile be self-governing with responsibility over internal defence, finance and public services. His justification was that the fight against communism could not be won if Malayans felt that they were 'being asked to fight other people's battles'.[3] Anticipating counter-demands, he declared his readiness to leave external defence and external affairs in British hands during the interim period. Although the separation of internal from external defence and the provision of a transitional period before full independence would apparently constitute an ideal formula to reconcile several competing demands, the practical translation of this formula was problematic, and acknowledged as such by the Tunku.[4]

The difficulty arose, first, because those hitherto engaged in Malayan defence had always perceived the communist threat as a blend of invasion and insurrection which made illogical any separation between external and internal security; and, second, because the role of the CSR was never precisely defined. While serving as a welcome supplement to the anti-guerrilla effort, the reserve was also perceived, especially by the Australian Government, as basically intended for regional defence and for the external defence of Malaya. Part of the agreed formula incorporated in the constitutional conference report reflected this difficulty and the attempt to circumvent it. The CSR was only directly referred to within the context of 'the external defence of the territory and for the fulfilment of Commonwealth and international obligations'.[5] But the CSR was also used in the anti-guerrilla war. While Britain retained responsibility over external defence and external affairs during the interim period, elaborate arrangements were made for the transfer to Malayan political control of operations during the remainder of the Emergency. Henceforth a Malayan 'Minister for Internal Defence and Security' would replace the appointed Secretary for Defence in internal defence and security matters. The Malayan Minister would preside over a new policy-making body – The Emergency Operations Council (EOC) – which replaced the committee formerly presided over by the Director of Operations, who now became a member of the new council. The EOC and the post of the Director were not expected to outlast the Emergency.

Yet the same paragraph which dealt with Emergency operations significantly subsumed the CSR under the amorphous label of 'The Forces required for the prosecution of the Emergency'[6] which would continue to 'remain under the operational command of the Director of Operations'. The role of the CSR in the continuing Emergency was not made formal until September 1957, when Malayan independence made that imperative.[7] It was then stated that overseas Commonwealth forces engaged in Emergency operations would come under the general direction – but not command – of the Director of Operations. Hence commanders of the Commonwealth forces remained 'responsible to their national authorities for the exercise of commands'.[8] They possessed 'a right of appeal to their national authorities' despite their membership of the EOC.[9] Moreover, these forces could not be used in operations of which their national Governments disapproved or considered militarily unsound. Although these provisions were cast in a post-independence context, they applied throughout the interim period. But they were not outwardly defined.

In a sense the net effect of the interim arrangements simply meant that the elected minister now became more closely associated with the Emergency operations and where political questions arose his voice would be dominant. But these arrangements also reflected attempts at political expediency by highlighting the political change and playing down the operational continuity. If the mechanism of Commonwealth safeguards proved politically irksome to the Tunku, who, ideally, would have preferred full political control over all forces engaged in the Emergency, efforts were directed at minimising adverse political consequences from the interim arrangements.

The clause in the 1956 report which stated that Britain was bound to consider the arrangements of United Kingdom and Commonwealth forces for Malayan defence 'against the background of general defence policy and cannot, therefore . . . make their dispositions subject to the approval of the Federal Government'[10] was balanced by the provision that the Federation would be informed of any proposed substantial changes in the size and character of the forces. When Holland announced in August 1956 that Britain had asked New Zealand to increase substantially the size of its force in Malaya, the Tunku underlined a consultative element (which was not apparent in the 1956 report) by explaining that the Federation would be approached at the appropriate stage 'for its agreement in accordance with the London understanding'.[11] By the time the document on the use of overseas forces in the Emergency was published (just after independence), it had become politically desirable and operationally feasible to restrict their use to the states of Johore, Perak and Kedah where they were most needed. To minimise any adverse reactions to their continued association with matters of internal security, they were to be used only where Federation forces were unavailable.[12] But with the slow build-up of Malayan forces and continuing demands on military resources, the Tunku could not fulfil the wish, confidently expressed in the previous July, to be able to deal with Communism with the Federation's resources only by the time of independence.

The 1956 constitutional conference smoothly transferred to Malayan administrative control the locally financed Malayan forces. The Federation forces were detached from the United Kingdom forces and placed under a British seconded officer responsible to a Federation Armed Forces Council with the Minister for Internal Defence and Security as chairman. Malayan naval and air forces, as they came into existence, would also be administered by this council which would be permanent and separate from the EOC. The strength of the Federation army would be further increased by two battalions with British finance.[13] As with the police forces, which had a similarly high proportion of British officers, the pace of Malayanisation should not disrupt operational efficiency. Although Britain freely controlled external defence during the interim period, consultation was facilitated by including the Minister for Internal Defence and Security on the External Defence Committee (chaired by the High Commissioner) established to discuss and advise on questions of external defence. This committee would lapse when Malaya attained independence. The parties also agreed that independent Malaya should enter into a defence agreement with Britain on the general principle that, in return for assistance in external defence, Malaya would grant Britain 'the right to maintain ... the forces', which would include the CSR, and facilities 'necessary for the fulfilment of Commonwealth and international obligations'.[14] Details of the proposed treaty were left to the deliberations of a working party (on which Britain and Malaya were equally represented) chaired by the UK Commissioner-General in Southeast Asia. Australia and New Zealand, because of their association with Malayan defence, would send observers to the working party.

The agreed general principle to be applied to defence arrangements after Malayan independence was welcomed by Casey. While it was premature to speculate on Malaya's membership of SEATO, Casey indicated Australian expectations by stating that, whatever the final agreement, the Australians would still be part of SEATO's strategic reserve.[15] At the same time, given the frequent sniping by the ALP at Australia's commitment of forces to Malaya, and, equally, the concern among some members of his own party that Malaya might demand the withdrawal of foreign troops, Casey quoted in Parliament the Tunku's statements of 8 February and 14 March favouring the continued stationing of British and Commonwealth forces in the Federation.[16]

While recognising the political costs of continued use of overseas forces in the Emergency and external defence, the Tunku was nonetheless realistic in facing up to existing deficiences in local capability. He felt that given such deficiencies, Malaya should at least agree to provide facilities and bases for stationing Commonwealth forces. Moreover, the country could avoid a heavy defence expenditure which would otherwise be incurred at the cost of social and economic advancement.[17]

Economic considerations were even more pressing for the British.

By mid-1955 the economy had become 'badly overheated', unemployment was at its lowest since 1945, a balance of payments deficit of about £100 million was threatened, gold and dollar reserves were falling rapidly and there was inflation at home. The Prime Minister, Sir Anthony Eden, decided after the May general elections that defence economies were necessary. In October 1955 Eden informed the Conservative Party Conference that service personnel would be reduced by 100,000 over two and a half years. Mid-1956 saw frequent official expressions of, and newspaper comments on, the hope for effective cuts in defence expenditure. Further ministerial review of long-term policy in July 1956 resulted in a general directive on manpower setting a ceiling of 445,000 for the three services to be achieved by April 1960.[18]

The developments had repercussions on Malaya. During the constitutional conference in January 1956, the British were reluctant to meet Malayan demands for a 'launching grant' into independence and an interest-free loan to finance development plans. Indeed, the British were uncommitted when *The 1956 Constitutional Conference Report* was published. Britain was prepared to consider special financial assistance to Malaya, over and above existing military aid, should the Emergency continue after independence, but the recognition that 'the attainment of full self-government implies the principle of financial self-sufficiency' was also asserted.[19]

Anglo-Malayan wrangling over financial issues surfaced during the finance and defence talks between 18 December 1956 and 10 January 1957 – an awkward coincidence with the immediate aftermath of the Suez crisis which presented Britain with its biggest financial problem since 1945. Given its own economic difficulties, Britain could only offer the Malayans about a quarter of their original demands of M$775 million for development and M$330 million for the armed forces.[20] Even this was not forthcoming until after a series of tough negotiations.

The considerable press attention attracted by the financial wrangling almost obscured the other negotiations on the terms of a defence treaty. The latter was generally acknowledged at the time to have an easy passage. Before he left London, the Tunku commented that the draft of AMDA was satisfactorily completed. Indeed, the previous week, he had even hoped to initial the defence agreement before his departure.[21] Yet he was to testify several months later that 'the discussions had taken a long time. The first meeting of the

Working Party was held in Kuala Lumpur on 16th April, 1956, and the last meeting – on 20th March, 1957 [i.e. two and a half months after the London talks], but the discussions between the two parties went on by correspondence until 23rd August, i.e. right to the very last week before Merdeka Day.'[22]

The constraints implied by Britain's economic condition and the constitutional position in Malaya forced some revision of expectations in both countries. Whereas there was no British questioning of the commitment to defend Malaya, or of Malayan willingness to provide overseas bases, the finer points of any document covering the external defence of an independent country had to take into account its wider foreign policy orientations which, technically, could not be expressed until after independence. Malaya's case was further complicated by the changing strategic emphasis (partly influenced by Britain's own straitened economic circumstances) confronting the providers of its security. If the outlines of AMDA were formed by January 1957, its refinement would have to await further political and strategic developments.

Britain's economic difficulties affected the financial negotiations but not the important British commitment to Malayan defence – a part of Britain's still substantial policing role. The 1956 Defence White Paper, while cautioning against assuming a heavy overseas defence burden, also insisted on supporting 'our standing as a world power'.[23] This theme re-emerged in the April 1957 Defence White Paper presented by the new Defence Minister, Mr Duncan (later Lord) Sandys. Britain would provide an effective nuclear deterrent and 'defend colonies and protected territories against local attack and undertake limited operations in overseas emergencies'.[24] The ends of policy remained unchanged even if economic imperatives affected the means: conscription would cease by 1960 and a volunteer force would be limited to 375,000. Manpower savings were compensated by increased mobility and striking power. Thus the 'whole familiar gamut of British military roles within increasing economic constraints' was continued.[25]

Though the Malayan commitment was unquestioned, the general economic preoccupations with military means were sufficiently disturbing for the Tunku to seek, during the January talks, a guarantee that sufficient Commonwealth troops would remain after independence to continue anti-terrorist operations.[26] On 14 March, the Tunku anounced that British forces in Malaya would be halved after independence. On the same day, Lord Home, Secretary for Commonwealth Relations, assured the SEATO Council in Canberra that the reductions would be 'neither far reaching nor sweeping'.[27]

Yet Britain clearly desired a larger Australian contribution to Malayan defence. As Casey, who participated in the Canberra talks, put it, the discussions on 14 March (attended by, among others, Menzies, Lord Home and Lord Carrington, then British High Commissioner to Australia) were 'not very pleasant – by reason of the fact that out defence effort very obviously struck the British as so meagre'.[28] When Sandys subsequently visited Canberra in August to explain his White Paper, he not only requested more Australian forces for Malaya but also proposed an integrated ANZAM command which would incorporate all the elements of the CSR. Such a structure would possess organisational advantages, although the Australian Chiefs of Staff were sceptical. But, as Casey argued during their meeting on 26 August, Washington would view that as resulting in too narrow a definition of the Australian commitment, if not actually undermining the Australian effort within SEATO. Casey also feared the difficulty of extricating the Australians once they were absorbed into the larger United Kingdom force.[29]

Sandys' visit, nevertheless, resulted in Australian–New Zealand adjustments which fed into the Malayan area. The 1957 New Zealand contribution of an infantry battalion, while serving to balance British force reductions and demonstrating more clearly a New Zealand commitment, was also perceived as part of the longer-term adjustment to the British emphasis on increased mobility.[30] Similarly, although Australia did not accept increased responsibilities in Malaya, it responded to Sandys' White Paper by increased land and air mobility and by offering to create a mobile brigade based in Australia.[31] At the same time, following Britain, the decision was taken to phase out national service over the next four years.

Since Malaya was the one place with Australian and New Zealand forces in being, this co-ordinated shift in emphasis enhanced in antipodean perceptions the significance of a SEATO-orientated Malaya. Hence the New Zealand External Affairs and Defence Minister, T. L. MacDonald, stated that their Malayan-based battalion would play 'a fire brigade role in the case of Communist aggression anywhere in the area'.[32] Menzies in turn forthrightly declared that Australian forces deployed in Malaya would 'be constantly related to SEATO defence'.[33] Australian adjustments to the Sandys policy had included standardisation with the Americans in arms and equipment, implicitly doubting Britain's logistic capability in Southeast Asia in a general war.[34] Menzies' remarks reflected attempts to demonstrate Australia's good faith in SEATO to the Americans.

But just when the wider strategic considerations of 1957 were beginning to define for Australia and New Zealand a clearer SEATO view of their Malayan commitments, constitutional developments in Malaya had reached the stage when the Malayans could express precisely the opposite attitude towards SEATO. Ironically those very ANZAM commitments to Malaya diminished in Malayan eyes the need for any SEATO association. Among the problems confronting the AMDA working party, which began negotiations even before Malaya had a foreign policy, was how to devise a formula to reconcile the ANZAM interests (embodied in the CSR) with Malayan military requirements without prejudicing the future attitude of an independent Malaya towards SEATO.

Britain's official position towards the question of Malaya's SEATO membership suggested a certain distinction between its immediate commitments in Malaya and the issue of regional defence. The Colonial Secretary, Lennox-Boyd, was careful to stress that Britain had given no advice to the Federation Government regarding SEATO membership – that choice was left to a future independent Malaya.[35] As the new British High Commissioner, Mr (later Sir) Geoffroy Tory, subsequently confirmed, the treaty would not be affected if Malaya decided against SEATO membership.[36] If this had been a private guideline for the working party, then it is conceivable that some impression, at least, of Malaya's future position on SEATO might have been conveyed to the British negotiators. Although the Tunku appropriately refrained from taking a public stand on SEATO up to the eve of independence, he hinted at the matter by saying that Britain would be in Malaya only to fight the communists and not to defend Southeast Asia as a whole.[37] The fact remained that, in Malayan perception, membership of SEATO was strategically unnecessary, politically unpopular and generally ineffective.[38] The last point was made by the Tunku himself in 1960 when he raised serious doubts about the efficacy of SEATO as a collective defence organisation.[39] In addition, the Malayan negotiators could not have been ignorant of the Australian and New Zealand attitudes towards their components in the CSR, since Australia and New Zealand had 'been fully consulted at every stage'.[40]

The formula devised by the AMDA negotiators had to satisfy various competing demands. The result was an extension of the ambiguity which had prevailed since 1955. Article III of the treaty reflected the wider strategic interests of the Commonwealth partners by stating that in return for the United Kingdom's assistance in external defence (Article I) and in the training and development of the Federation's armed forces (Article II), the Federation would grant the United Kingdom the right to maintain in Malaya 'such naval, land and air forces including a Commonwealth Strategic Reserve ... for the fulfilment of Commonwealth and international obligations'. To the ANZAM partners, these 'obligations' obviously referred to SEATO commitments. Yet Article VIII, in a clear concession to Malayan interests, declared that where a threat to the peace, or an outbreak of hostilities, occurred other than in Malaya or in British dependencies in the Far East (the area of commitment covered in Articles VI and VII), prior Malayan agreement must be obtained before United Kingdom forces could be committed to active operations involving Malayan bases. This seemed to give the Federation the power of veto over the use of the CSR in SEATO operations, which was how Dato (later Tun) Abdul Razak, the Defence Minister-designate, saw it.[41] However, a *de facto* Malayan association with SEATO could be read into the escape clause in the same article which stipulated that the British right to withdraw forces from the Federation would be unaffected. Thus, if necessary, the forces could be withdrawn to, and redeployed from, Singapore – a conveniently placed British colony which, according to Sandys, Britain had no thought of quitting.

In 1958 the Tunku admitted an indirect SEATO link, but chose to focus on the area of commitment in which Malaya would be involved if one of the British Far East dependencies (say Singapore or North Borneo) were attacked because of British involvement in a SEATO war.[42] A distinction was made between British Far East territories (especially Singapore and North Borneo, and, more distantly, Hong Kong) with which Malaya had strategically identified itself, and the wider SEATO area where a threat might not involve Malayan security directly and hence towards which Malaya could remain non-involved. The Tunku sought to dispel the fear that the 'Far East Commitment' would involve Malaya on the British side in an anti-colonial conflict (a point later echoed by J. D. B. Miller)[43] by dismissing Malayan involvement in any internal conflict which did not threaten Malaya.[44]

Indeed, Malaya was not even committed to defend Australia and New Zealand, let alone Britain. The fact that Britain, alone of the ANZAM partners, was the high contracting party allowed Australia and New Zealand to hedge their commitments in Malaya against a British guarantee to defend Malaya in the first place. Although, in Holyoake's view, the intention to be associated with AMDA was 'to ensure that our forces are placed on the same footing as the other overseas forces there',[45] one should distinguish the equality of status of the forces from an equality of roles. The role of the associates could be subtly different from that of the anchor power and this is worth recalling when we consider ANZAM responses when AMDA was severely tested.

Article IX of the treaty, which obliged Britain to consult the Federation Government when major changes in the character or deployment of the forces kept in Malaya were contemplated, went beyond paragraph 15 of *The 1956 Constitutional Conference Report*, which applied to the interim period and obliged Britain only to inform but not to consult. This might or might not have been inserted to give the Federation a veto over any possible deployment of nuclear weapons in Malaya. However, the response following Sandys' remarks in Australia on the eve of Merdeka was to make explicit what the Federation took Article IX to mean. Sandys had gone to Australia and New Zealand to explain his new defence policy and in Canberra publicly disclosed that 'British forces in Malaya are to be cut slightly, but their fire-power will be increased by the availability of nuclear weapons'.[46] This statement, when seen against the revelation that Canberra bombers then being sent to Malaya were actually equipped to carry nuclear weapons, alarmed the Malayans. Abdul Razak briskly disavowed any intention of 'making Malaya an atomic base for anybody' and emphasised the need for prior consultation and agreement.[47] Sandys subsequently made a partial retraction by stressing that no decision had been made about the location of atomic weapons while affirming the 'British angle' of 'regarding SEATO as a vital factor in the defence of the free world'.[48]

Although Sandys' initial statement might have been a trial balloon, Malayan responses showed that something which might fit neatly into a wider strategic framework could have disturbing political effects. The reason was that Commonwealth defence co-operation with Malaya represented an overlapping rather than a complete convergence of interests – a situation which had been apparent even among the ANZAM members in 1955 but which had now to be institutionalised. As the endless controversy over the SEATO role of the CSR showed, the essence of AMDA lay in its *de facto* acknowledgement of an ANZAM strategic imperative while in a *de jure* sense enabling the Federation to express contrary reservations according to its own political priorities. Thus the several public Malayan protests between 1959 and 1962, when statements from the SEATO powers indicated they regarded Malaya as being involved in SEATO defence planning, are to be seen against the actual withdrawal of an Australian Sabre jet squadron from Butterworth to Singapore and its redeployment to Thailand during the May 1962 Laos crisis. This curious feature arises out of the fact that AMDA was a treaty between equals (with interests that could be differentiated) in status but not stature, while the circumstances in which it was negotiated necessitated a special emphasis on the former equality. AMDA remained in effect a security guarantee and, in so far as Britain remained the anchor power in this physically unequal alliance, opponents of the treaty could portray Malaya as a 'protectorate'.[49] Indeed, as late as 1963, Opposition charges were still being raised that 'the satellite status of Malaya' was being prolonged by 'the strangle-hold of the British War Office' on Malaya's defence.[50]

This politically exploitable unequal alliance and the psychological reactions to a treaty which emerged immediately after independence were apparent to the Tunku who felt that 'if the allegation [that overseas forces are in Malaya as an Army of Occupation] can be made, even on the flimsiest of pretexts, it can wreck the working of the Agreement' and undermine future Anglo-Malayan relations. AMDA, therefore, 'must reflect both in word and spirit the full Independence 'and Sovereignty of the new Malaya'.[51] In this sense AMDA was an exercise in how not to offend a newly independent country's susceptibilities.

It was not just left wing or Opposition criticisms that bothered the Tunku – parliamentary approval was assured by the overwhelming Government majority. More significant was the strong feeling of the Malay nationalists, a vocal faction of whom came from UMNO itself. Their pride about Malaya's new status, and the apprehension that AMDA would make it a 'half-baked' independence, developed into an UMNO grass-roots revolt in late September. Criticisms of the indirect SEATO link grew into protests against land alienation and demands for a time limit to AMDA. The Tunku was sufficiently concerned to make the crisis an issue of confidence and although the revolt was dealt with firmly, he tactfully agreed to review the treaty within a year.[52]

These events, coming after the publication of the defence agreement as a White Paper, indicated the political climate in which the AMDA negotiations took place. As the Tunku revealed, the protracted negotiations stemmed from attempts at resolving those treaty provisions which might possibly compromise Malayan sovereignty. Apart from the elaborate reconciliation of Article III with Article VIII, the issues prolonging the negotiations included jurisdiction over the overseas forces and review and termination of the agreement.[53]

The negotiators were divided over the question of jurisdiction over foreign troops in Malaya. The British preferred the international practice of giving jurisdiction to the service courts over offences arising from actions committed in the course of official duties. The Malayans, however, insisted that the Federation's civil courts should continue (as they had before independence) to exercise this jurisdiction. This Malayan preference was first voiced at an UMNO conference in Kuala Lumpur on 17 January 1957, and again at the UMNO general assembly at the end of June. Anglo-Malayan differences were reconciled by the formula of concurrent jurisdiction except where offences were punishable by the laws of either the Federation or the United Kingdom alone, in which case exclusive jurisdiction would apply.

That either party was free to suggest a treaty review from time to time emphasised the mutuality of the arrangement. But to meet Britain's need for security of tenure over its bases initial leases of 30 years were granted with the provision for further renewals as required for the implementation of AMDA.[54] On balance the bargaining over AMDA gave a maximum of security to Malaya in return for a minimum of obligations. But any claim of a 'diplomatic triumph' for the Federation must be seen against the backdrop of circumstances which called for adjustments as much to strategic continuity as to political change.

The treaty was not signed (and hence there was no formal document governing the presence of British Commonwealth forces in Malaya) for over a month after Malayan independence to allow the Malayan Parliament an opportunity to debate it. According to Casey, London was sufficiently concerned to suggest an Exchange of Letters to cover the time-gap. The Tunku was offended by the proposal which suggested a lack of British confidence in him.[55] The actual signing of AMDA on 12 October 1957 was an Anglo-Malayan affair. Having announced their intentions, Australia and New Zealand did not make formal their association with the treaty until 1959.

One notable aspect of the AMDA negotiations was the complete absence of Singapore. The desirability of associating Singapore with these negotiations from the very beginning was voiced by the former Colonial Secretary, James Griffiths, and indeed appreciated by Lennox-Boyd.[56] But Singapore, separated from the mainland by the Malayan Union of 1946 and thus maintained after the Union was replaced by the Federation in 1948, was to take a different and separate path to independence. Any possibility of a union with Singapore was dispelled by the Tunku in 1956 while the conclusion of AMDA enhanced further the advantage of Singapore as a colony to the British. But events in Singapore in the late fifties were to put these advantages in doubt and it is to the vexing politics of the Singapore base that attention must now be turned.

4. THE EXTENSION OF AMDA

AMDA's extension was necessitated by the formation of Malaysia which embodied Malaya, Singapore and the British-administered territories of North Borneo (later renamed Sabah) and Sarawak. Malaysia was born mainly out of the changing political circumstances in Singapore whose separate constitutional development had been influenced both by socio-economic factors and by its strategic importance to Britain.[1] Singapore's strategic importance to the ANZAM partners was enhanced after AMDA was formed. Singapore provided the loophole through which units of the CSR, based in Malaya, could be redeployed for SEATO purposes. Its strategic importance attracted much interest among the ANZAM partners during the constitutional negotiations of 1956 which collapsed on account of the insurmountable difficulty of separating external defence from internal security.

Internal instability in Singapore in the mid-fifties strengthened Britain's insistence on control over internal security matters to ensure unhindered use of the bases and also created a Malayan interest in Singapore. Although, in 1956, the Tunku saw the protection of Malayan interests in the exclusion of Singapore from the Federation, a network of internal security (and later defence) co-operation between the two territories gradually emerged. The practical realities of their close association were demonstrated by the Singapore riots of October 1956, and given further recognition in 1957 by Malaya's participation in Singapore's Internal Security Council – an arrangement that broke the earlier deadlock in Anglo-Singapore negotiations and effectively placed the casting vote in Malayan hands. There was, moreover, an intrinsic Malayan interest in Singapore's internal security given its proximity and a shared problem of communist subversion.

By 1959 political trends eventually leading to the establishment of Malaysia were already emerging. In Singapore the electoral victory of the People's Action Party (PAP), with its strong commitment to merger with the mainland, saw the beginning of a sustained campaign to woo the Tunku, while the appearance of a 'leftward drift' in Singapore politics (and the eventuality of the decolonisation of Singapore) subsequently persuaded the Tunku to accept merger through Malaysia.

While 1959 was a year of important political change which led to AMDA's extension, it was equally significant in terms of the reaffirmation of strategic continuity and of the validity of AMDA. The improving counter-insurgency situation in Malaya led, in early 1959, to a shift in the emphasis of the CSR's role towards garrison duties. As a 'strategic reserve' its SEATO connections became even more discernible. Reflecting their continued interest in regional defence and their junior roles, Australia and New Zealand associated themselves formally with AMDA in April 1959. This appeared to anticipate the outcome of the promised review of AMDA the following month.

AMDA was not affected by the Anglo-Malayan defence review. The useful ambiguity of Article VIII of AMDA served the complementary (but not wholly congruent) interests of Malaya and the three external powers, while the Singapore base itself made that ambiguity practicable. The impending incorporation of Singapore in the enlarged Federation of Malaysia confronted the allies with the problem of 'squaring the circle' of political change and strategic continuity, particularly with regard to the special importance of Singapore to the external powers. This was the central problem of the extension of AMDA.

AMDA's extension was linked to political change in Singapore. The isolation of Singapore from Malaya's constitutional development reflected the priority of British strategic interests in the island. Singapore had been separated from the Malayan Union proposals of 1946 and remained separated after the short-lived Union was replaced by the constitution of the Federation of Malaya on 1 February 1948. By the mid-fifties Singapore assumed an even greater importance to Britain. It possessed the 'only dry-dock between Japan and Sydney large enough to hold an aircraft carrier'[2] and contained the headquarters for British Far East Land Forces (FARELF). It also embraced the Far East Station of the Royal Navy (RNFE, sited at Woodlands), while the RAF in the Far East was subordinated to HQ Far East Air Forces (FEAF) sited at Changi.

Each of the above commands was responsible not only for Singapore but also Malaya, Hong Kong, Fiji and the Borneo territories. Functionally, the base was 'a place where troops, ships, aircraft, heavy equipment, supplies and facilities for maintenance and repair can be kept for military operations elsewhere'.[3] FEAF controlled Seletar base, the general aircraft-servicing station for the whole area, and Tengah airfield. ANZAM navies also benefited from facilities provided by Singapore's dockyards. New Zealand and Australian aircraft had been attached to the RAF at Changi as early as 1949 and 1950 respectively. With the CSR's formation, operational employment of its land, air and naval components came under the British command structure based in Singapore. Regional developments, culminating in the formation of SEATO in 1954, enhanced Singapore's regional importance. Indeed, at SEATO's founding conference, Britain pressed strongly for the siting of SEATO headquarters in Singapore as opposed to the rival Philippine preference for Manila.[4] Singapore's strategic importance gave Britain a special interest in the security of the bases there – an interest reinforced by Singapore's internal unrest of the mid-fifties when communist agitation intensified along a broad front.

British anxieties over the continued use of Singapore for external defence and over Singapore's internal security (a deterioration of which could impair the functioning of the bases) were related. This connection largely obstructed the attempt by Mr David Marshall (Singapore's first locally elected Chief Minister, who headed a form of limited local government) to gain control over internal security during constitutional discussions with Britain between April and May 1956. The objective of the all-Party delegation (which included Mr Lee Kuan Yew of the PAP) led by Marshall to London was to achieve internal self-government. In reality, the quest for 'independence' was circumscribed by certain concessions to British interests. The delegation was mandated to offer Britain an agreement whereby 'the United Kingdom . . . would exercise control over external defence and give guidance in foreign relations other than trade and commerce'.[5]

Marshall, however, defined Singapore's external defence not in terms of 'defending Singapore' but in terms of 'utilising Singapore for the defence of other members of the Commonwealth including the United Kingdom'.[6] Singapore's vital position in 'free world strategy' made it 'unreasonable and impractical' to deny Britain its defence facilities in the island.⁷ Likewise, wherever external affairs affected Britain's external defence commitments, Singapore would act in consultation with London. Bluntly put, Marshall's offer of the 'agreement' with the United Kingdom was, as Lee Kuan Yew observed, a euphemistic acknowledgement that Britain would not grant complete independence because it would mean 'upsetting international arrangements and international bases'.⁸ There was also the equally realistic factor of Singapore's economic dependence on the British presence since 'one-sixth of our labour force is employed by the armed forces'.

Britain's apprehension over Singapore's internal security was underlined in Lennox-Boyd's speech at the opening of the conference on 23 April. Having referred to Singapore's importance as a bastion in the free world's defence system and to the threat of subversion it faced, he pointed to the impossibility of dissociating active interest in internal security from responsibility for external defence.⁹ The protracted constitutional talks in London broke down over the structure of the joint machinery necessary to oversee the vital areas of external affairs, external defence and internal security where a conjunction of British and Singapore interests existed. Marshall's insistence on control over internal security could not be reconciled with Britain's inclusion under external defence of 'the preservation or restoration of ... public order and the maintenance of essential supplies and services' which related to the provision and management of facilities at British bases.¹⁰ Possibly, too, the British regarded Marshall as too unreliable to be placed in sole charge of internal security, remembering his reluctance to summon British troops during the 'Hock Lee' riots in May 1955. The conference ended without agreement on the composition of a Defence and Security Council. Marshall returned to Singapore on 26 May and on 6 June resigned his Chief Ministership.

As Darby has argued, Singapore proved the prevalence of the view (expressed by Harold Macmillan in 1955) that the principle of self-determination could not be indiscriminately applied, particularly to certain small territories of major strategic significance.¹¹ Selwyn Lloyd, the Foreign Secretary, echoed this view when he spoke of the necessity to 'retain certain positions of strength at whatever cost'. He specified Cyprus, Aden and Singapore and added: 'We need Singapore now more than ever.'¹² The strategic reserve which necessitated advance bases overseas was still relevant and, coupled with the uncertainty of British tenure at the Trincomalee and Katunayake bases in Ceylon and the probable non-membership of independent Malaya in SEATO, emphasised Singapore's importance to the overall British defence posture. Neither the political costs (defined by internal developments in Singapore) nor British economic constraints were sufficiently high for a re-evaluation of the strategic benefits yielded by Singapore.

The London conference was also closely monitored by Australia whose traditional strategic interest in the Singapore base had tempered its support for constitutional advance. While sympathising with Singapore's aspirations, Casey openly supported British insistence on retaining the powers over internal security and recognised the 'very considerable dangers ... in a too precipitate advance towards self-government'.[13] Denying Marshall's allegation that Canberra had not ascertained Singapore's views on the British proposals, Casey mentioned 'active' discussions which both he and, subsequently, the Australian Commissioner in Singapore had had with Marshall before the London talks.[14] Casey reported his discussions with Marshall to the Cabinet and, on the basis of that, Menzies cabled his views to London. In contrast, the New Zealand Prime Minister, Holland, appeared more sympathetic towards Marshall. In May 1956 Holland and his Secretary for External Affairs, A. D. McIntosh, *en route* to the Prime Ministers' Conference in London, met Marshall in Singapore. Afterwards Holland expressed 'full agreement with the aspirations of the people of Singapore'.[15]

The failure of the Singapore constitutional talks strengthened the feeling among the Singapore delegation that merger with Malaya might resolve the internal security issue with Britain. But it was precisely the internal instability in Singapore which initially persuaded the Tunku against merger. Nevertheless, Malaya found itself increasingly involved in Singapore's internal security. The violent Singapore riots (which reached a peak on 26–27 October 1956) triggered by the systematic measures against the left-wing by Singapore's new Chief Minister, Mr Lim Yew Hock, saw a substantial redeployment of troops from the Malayan jungle to Singapore and a heightened awareness of an interconnection of security matters between the two territories.

Another interconnection was formalised by Malaya's participation in the Internal Security Council (ISC) – an improvement upon the rejected Defence and Security Council. Equal representation for

Britain and Singapore on the ISC effectively gave the casting vote to the seventh member, who would be a Malayan minister. The strongly anti-communist character of the Federation Government was sufficiently reassuring for Britain to accept a minority position within the council. This acceptance in turn resolved the earlier constitutional deadlock and Anglo-Singapore negotiations resumed between March and April 1957. The ISC facilitated access to all information, consultation and decision making on all issues regarding order and public safety in semi-independent Singapore. Responsibility for summoning British troops to aid the civil authorities rested with the local government, but Britain's retention of the right, *in extremis*, to suspend the constitution meant that in the final resort it could summon its forces to re-establish order.[16]

Malayan participation in the ISC eased the constitutional deadlock over Singapore and institutionalised a Malayan interest in Singapore's internal security. But a pattern of local defence co-operation between Malaya and Singapore was also developing. In September 1957 Kuala Lumpur agreed to take over, without charge, the Royal Malayan Navy which had been based and controlled in Singapore since 1948. This move complemented the formation of a Singapore battalion, the redistribution of efforts being cast in a pan-Malayan context.[17] Lim Yew Hock, himself with merger in mind, partly justified the formation of the Singapore Infantry Regiment in terms of a future contribution to common defence.[18]

Singapore's external defence, as with external affairs (except for the delegated areas of trade and commerce), remained under British control. The 1957 Constitutional Agreement[19] instituted a consultative Intergovernmental Committee under UK chairmanship on those matters of defence and external affairs affecting Singapore. The reality of British sovereignty over external defence was acknowledged by Lim Yew Hock who, in the wake of controversial speculations (stirred by Duncan Sandys' visit in September 1957) that Singapore might become a nuclear base, admitted that Britain could establish such a base despite local opposition.[20] The speculation followed Sandys' affirmation in Sydney, later repeated in Singapore, of Britain's military tenure in the island. His assurance to Australia should be read in the light of anxiety in Britain and Australia over the political future of the Singapore base leading to continual speculation over an alternative base in Australia.[21] Richard Casey had expressed similar anxiety to Lord Home at a London meeting in September 1957.[22]

Although, for several years at least, the British base was constitutionally secure, there was unease over perceived uncertainties posed by impending elections under the new constitution. The only viable alternative to Lim's Labour Front Government was the PAP, led by Lee Kuan Yew who was regarded with suspicion because of his accommodation of pro-communist militants in an anti-colonial front. Lee's strategy of 'riding the tiger' was not fully appreciated in Kuala Lumpur and Canberra. The PAP's success in winning thirteen of the fourteen PAP-contested seats at the city council elections in December 1957 heightened anxiety. Ong Eng Guan, the PAP treasurer, became Mayor and, in the midst of his anti-colonial antics, the British Prime Minister, Harold Macmillan, visited Singapore. Macmillan himself noted 'an atmosphere of uncertainty and alarm'[23] and doubted whether Lim Yew Hock could withstand the communist pressure.

It remained for Britain to assure both Australia and New Zealand (in New Zealand a general election, held just two months previously, had brought into office, by a majority of two, a Labour Government under Mr (later Sir) Walter Nash) of British intent concerning defence dispositions, particularly with regard to Singapore which, with the British decision to close down the Hong Kong Royal Dockyards, was acquiring increasing strategic significance. In both Australia and New Zealand, to which Macmillan proceeded after Singapore, defence issues dominated the discussions. In Australia, Macmillan was 'strenuously cross-examined; not only by Menzies but also by all his ministers'.[24] Macmillan's visit revived speculation that he would seek a greater Australian share in the Malayan commitments. Such a request, if made, would have been refused, given Australia's previous refusal during Sandys' visit in August 1957. New Zealand, for its part, with increasing economic difficulties, was tailoring its defence programme to the Sandys White Paper by an emphasis on reduced manpower and the abolition of conscription. Macmillan admitted in Australia that the problem of Southeast Asian defence had been discussed and hoped 'that you are content with what we are doing'.[25] He publicly assured the Australians that Britain would retain substantial and balanced forces in Southeast Asia and the Far East. This assurance was repeated in a Defence White Paper.[26]

Attention, however, was increasingly attracted to the internal political situation in Singapore. Indeed, Macmillan was asked in Parliament whether the foundations of Britain's Far East defence lynchpin ought not to be on politically secure grounds. He merely replied that the Singapore Government had no responsibility for defence.[27] An expectation of turmoil was also partly hinted at in Casey's observation that 'the British felt they might (if a PAP Government came to power) have to ask Australia and New Zealand to alter present restrictions on the use of their troops for internal security'.[28] The importance of Singapore to the defence of Southeast Asia was, according to Casey, repeatedly stressed during the 1959 SEATO conference in Wellington. Britain in turn was equally ready to reassure.

Beneath the determination that Singapore must remain the main British base lay an apprehension, particularly in Australia and New Zealand, over its future role and status. It has also been accepted that Australian policy makers distrusted Lee and made little effort to communicate with him.[29] Tom Bellows, without citing sources, suggests that the British, on the other hand, were, for some time before the May elections, beginning to make a realistic distinction between the moderate Lee group (who could be relied upon) and the pro-communists in the PAP.[30]

No matter how anti-colonial the PAP might have been in appearance, they faced a number of constraints which included Britain's power to suspend the constitution, the fear of antagonising conservative Malaya (with which the PAP had pledged to merge), the need to retain business confidence and, finally, Singapore's economic dependence on the British military presence. In a letter to the *Straits Times* Lee clarified his belief that in the long run the British bases must go when Singapore attained independence through merger with Malaya, but that until then defence and the bases should remain in British hands.[31] Indeed, Lee approached the British Labour Party's Shadow Colonial Secretary, James Callaghan, for '3 or 4 years' previous notice if there was any change of policy'.[32]

Following the PAP's electoral victory, the British military announced extensive military building projects in Singapore, thus underlining the relative 'permanency' of their presence. Indeed General Sir Richard Hull said: 'We are not building these just temporarily. This is a permanent base.'[33]

By late 1959 strategic mobility was being emphasised by the British in Singapore. This came at a juncture when the elected Government was neither constitutionally equipped nor economically inclined to telescope long-term aspirations into short-term radical action against the bases. While a Singapore-based 'heli-commando' naval force was materialising, approval was given to extend the Tengah airfield at a cost of £2.5 million. As *The Times* observed, Lee's Government accepted the Tengah expansion without demur, which suggested a continuing tolerance of the bases after full independence since the financial burden would remain with Britain.[34] Indeed, the new PAP Government, conscious of its burdens in financing its Five Year Development Plan, was not disposed to accept too rigid a financial distinction between external and internal defence responsibilities. It would prefer Britain to pay for the locally raised forces as well. Negotiations with Britain were taken up in September and the financial agreement was announced in October 1960.[35]

The PAP, following its electoral victory, was intent on establishing financial confidence and political credibility, particularly in its relations with the Federation. It was strongly committed to merger with Malaya on economic, military and political grounds and because of concern over 'the leftward trend' of Singapore politics. The PAP victory in 1959 set the trend for the events which contributed to AMDA's extension. PAP attempts to create the conditions for unification were manifested in the inculcation of 'a truly Malayan spirit' in Singapore and in efforts at arguing the case for a common market. In internal security matters the PAP was also determined to prove itself a credible partner with the Federation within the ISC.

The PAP, on winning 43 of the 51 parliamentary seats contested, had refused to take office until eight of its members, including left-wing trade union leader Lim Chin Siong, were released from detention – a development which the Federation found disturbing. The 'difference in approaches to security problems between a non-Communist Socialist Government and an anti-Communist Federation Government' with its experience of militant communist insurrection, was acknowledged by Dr Toh Chin Chye in a lengthy statement nineteen weeks after the PAP took office. It explained that, while the Singapore Government was duty-bound to defend 'the rights of left-wing non-Communist Party forces and to encourage their growth', it would not act as 'a buffer to protect pro-Communist Party forces against the Federation Government'. Indeed, it promised to be 'less inhibited' in taking measures against pro-communist activities,[36] with the result that the Preservation of

Public Security Ordinance, which provided for detention without trial, was extended by another five years.

There were in 1959 much clearer indications in Singapore of a unification with Malaya and, consequently, an extension of AMDA. In Malaya, the de-emphasis on the counter-insurgency role of the CSR (and, conversely, the re-emphasis on the garrison role) had become more evident. By early 1959, Malaya had experienced a marked improvement in internal security and plans were made to end the Emergency. Gradual changes were also introduced into the training and duties of Commonwealth forces in Malaya. For areas southwards, from Ipoh to Singapore, a return to training in limited, but more open, war was ordered. It may be recalled that deployment of the CSR in anti-terrorist operations in Malaya was subject to an agreement separate from AMDA. These same forces, however, were also stationed under the terms of AMDA. From Kuala Lumpur's viewpoint, they were essentially for external defence, while the ANZAM partners generally tended to draw a SEATO connection. Hence, ambiguity and controversy had arisen over their role within AMDA.

By 1959, however, the CSR was assuming increasingly a garrison role which would have categorised it as a truly 'strategic reserve'. This operational shift again triggered an incipient tension between two different conceptions of the CSR's role. Notwithstanding the dwindling opportunity for jungle warfare training with the end of the Emergency, the kind of military experience hitherto available in Malaya (where troops generally operated at platoon or company strength) was inappropriate to a mobile strategic reserve. Furthermore, even if suitable training areas existed in Malaya for large-scale manoeuvres, the Federation Government would be disinclined to host SEATO-connected exercises. There were two aspects of the 'SEATO problem' which emerged: the end of the Emergency shifted the operational emphasis of the CSR to the SEATO role and with that the possible arousal of Malayan sensitivity, and there was concern lest the vicissitudes in Anglo-Malayan relations jeopardise SEATO training itself.

The British, while discounting withdrawal from Malaya, were also looking for a suitable site for training a strategic reserve. Following an observation tour of North Borneo in early 1959 and discussions between FARELF and the North Borneo Government, the vast undulating country in the Kota Belud district – ideal for mechanised warfare training – was confirmed as a 'training area for British army units stationed in Malaya and Singapore'.[37] The first SEATO amphibious exercises involving ANZAM and US forces was conducted in June 1959 on beaches between Kota Belud and Kudat. In 1961 SEATO exercises – involving Thai, Philippine, ANZAM and US forces – were again held near Kota Belud.[38] By 1962, with the likelihood of North Borneo's incorporation in Malaysia, there were no more reports of such exercises.

But in 1959 British North Borneo was a convenient back yard for CSR training in SEATO-type contingencies. On Malayan soil, a greater diplomatic finesse at understating the obvious was necessary. Among ANZAM components in Malaya, the air element was least amenable to ambiguity if only because the strategic assumption behind the siting of the Butterworth air base at the northern end of the peninsula made it an obvious manifestation of regional intent. Both the extension to the Butterworth runway and the reinforcement of the base by more Australian jet bombers and fighters fitted into the SEATO-orientated forward defence postures of Australia and New Zealand. As the Commanding Officer of No. 2 Canberra Bomber Squadron RAAF rather incautiously told Penang Rotarians in March 1959, Australian air forces in Butterworth were in immediate readiness to fulfil SEATO obligations.[39] The Malayan Ministry of External Affairs promptly dissociated Malaya from any SEATO involvement.[40]

The Tunku had been perturbed the previous March by Walter Nash's statement that 'Malaya would gain, not lose, by becoming a member of . . . [SEATO]'. Nash (who was in Kuala Lumpur with Casey for the ECAFE conference) also intended to discuss SEATO with the Tunku. The Tunku retorted that if Nash broached the subject he would be informed that Malaya's attitude remained unchanged.[41] Casey, who said that he 'would not be impertinent enough' to raise the matter, later recorded that the Tunku concurred that Nash's public remarks were politically embarrassing, 'at least this side of the election . . . [and that the Tunku said that] his opposition was gunning for him on the question of SEATO'.[42]

1959 saw elections in Malaya, a possible end to the Emergency and the promised review of AMDA. There were speculations that Malayan demands would mount for substantial withdrawals of Commonwealth troops. Certainly left-wing and PMIP opposition to foreign troops in Malaya resurfaced during the election campaign.

Both Nash and Casey carefully indicated that the continued presence of their forces in Malaya beyond the Emergency rested with the Tunku. However, the Tunku did not seem to question the continued usefulness of Commonwealth forces. Indeed, the Anglo-Malayan defence review, scheduled about two months before the general elections of August 1959, seemed timed to minimise local politicking over AMDA. As it transpired, the defence review was mainly of Malaya's defence requirements after the Emergency ended rather than of AMDA itself.

The month before the AMDA review, an Exchange of Letters was concluded between Malaya and Australia and New Zealand by which the two external powers associated themselves with those provisions and annexes (together with letters exchanged between Malaya and Britain) of AMDA which applied to the CSR. A gap of nearly two years had lapsed between the signing of AMDA and this Exchange of Letters. A few surmises might be advanced for the delay.

First, as various Australian and New Zealand pronouncements in 1958 and early 1959 suggested, there was the continuing hope that Malaya might, at some stage, associate more openly with SEATO and, in so doing, sanction the regional role of the CSR. Australia and New Zealand could well have waited for firmer indications of the Malayan position at the promised review of AMDA. And if there was any uncertainty about the future of AMDA, that too would caution against a precipitate association with the treaty. Their association with AMDA shortly before the treaty was reviewed indicated that they did not expect radical changes. Second, the ending of the Emergency had some bearing on the timing of their association with AMDA. The shift in emphasis from counter-insurgency to a garrison role for the CSR occurred against a background of Malayan Opposition demands for foreign troop withdrawals. Owing to continuing Malayan antipathy towards SEATO, there was now some urgency to formulate a legal basis for the presence of antipodean forces already in Malaya.

A New Zealand official, in Canberra at the time of the Exchange of Letters, recalled that much thought was spent in drafting those rather 'cryptic documents'.[43] Indeed, the actual status of the Australian and New Zealand forces could not be perceived without direct references to those provisions of AMDA which related to the CSR. The Exchange of Letters simply stated that 'the various provisions applicable to the Commonwealth Strategic Reserve, in particular the provisions dealing with the status of forces, apply in respect to these [Australian and New Zealand] forces'.[44]

Significantly, no 'rights' or 'obligations' were mentioned. Their associate status underlined the fact that Britain alone had defence obligations to Malaya and that Australia and New Zealand were merely 'junior partners' whose 'commitments' to Malayan defence could only be inferred from the fact that their forces constituted part of the CSR which was based *in* Malaya. Their association with AMDA meant that their contributions to Malayan defence depended in the first place on British willingness to play the role of guarantor. However, as will be shown in subsequent chapters, the flexibility of action and the reservation of positions which Australia and New Zealand could derive from their associate status were not always readily acknowledged by Kuala Lumpur, especially in times of crisis. Ironically, the fact that the status of their forces in Malaya could only be fully appreciated by reference to AMDA made it even easier for the Malayan press and public to confuse the antipodean roles with the British one.

If in 1959 Australia and New Zealand were mainly concerned over the future of their forces in Malaya, the Tunku clarified his attitude while visiting Australia in early November 1959 when he met Menzies for the first time. He subsequently added that he did not intend to ask Australian troops to leave now that the Emergency was virtually over – they provided a sense of security and helped release funds for development purposes. But he was equally clear in stating that SEATO was not popular with Malayans.[45]

Although the Tunku had told Menzies that 'one day ... these pacts [including AMDA] may be abrogated',[46] there was no question of any revaluation of Malayan policy *vis-à-vis* AMDA in the foreseeable future. This was reaffirmed to Menzies during his return visit to Kuala Lumpur in December 1959 when he reported to the Malayan Cabinet 'some objections' he had heard 'in another country'.[47] Menzies indicated Australia's readiness to withdraw its troops should the Malayan people similarly object to their presence. In return the Tunku reiterated his government's positive attitude towards the Australian troops. The following month Malaya's Defence Ministry announced the continuation of the Commonwealth military presence beyond the Emergency. Nonetheless a massive redeployment in line with their diminishing anti-terrorist role of the Commonwealth forces was necessary. By 1962 Commonwealth Land Forces would vacate all their bases in Kuala Lumpur, Sungei Besi, Sungei Patani, Ipoh and Taiping and re-establish themselves in Johore and Malacca, with the cantonment at Bukit Terendak (Malacca) as their main base. Most of the vacated bases would be given to the Federation Army.

The changing emphasis of Malaya's defence requirements in 1959 resulted in an exchange of ambiguities over the roles of the CSR. Just when emphasis was being shifted from the internal security function of the CSR, the contention over its external defence and regional roles became even sharper. The built-in flexibility of AMDA, designed to accommodate Malayan and ANZAM defence interests, was stretched by the increasing ANZAM attempts to give a clearer regional definition to Malaya's external defence. Among the ANZAM partners, recognition of the Australian role in regional defence was reflected in the decision to place the 28th Commonwealth Brigade Group in Malaya (the main unit to be at Terendak) under an Australian commander.

In 1957 both Casey and Selwyn Lloyd saw the unlikelihood of Malayan participation in SEATO before the 1959 elections.[48] Hopes of such participation were unfulfilled after the Alliance won a comfortable 74 seats out of 104 in the August Federal elections. The Tunku, though vaguely accommodating, was as unresponsive as ever in his public statement (made while visiting New Zealand in January 1960) over the indirect SEATO association. AMDA's flexibility would continue to provide an accepted framework for an evolving Malayan–ANZAM defence relationship. This had an important bearing on the subsequent inclusion in an extended Anglo–Malaysian Defence Agreement of what was considered the most important SEATO base among the ANZAM partners.

Notwithstanding the Tunku's claim of the gradual development of the Malaysia idea in his mind[49] and the strenuous lobbying by Singapore ministers, his eventual consent to merger was largely influenced by internal instability in Singapore and the perceived effects of that on the Federation. The decisive defeat of the PAP candidate at the Hong Lim by-election in April 1961 by former mayor Ong Eng Guan helped crystallise the Tunku's apprehension (which the PAP itself partly encouraged) about the political prospects of the PAP. This apprehension (later confirmed by another PAP defeat in the Anson by-election) was compounded by the approaching deadline for the review of Singapore's constitutional arrangements which, presumably, would pave the way to full independence. The Tunku feared that an independent Singapore would disallow continued Malayan representation on the ISC.[50] With the loosening of British control in Singapore, communist activities there might endanger Malayan security. The Tunku was persuaded that a situation in which an independent Singapore and the Federation would take divergent paths must be prevented. He hoped that the Malaysia proposal, with the inclusion of the Borneo territories, would diminish the security dilemma while preserving the racial 'balance'.

For AMDA, the Malaysia proposal meant a delicate exercise in accommodating the Singapore base – itself the *raison d'être* of AMDA's extension – in a defence framework that had hitherto satisfied the overlapping interests of the partners because Singapore's exclusion made it practicable to differentiate regional defence from the external defence of Malaya. The Laos crisis in April 1961 amply demonstrated the significance of AMDA's Article VIII, which was deemed to provide 'the loophole of technical withdrawal' for the CSR's redeployment (from Singapore) at short notice for SEATO purposes. This was despite the Tunku's insistence that Malaya had to consent before forces could be withdrawn and the inference that, in the circumstances prevailing, permission would be denied.[51] Similarly, during a further Laos crisis in May 1962, CSR air detachments were dispatched (those based in Malaya having first been withdrawn to Singapore) to Thailand which was allegedly being threatened by the proximity of communist forces and their operations in neighbouring Laos. On this occasion, Harold Macmillan stated that it was 'not proper that [the Tunku] should be consulted, or wished to be ... [although he had] of course been informed'.[52]

An expanded Federation whose leaders, both in Malaya and Singapore, had been consistently anti-SEATO would appear to close 'the loophole of technical withdrawal'. The Malaysia proposal did not, however, alter the basic strategic interests of the allies. As the Tunku put it, Britain had affirmed that 'with the situation as it is in Southeast Asia ... there is an absolute necessity for Britain in connection with this [Singapore] base to maintain confidence in this part of the world'.[53] Any alternative to the Singapore base was economically prohibitive and politically counter-productive to the confidence which Britain was trying to maintain, particularly *vis-à-vis*

Canberra and Wellington. Both Australia and New Zealand had a strong interest in seeing Britain remain in Singapore and thus underline its stake in the region. Nor, given the economic considerations, would the Singapore Government agitate for British withdrawal from the bases.

The economic argument was equally pertinent to Malaya, which had always recognised the close relationship between economic and defence interests. It was not disposed to accept a larger defence burden (which could not be avoided if Britain withdrew) at the expense of economic development. In October Tun Razak reiterated the economic rationale behind Malayan partnership in AMDA, reaffirmed Malayan commitment to the 'Commonwealth effort in the protection of our territories and the United Kingdom territories in this area' and broadly referred to the continued relevance of AMDA in the context of merger.[54] Furthermore, the Singapore bases were equally relevant to Malayan defence. Indeed, the Tunku had already stated after the first of the merger discussions in Kuala Lumpur that Britain would be allowed to continue using the bases in Singapore, and Lee Kuan Yew concurred that 'workmanlike solutions' could be arrived at to cover British interests in Singapore in the event of merger.[55]

There were two problems which required 'workmanlike solutions'. While the Malaysia proposal did not involve an expansion of the AMDA treaty area, AMDA provisions governing the use of bases in Malaya could not simply be extended to cover the Singapore bases without affecting their SEATO role. AMDA's Article VIII in effect linked Malaya indirectly with SEATO. It could operate because Britain retained control over the Singapore bases. But where Article VIII applied specifically to bases in Malaya, the Tunku could claim political sovereignty by arguing that the Federation had veto rights over the use of Commonwealth forces based in Malaya for operations outside the treaty area. To simply extend Article VIII to the Singapore bases would give too explicit a political control to Kuala Lumpur at the expense of the wider strategic interests of the guarantor power. In this sense the problem was similar to that faced by the AMDA negotiators who had had to devise a political formula to harmonise strategic continuity with political change. The difference was that whereas in 1956 the focus was on the Malayan acquisition of political sovereignty, the Malaysia proposal now focused on the British loss of it over Singapore. The problem was the psychological resistance to any attempts, in terms of Malayan public relations, to 'de-SEATO' the Singapore bases. Unlike the Malayan bases, Singapore was, in general public recognition, though not in a strict technical sense, 'a SEATO base'.

British reaction to the Malaysia proposal where it related to the future of the Singapore bases was understandably cautious. Although Macmillan had welcomed the Malaysia proposal in the Tunku's memorandum, his reply on 3 August 1961 sought 'to restrain [the Tunku's] impetuosity'.[56] Initially, the British faced a dilemma between the greater stability which Malaysia promised and the uncertainty of effective control over the Singapore base as a consequence of unification. The Tunku himself detected 'a note of anxiety' in the exchange of correspondence with Macmillan.[57] Indeed, Macmillan's letter had stressed that 'nothing should be said which might cast doubt on the maintenance of British defence capabilities in the area'. Furthermore, the interests of Australia and New Zealand had to be reckoned with.[58]

By Lee Kuan Yew's account, the British had not, until the beginning of October 1961, initiated negotiations with the Tunku on the Singapore bases – indeed the merger issue had not reached Cabinet level in Britain.[59] Moreover, the Tunku was (as Lee said) 'cheesed off' by Britain's attitude towards 'these defence matters' when he approached the British Government. Lee accused the British of 'wanting merger and at the same time insisting on the status quo of the military bases in Singapore'.[60] The Tunku himself was loath to initiate direct talks until Britain agreed on the basis for discussions. Lee's impatience was reflected in his threat on 30 September to 'generate heat' against the British. He also put pressure on the British Commissioner in Singapore, Lord Selkirk, to 'start talking' with Federation officials.[61] On 2 October Selkirk called upon Lee and the following day summoned his military advisers to discuss the future of the base. On 3 October the Tunku was invited by Macmillan to visit London for discussions and he set the date for November 1961.

Malaya and Singapore themselves resolved very quickly the broad defence issues arising from the Malaysia proposal in discussions in August. Lee's outburst in September against British foot-dragging was made following the joint communiqué confirming the acceptance in principle of, *inter alia*, Federation control over external defence, external affairs and internal security.[62] The two parties also agreed to bring about merger in or before June 1963 and, having decided that defence was the responsibility of the future Central Government, the Tunku was left to negotiate the status of the Singapore bases with Britain. For the British, this arrangement happily presented, in the person of the Tunku, a negotiator whose flexibility had made possible much of the useful ambiguity in AMDA. The prospect of mutual accommodation seemed good.

Up to the evening of the Tunku's departure for London, his comments on the future of the Singapore bases had consistently reflected the desire for their retention. Again on 16 November he was optimistic that the bases would continue to serve Commonwealth purposes and the defence of 'these territories' against aggression – after all, bases in Malaya were similarly used.[63] He felt, however, that Singapore could never be used as a base of operation 'in time of war' since the whole city would be 'smashed to smithereens' by a few bombs.[64] Apparently he hoped to differentiate the limited defence of Malaysia and the peacetime role of the bases from an extended SEATO scenario in which Malaysia could be drawn into an escalating conflict. The Foreign Office, for its part, emphasised Britain's commitments to its SEATO allies. These obligations would be in the forefront of any discussions about the future of Singapore and other British territories in Southeast Asia.

Of Britain's SEATO allies, Australia and New Zealand had special interests in the outcome of the negotiations. Both hoped for a balance of military advantage to emerge from their interests in SEATO and their equally strong interests in an enduring political settlement. Menzies acknowledged that if the Malaysia plan proved practicable it would enhance stability and progress in an area in which Australia was deeply interested. There was, however, some public anxiety in Australia over the future use of Singapore for SEATO purposes, with the *Sydney Morning Herald* advocating a joint Anglo-Australian base at Darwin.[65] New Zealand was explicit in expressing its expectations on the base issue. Its Defence Review in September clearly mentioned SEATO as one area 'of primary strategic interest' and declared that, with the anti-terrorist war virtually won in Malaya, the ground elements of the CSR would assume 'the role which that title implies – that of a contribution to a standing force ready to counter aggression in Southeast Asia'.[66] On 3 November New Zealand's Defence Minister, Dean Eyre, expressed certainty that the formation of Malaysia would not diminish SEATO's strength. The Federation was inclined to let Britain find a solution to these divergent demands. As Tun Razak indicated, 'Singapore is a British problem. It will be up to them to suggest a satisfactory solution.'[67]

The conference was opened on 20 November 1961 by Macmillan, who fully accepted the principles of the Malaysia plan without minimising the difficulties of working out the details. The Tunku emphasised that speed was essential to the negotiations. Neither party could afford to await the normal processes of political evolution.[68] The future of the bases was dealt with the following day. Razak's reply to the opening remarks (by Sandys and Defence Secretary Sir Harold (later Lord) Watkinson) reportedly reaffirmed that the base problem could be solved provided Britain appreciated that the defence of Southeast Asia against communism was equally a political and a military matter. Neither Malaya nor Singapore was prepared to allow the Singapore base to be used for SEATO purposes but, given Britain's Commonwealth commitments, the Federation would contemplate an extension of the existing terms of AMDA.

The negotiations were speedily concluded one day ahead of schedule. The Malayan delegation readily accepted the British formula on defence arrangements as laid out in Annex B of the Joint Statement signed on 22 November. Moreover, the tedium of renegotiating AMDA was avoided. Annex B merely extended the 1957 Agreement 'to apply to all territories of the Federation of Malaysia'.[69] This extension, however, was 'subject to the proviso' that the Malaysian Government would afford the British

> the right to continue to maintain the bases and other facilities at present occupied by their service authorities [in Singapore] and will permit the United Kingdom to make such use of these bases and facilities as the United Kingdom may consider necessary for the purpose of assisting in the defence of Malaysia and for Commonwealth defence and for the preservation of peace in Southeast Asia.[70]

The British press quickly seized upon this wording as evidence that Britain would have unhampered use of the Singapore base for SEATO purposes, while the Tunku, perturbed by their bold headlines, sought to clarify that 'the terms under which Britain is allowed to use the Singapore bases are no different than those which exist at present under ... [AMDA]'.[71] Although Article III of AMDA was specifically referred to by the Tunku, nowhere in that Article was 'the preservation of peace in Southeast Asia' mentioned as a role of the CSR. Yet the 'international obligations' which the CSR was to fulfil were even then sufficiently ambiguous to give Malaya a SEATO association. The new provisions, with respect to the Singapore bases, show more clearly that SEATO was in British minds when they considered the 'preservation of peace in Southeast Asia'. This was certainly how Duncan Sandys saw it.[72]

Strictly speaking, Singapore was always a British but never a SEATO base and the British could easily concede that they had no right to transfer its control to any other treaty organisation. Nor could any other power be invited to use the base without Malaysian consent. What really mattered was Britain's use of the base to discharge its SEATO obligations, and the controversy increasingly centred on the issue of political sovereignty as Malaya was forced to fall back on its claim to sovereign rights when it became apparent that Singapore had a SEATO connection. Malayan emphasis was directed at the right to be consulted. The most direct statement of this came from Razak, who said: 'The sovereignty of the Base lies with us. The British Government cannot make use of the Base without consulting us.'[73] But what would happen if Malaya was consulted but not heeded? Sandys had explicitly said that 'we must be free to use our forces in the area in whatever way we consider most effective'.[74] The revealing answer came from the Tunku when closely questioned in Parliament by S. P. Seenivasagam. While still rigorously denying that Singapore was 'a SEATO Base', he replied that, 'if the consultation does not produce the result which would enable . . . [Britain] to use the Base for the purpose she wants, then *perhaps* [emphasis mine] it would be in her interest to accept . . . [Malaysia's] views'. But he also concurred that this meant in effect that Britain had the right to use the base without Malaysian consent.[75]

It could be argued that, in the extreme case of a regional flare-up where Malaysia's security was at stake, its government could not afford to be particular about sovereign rights. But there were also conceivable 'SEATO situations' in which Malaysia, whose central interest might not be affected, would wish to differentiate its stand. In such an instance it would appear that both the legal argument of Annex B and the hard strategic facts of life would tend to favour Britain as the provider of Malaysian security. Subsequent Malaysian insistence on the necessity for consultations should be interpreted in this light. The act of consultation was significant because it was the one, if not the only, means whereby some appearance of Malaysian 'control' could be maintained, particularly when, as the Tunku himself stressed, treaties were 'not all that important'.[76]

The 1961 Agreement which extended AMDA as a result of the formation of Malaysia was, in short, an extension of the practical ambiguity of AMDA. In its deliberate flexibility, Annex B reflected much of the style that went into the negotiation of AMDA. As the Tunku explained: 'Britain has one interpretation and we have a different one. The wording is such that it gives both of us a chance to explain to our Parliaments.'[77] The useful ambiguity of the 1961 Agreement was equally satisfactory to both New Zealand and Australia, whose rationale of forward defence would have been threatened by a rigid differentiation of the role of the Singapore base. With the successful conclusion of the 1961 Agreement, the preliminary phase of AMDA's extension was completed. Its *de facto* extension, including the formal association with it of the antipodes, was to be completed in a crisis when AMDA itself was put to the test and when the overlapping circles of interest which AMDA comprised were stretched by external forces.

5. THE EXTERNAL TESTING OF AMDA

Among other things, the Malaysia proposal involved additional defence burdens for Kuala Lumpur. Rapid expansion of local military forces and Malayanisation of the senior army posts were necessary. A three-year blueprint for the defence of the Malaysian region (announced in September 1962) envisaged a doubling of the air force's manpower, a near doubling of that of the navy and an increase by a third of that of the army.[1] The expansion was concentrated on peninsula-based forces. There were no immediate plans to station Malayan units in the Borneo territories, nor was a third battalion suggested for Singapore. Indeed, this military expansion, compared to the doubling of territorial responsibility, was modest. The M$90 million defence expenditure for 1962 represented a mere 9% of Malaya's expenditure on current account. Furthermore, the projected expansion depended heavily on anticipated external financial assistance.

The establishment and financing of a Malaysian force was discussed *inter alia*, in London in July 1962, when it was agreed that the new Federation would be inaugurated on 31 August 1963. However, discussions on the financing of Malaya's defence were inconclusive and further talks were scheduled for September. Apparently Britain fell short of Malaya's expectations and, on returning to Kuala Lumpur, the Tunku indicated that contributions from Australia and New Zealand would be welcomed.[2] Rapid development of the Malayan armed forces within the very short period before 31 August 1963 proved to be a major problem. But there was an absence of undue Malayan anxiety on account of Britain's extended protective role. Indeed, despite the political consequences for Kuala Lumpur of overreliance on British protection at that juncture, pressing economic priorities and the time needed to establish a credible indigenous defence force for the vastly increased territories necessitated a continued assumption by Britain of the main burden of Malaysian defence.

More importantly, the 'threat factor' which Kuala Lumpur had identified in its rationale for territorial enlargement was essentially the containment of communism (backed at long range by China) in Singapore. There were early ominous signs from Indonesia – the Indonesian Communist Party (PKI), which enjoyed a position of influence with Sukarno, was first to denounce Malaysia in a resolution passed at the end of December 1961. But, despite the official Philippine claim to North Borneo in June 1962, an external threat was remote for most of 1962 since Indonesia did not officially oppose the Malaysia plan until after the Brunei revolt.

Britain, in turn, had reassuringly spelt out in the February 1962 Defence White Paper its intention to carry out its 'obligations for the protection of British territories overseas and those to whom we owe a special duty by treaty or otherwise'.[3] Britain reaffirmed its 'responsibility for assisting in the forward defence of Australia and New Zealand', with whom were shared 'a close concern for the defence of . . . Malaya for which Britain accepted obligations' under the 1957 Agreement.[4] The White Paper also reproduced the provisions for AMDA's extension with the advent of Malaysia.

The future of the Singapore base and the Commonwealth military presence were two aspects of the Malaysia plan with special relevance to the antipodes. Sir Garfield Barwick, who became Australia's External Affairs Minister in December 1961, was assured of Kuala Lumpur's desire to retain a Commonwealth force during his visit there between 28 June and 1 July 1962.[5] The defence implications of the new Federation had been discussed in Singapore among ANZAM Defence Ministers on 23 March 1962. Although the question of an alternative base in Western Australia was obliquely raised, the meeting concurred on the need to retain the Singapore base.[6] Nor, as the British Defence Minister, Sir Harold Watkinson, indicated, was there to be any change in the external role of the base.[7] However, the internal security function of British forces in Singapore would change as this responsibility would pass to the Central Government.

Although the British Governors of North Borneo and Sarawak had reservations initially over rapid decolonisation, it was hoped that Malaysia would 'contribute to regional stability'. Such a federation had certain attractions for Britain, increasingly reconciled to colonial disengagement yet tenaciously upholding its peace-keeping role and with substantial economic interests in the area. Malaysia would unify the disparate and seemingly unviable territories under a proven indigenous leadership while the extended AMDA would enable Britain to discharge its responsibilities for Malaysian and regional defence. The containment of internal unrest would be increasingly Kuala Lumpur's responsibility, but external security would be necessarily underpinned by Britain. AMDA made explicit an assumption that the new state should be provided with a stable external environment.

Intertwined with post-colonial obligations were wider strategic considerations stemming partly from Britain's view of itself as a 'Great Power' and reflected, for example, in the remark by the Shadow Foreign Secretary, Gordon-Walker, that 'we have a common interest in maintaining the balance of stability in this part of the world'. More forthrightly, the Shadow Colonial Secretary, Arthur Bottomley, commented that: 'Malaysia is being created to contain Communism.'[8] Bottomley also saw Britain's role in terms of its moderating influence on Kuala Lumpur, particularly with regard to the evident tension between Kuala Lumpur and Singapore.[9] These different views of Britain's role all assumed a continuing and substantial British presence.

Conversely, it may be argued that Britain's act of decolonisation was a prelude to an abandonment of the East of Suez role. According to Milne and Ratnam, one reason why Donald (later Tun Mohammed Fu'ad) Stephens (a prominent North Borneo leader, subsequently its first Chief Minister) switched to supporting Malaysia was that 'some months after the Tengku's ... proposal, a British Conservative leader had told him that a withdrawal would occur by about 1972'.[10] A similar view (with deadlines unmentioned) was conveyed to a visiting Australian parliamentary delegation in 1963 by Lord Selkirk, the British Commissioner-General for Southeast Asia. The Australians were urged to assume greater responsibility for the stability of the area.[11]

Among the British Labour Opposition, a certain scepticism existed over the generally accepted value of the East of Suez role. This early scepticism (expressed by some Labour MPs who later played important roles in Government) went beyond the means of policy to a questioning of objectives. Denis Healey wondered whether certain substantial British overseas commitments were not politically or strategically irrelevant in the contemporary context.[12] Moreover, as Healey later argued, there was the dubious assumption 'that the status quo could be buttressed by alliances and large-scale military aid'.[13] Christopher Mayhew felt that the British role in Singapore needed clarification. If Britain had an internal security role in supporting Lee Kuan Yew, what would the political repercussions be? And if Britain was there for the external defence of Malaya and Singapore, how real was the immediate threat and did it justify the expenditure on the Singapore base?[14] Other prominent Labour MPs who in the 1960–1 period criticised the overseas role on the basis of over-stretched commitments included George Brown and Richard Crossman. Indeed: 'On the Labour side, only George Wigg ... firmly defended the East of Suez emphasis.'[15]

Much of the criticism in Britain against the East of Suez role hinged on some vague long-term hope of phasing out commitments. Those who either pointed to, or argued for, an eventual British withdrawal had differing motives: Donald Stephen's Conservative informer might have sought to influence his attitude towards Malaysia. Lord Selkirk hoped to extract firmer Australian contributions to Malaysian defence. And Labour critics could have been motivated by a desire for a higher priority for European defence or for social services. However, these publicly expressed attitudes reinforced local awareness that the British commitment could not be indefinite. Indeed, Tun Razak stated in London in May 1963 that Malaysia had no such expectations, although 'for the interim period – perhaps until 1970, we will certainly require aid'.[16]

But long-term aspirations and medium-term objectives were not necessarily in conflict. For the purpose of stabilising the Malaysian environment, the important factor was *medium-term* British defence objectives. And here both the stress on strategic mobility and the capacity for operational deployment in the 1960–1 period suggested an increased interest in the East of Suez commitments. The 1962 Defence White Paper saw the problem in terms of sustaining commitments in spite of the possible loss of overseas bases. The answer was greater mobility. In the event, the external challenges with which Malaysia was faced during its early years enhanced Britain's commitment to AMDA. For a time the early criticisms of the East of Suez role paled into the background.

From the Tunku's public proposal of Malaysia on 26 May 1961, events moved rapidly towards the realisation of the plan. On 28 July 1961 a Commonwealth Parliamentary Association Regional Meeting was held in Singapore where the idea of federation was discussed by leaders of the five states concerned. By February 1962 the

Malaysia Solidarity Consultative Committee, which grew out of the meeting in Singapore, had endorsed the plan. Subsequently, a Commission of Enquiry under Lord Cobbold assessed and reported favourably (if with some qualification) on the views of North Borneo and Sarawak on federation (the Sultan of Brunei being consulted separately). Terms of union were discussed by an Intergovernmental Committee under Lord Lansdowne and, when the four states (Brunei having opted out) and Britain had reached agreement, the Malaysia Act and attendant legislation were passed in July 1963.

These rapid developments were followed before their completion by certain external responses which challenged the Malaysia concept and, with the realisation of Malaysia, threatened its security. Of three crises which faced the nascent Federation, the Brunei revolt and, more crucially, Indonesia's Confrontation policy had a direct bearing on AMDA and its associates. Less important from the defence angle, but central to the transfer of power in the region, was the Philippine claim to North Borneo (later renamed Sabah).

This was the first of the three crises to occur. Briefly, the Philippine claim centred on the contention that the predecessors of the British North Borneo Company (whose territorial assets had been incorporated as a British Crown Colony in 1946) were private lessees and could not have acquired sovereignty through a contract signed with the Sultan of Sulu in 1878. The claim, dormant since 1946, was resurrected at the imminent prospect of the incorporation of the territories within Malaysia. The election to office in November 1961 of President Macapagal (with a record of previous involvement with the claim) and the crusading by the *Philippine Free Press* throughout early 1962 together contributed to subsequent official Filipino association with the claim.

Initially, Kuala Lumpur treated the claim as an issue in Anglo-Philippine relations, but with the creation of Malaysia Kuala Lumpur acquired a crucial interest in the dispute. And as it interacted with the Confrontation crisis, the Tunku was drawn into tripartite diplomacy with the Philippines and Indonesia. Yet, as a crisis in Malaysian–Philippine relations, the claim did not extend beyond the diplomatic arena. And, although it culminated in the rupture of diplomatic links between Kuala Lumpur and Manila in September 1963, it was not until 1968 that it was perceived as a major threat to the territorial integrity of Malaysia and hence of direct concern within AMDA. Whatever the defence implications of the initial phase of the dispute, these related to SEATO (to which Britain and the Philippines belonged) rather than to AMDA. But the Philippines itself had stressed that the claim was to be pursued pacifically with due regard to SEATO. Although the leader of the Brunei revolt, A. M. Azahari, was in Manila when the rebellion erupted and received unofficial financial support and sympathetic hearing from high officials, the Philippines remained uncommitted to Azahari whose plans for a unitary Bornean state ran embarrassingly counter to the Philippines' claim to Sabah.

The substance and political motives behind the Philippines' claim and the resulting diplomatic manoeuvrings will not be discussed here. Such manoeuvrings, however, overlapped with the Confrontation crisis at certain points and will be discussed where they had a bearing on the latter crisis. The brief reference here to the claim provides a background to, and a comparison with, the circumstances of a crisis following the revival of the issue in 1968 when it did pose a problem within AMDA.

Even as the Sabah claim was being made, a violent but unsuccessful challenge to Malaysia was initiated in Brunei where a major source of opposition was the Brunei Party Ra'ayat founded by Azahari in 1956. By winning most of the contested seats in the first district council elections on 30 August 1962, it had secured all the indirectly elected seats in the Brunei Legislative Council. An important ingredient in Azahari's opposition to Malaysia was his advocacy of the reunification of Borneo under the Brunei sultanate. As the campaign for Malaysia intensified, so Azahari's movement progressed.

At 2 a.m. on 8 December 1962 (Azahari having departed for Manila) armed rebellion, mounted by the so-called North Borneo National Army (TNKU) erupted in Brunei. The insurgents rapidly seized control of the Seria oilfields, where they took several European hostages, and attacked the police station and other Government buildings in Brunei town. Incidents also occurred in adjoining areas of North Borneo and Sarawak.[17] An attempt to capture the Sultan and make him legitimise the revolution failed, whereupon the Sultan proceeded to summon British assistance. A 1959 treaty obliged Britain to assist in restoring law and order in the protectorate. Kuala Lumpur was also involved: first, because of the political ramifications for the Malaysia proposal; second, because of the precedent set by the practical assistance rendered by Malaya to the

Brunei civil service and to the training of military personnel; and third, because Brunei, as a British protectorate, fell within the treaty area (Article VII) of AMDA.

Azahari's connections with Malaya's Party Ra'ayat and Labour Party, as well as with the Singapore Barisan Sosialis, and his frequent visits to Singapore, Malaya and Indonesia during 1961–2 attracted Kuala Lumpur's and Singapore's attention. Lee Kuan Yew suspected Manila's and Jakarta's involvement and promptly flew to Kuala Lumpur for consultations. Malayan Intelligence had possessed foreknowledge of the revolt and on 2 December the Tunku had accordingly informed Lord Selkirk, who immediately visited North Borneo, Sarawak and Brunei.[18] But as the *Straits Times* observed, the enquiry led 'to a smug reassurance' that was falsified in 48 hours.[19] Duncan Sandys denied Malayan allegations of British unpreparedness and claimed that the new warnings corresponded to earlier false alarms.[20] The absence of pre-emptive measures, however, suggested that the imminence of serious trouble was discounted. This did not represent a departure from the predetermined doctrine of strategic mobility. If Britain did not prevent the brushfire in the first place, it did, as events proved, rapidly extinguish it.

Limited resources and political expediency restricted Malaya's response to the despatch of 150 policemen to maintain public order. Even then, Denis Healey feared that Malaya's gesture might be misconstrued as coercion since the revolt had a strong anti-Malaysia ingredient and since the Sultan himself had not finally decided on accession to the Federation.[21] For Britain the uprising was a test of strategic mobility and of the efficiency of the newly unified services' command in Singapore. The first Gurkhas, together with 280 British troops, were flown out from Singapore within 12 hours of the insurrection. Their numbers reached 2,000 within two days. Seria was recaptured on 11 December, and from then on organised resistance disintegrated. The last two rebel strongholds in North Sarawak were captured on 15 December, but mopping-up operations continued in the jungle and swamp areas. British service casualties totalled 8 killed and 28 wounded, while the rebels lost between 50 and 60 killed and about 2,000 captured.[22]

The revolt, in so far as it was a definable issue within AMDA, called for a demonstration of support from the AMDA associates. And Britain did approach them for assistance. On 10 and 14 December, Holyoake and Barwick respectively announced their

Government's agreement to commit their transport aircraft in Singapore to ferry British troops and supplies to Brunei. To emphasise their concerted responses, Barwick reaffirmed the New Zealand and Malayan offers of assistance.[23] As open revolt paled into guerrilla insurgency, Britain switched to jungle warfare tactics and on 16 December Major-General W. C. Walker (who had directed the Malayan jungle war) assumed the newly created post of Director of Operations in Command of British Forces, Borneo Territories.

Although the Brunei revolt was short lived, it was admittedly costly to Britain in financial and manpower terms. The crisis had necessitated the dispatch of one battalion from the Strategic Reserve in England and the cancellation of the move of No. 247 Gurkha Signals Company to the Rhine Army and, as Denis Healey observed, had compelled Britain to place half the Strategic Reserve on alert and to plan to employ a full regiment of artillery – minus its guns – in an infantry role.[24] While Healey, George Wigg and Gordon-Walker saw these moves as evidence of the Strategic Reserve being dangerously overstretched, the Government, on the other hand, argued that the force was being used as it should be and that the redeployment merely illustrated its flexibility. Indeed, British forces in Europe, as Darby observed, 'were regarded as a manpower reserve for the world role and few senior officers saw anything imprudent in withdrawing certain of these units in an emergency'.[25]

Besides testing British mobility, the revolt also demonstrated the significant role of the Singapore base. Readily available forces in Singapore and the proximity of base facilities to the crisis area helped greatly to translate a strategic doctrine into strategic action. The response of Malaya and the AMDA associates reflected their varying interests. Kuala Lumpur's reaction was constrained by limited resources and by political expediency. Australia and New Zealand did not exceed their offers of transport aircraft. Even then, Australia was conscious of its position *vis-à-vis* the Philippines and Indonesia. Barwick quickly welcomed 'the clear and categorical assurances' by the Philippines of non-involvement and, with an eye on Indonesia, emphasised the importance 'for peace and confidence among neighbouring countries in the area that there be no interference in the settlement of what is essentially a domestic situation'.[26]

The early suppression of the revolt saved both Canberra and

Wellington from the prospect of committing their ground forces to Brunei. The revolt, however, served as a catalyst to a more dangerous crisis, in the wake of which the partners to Malaysian defence were called upon to make even clearer definitions of their interests and much greater allocations of military resources.

A growing acrimony had developed between Malaya and Indonesia following the Tunku's parliamentary statement on 11 December 1962 that the Brunei rebels had received support from the PKI and other 'foreign parties'.[27] The first official Indonesian reference to 'Confrontation' was made by Foreign Minister Subandrio on 20 January 1963.[28] Subandrio's statement (following the precedent of the use of coercive diplomacy adopted to wrest West New Guinea from the Dutch, against whom the term 'Confrontation' was initially applied) heralded 'a pattern of intense diplomatic pressure, press campaigns, mobilisation of public opinion and threat of military force'[29] against Malaysia. Indeed, Indonesian pressure subsequently extended to territorial incursions and limited guerrilla war.

Sukarno's coercive diplomacy sought to challenge the legitimacy of Malaysia and to abort its formation. But after the advent of the Federation the momentum of Confrontation had to be sustained, indeed intensified, partly to justify an existing policy and partly to excommunicate Malaysia from the international system. In terms of domestic Indonesian politics, Confrontation served the competitive requirements of Guided Democracy.[30] It is possible that elements of external ambition were interwoven with the policy of Confrontation; certainly there was an underlying resentment of major political and territorial change in the vicinity of Indonesia. Finally, Confrontation fitted into an aspect of the revisionist ideology of Indonesia which viewed international politics in terms of contention between the 'New Emerging Forces' and the 'Old Established Forces'. Malaysia was accordingly condemned for sustaining the British military presence through AMDA.

To the Tunku, Subandrio's reference to Confrontation amounted to 'a direct attack on Malaya'.[31] Malaya's own military strength at the beginning of 1963 could not be expected to meet effectively an overt, or covert, threat from Indonesia with its 300,000-strong army, a mainly Russian-equipped navy and a numerically formidable (at least on paper) air force of over 400 planes. Further defence problems were posed by the geography of Malaysia. The Borneo territories are separated by 800 km of international waters from peninsular Malaya, itself with a 1,280 km coastline which at points runs to within 32 km of Indonesia's fortified Rhio Islands. Malaya already had to deal with a 500-strong residual communist force along the Thai border. The formation of Malaysia would add another 1,552 km of land frontier, traversing equatorial forest, with Indonesian Borneo. The Tunku was thus obliged to stress the significance of the British commitment under AMDA.

Malayan apprehension was aroused first by Indonesia's refusal to declare non-involvement, then by the announcement of Confrontation followed by the extension of Indonesian bomber patrols along the Borneo territories to the approaches to Singapore and southern Malaya, and finally by reports of 'Indonesian volunteers' massing on the Borneo border. The Tunku was sufficiently alarmed to request that British Strategic Reserve troops be placed on the alert to fly to the Far East.

Within the first week of February two incidents involving Indonesian gunboats were reported, one off the southeast coast of Johore and the other in the Straits of Malacca. In the same week, Indonesian bombers twice flew within 64 km of Singapore but turned back when interceptors were deployed. Malayan attempts to pre-empt a possible internal conspiracy complementary to the external threat were manifested in the mass arrest during the early hours of 2 February of 107 (later rising to 118) pro-communist and left-wing suspects in Singapore.

Confrontation also necessitated a Malaysian strategic response. It is, however, difficult to make a clear distinction between Malaysian and British strategic thinking since in many respects British advisers played significant roles in Malaysian defence. Nevertheless, Kuala Lumpur's response, especially after Malaysia's formation, can be seen, first, in terms of the political expediency of demonstrating that Confrontation was the Federation's war; and second, given the British defence guarantee, in the need to trigger British action.

The Malayan response, which began with increased naval patrols in territorial waters and the cancellation of relief troops for the Malayan force then assisting in UN peace-keeping in the Congo, intensified when Subandrio, on 11 February, referred to possible 'incidents of physical conflict'.[32] Two days later Sukarno publicly associated himself with Confrontation. After a Cabinet meeting on 13 February, Tun Razak announced immediate steps to expand Malaya's armed forces. The immediate build-up of the three

Malayan services meant a 3% increase in their overall strength, then numbering between 12,000 and 15,000 men. At the end of May 1963 Parliament approved a M$75 million blueprint for the first phase of the build-up. For the first time since Independence, Malaya's defence expenditure exceeded 10% of its budget.[33]

The immediacy of the threat, however, called for swift British assurances of treaty commitments to Malaysian defence. Within a week of Razak's announcement on 13 February, the CIGS, General Sir Richard Hull, arrived in Kuala Lumpur to discuss British assistance. He was emphatic that Britain had every intention of honouring AMDA. In the testing months ahead, this pledge was echoed by the Commanders-in-Chief, the British High Commissioner and British Ministers.

Prompt British reaction might seem the mere observance of commitments in Articles VI and VII of AMDA. But in spite of Kuala Lumpur's response (in the period between the commencement of Confrontation and Malaysia Day), which suggested the playing of a *de facto* Malaysian role, the threat had been felt primarily in what were still effectively Britain's Bornean territories. Strictly speaking, Malaya's response during the first nine months of Confrontation followed the Brunei pattern of 'going to Britain's assistance . . . in pursuance of our obligations under the Mutual Defence Treaty'. Only after Malaysia was proclaimed was it 'no longer Britain's war'.[34] The Tunku, too, exploited this point in arguing for more defence aid from Britain.[35]

In fact, Kuala Lumpur's contribution to that period of 'Britain's war' was insubstantial because its military expansion had only just begun. However, Confrontation stimulated an accelerated expansion and engendered the need to dispatch Malayan troops to Borneo; first, to demonstrate solidarity with, and give reassurance to, the Borneo territories; and second, with the formation of Malaysia, to demonstrate that Confrontation had now become 'Malaysia's war'.

Britain's own reaction to the first attack in Sarawak by Indonesian-based guerrillas on 12 April 1963 had been swift and followed the pattern of strategic deployment in Brunei. At that time there were still about 3,000 British troops stationed in Borneo engaged in mopping-up operations against the Brunei rebels. The existing command structure facilitated the rapid dispatch of reinforcements from Singapore, which were also placed under General Walker. The

The external testing of AMDA 69

strong military response could have been motivated by the expectation of long-term and more serious direct Indonesian involvement.

Evidence of direct Indonesian involvement in the terrorist attacks in Sarawak since April was finally displayed in Kuching on 21 August 1963. The Colonial Office affirmed proof of Indonesian 'complicity' in seventeen major incidents in Sarawak over the past few months.[36] Indonesian 'complicity' ranged from the organising, equipping, training and provision of sanctuary to TNKU remnants, Azahari's rebels, the Clandestine Communist Organisation (whose members had come from Sarawak) and assorted Indonesian volunteer groups, to the increasing participation by regular Indonesian troops in the escalation of Confrontation.

While Britain underlined its commitment to AMDA, it also attempted to solicit a demonstration of solidarity, if not material support, from the AMDA associates. In February 1963, when General Sir Richard Hull bluntly declared in Kuala Lumpur the British intention of 'honouring AMDA', he was *en route* to Canberra to attend an ANZAM Defence Committee Meeting – a routine matter, which, however, excited unusual interest because of Confrontation. General Hull conferred with the Chairman of the Australian and New Zealand Chiefs of Staff Committees and with the Permanent Heads of the Australian Defence Department, of the Prime Minister's Department and of the External Affairs Department on 27 and 28 February.[37] The tension over Malaysia, the question of the future status and role of Australian and New Zealand forces within the CSR and the likely consequences of open hostilities were discussed. Hull pointed out publicly on 28 February that it was up to Australia to decide on its military commitment to Malaysia – the position then being that Australian troops would remain in Malaya until after 31 August (the original Malaysia Day) without commitments beyond that. For his part, Hull had emphasised that Britain was committed '500 per cent, if need be'.[38]

Hull attempted to put pressure on Canberra by openly revealing on 27 February, and again on 5 March, the nature of ANZAM. The Australian Government had feared that publicity might compel them to explain their commitments to the CSR. Hull revealed that ANZAM met on an *ad hoc* basis over matters in the Malayan area and that CSR deployment fell within its purview.[39] Given Indonesia's Confrontation, such disclosures created an expectation of impending decision over Australian forces in Malaya.

Following closely on the ANZAM consultations, Lord Selkirk arrived in Canberra on 3 March from a private holiday in New Zealand. At the same time, Mr T. K. Critchley, who had close contacts with Indonesian and Malayan leaders and who since 1955 had been the Australian High Commissioner in Kuala Lumpur, was recalled for consultation. Selkirk and Critchley had each spoken to the Tunku and to Sukarno in the previous week. Both diplomats were well placed to brief the Australian Government and to convey accurately the British and Malayan expectations of Australia's response. On arrival Selkirk immediately conferred with Menzies and, the following day, met External Affairs officials, including the Secretary, Sir Arthur Tange, who, on 14 February, had flown to Washington at short notice to solicit support for the Malaysia idea.[40]

On 5 March Selkirk and Critchley attended the first full session of the Australian Cabinet summoned to consider Confrontation exclusively. Confrontation presented Canberra with an awkward dilemma for, if pressed to take a less ambiguous position over Malaysia's defence, it would be obliged to make an invidious choice between supporting a traditional Southeast Asian ally and risking the antagonism of a much larger and increasingly restive neighbour with which a common land frontier was to be shared in West Irian/Papua New Guinea from 1 May 1963.

If strategic considerations had earlier created an Australian interest in continued Dutch occupation of West New Guinea (West Irian),[41] the *fait accompli* of Indonesian control of West Irian dictated caution lest Confrontation affect adversely Australia's security. This restrained approach was emphasised by Barwick who gave high priority to cultivating understanding of, and good relations with, Australia's Southeast Asian neighbours, of which Indonesia was the nearest and most powerful.[42]

For Australian policy makers, however, the tolerable position was contemplated as one in which they could avoid having to choose, i.e. support for Malaysia without jeopardising relations with Indonesia. Jakarta, in turn, showed itself adept at exploiting this dilemma: Confrontation, directed mainly at London and Kuala Lumpur, was not represented as an open quarrel with Canberra.

Faced with this dilemma, Canberra resolved on 5 March to support politically the Malaysia plan while underplaying its military implications. The role of Australian forces in the CSR was left ambiguous. Barwick reaffirmed that the creation of Malaysia was 'the best solution for the future of the Borneo territories' and deserved support 'as a major act of orderly decolonisation'.[43] The CSR and the future role of Australian forces in Malaysia were not mentioned.

The ECAFE meeting in Manila between 10 and 14 March provided Barwick with an opportunity to meet with Macapagal, the Philippine Vice-President, Palaez and Dr Subandrio. While disclaiming any mediatory role, Barwick gave 'positive encouragement' to Macapagal's proposal for tripartite talks between the Philippines, Indonesia and Malaysia.[44] But he added pointedly that he understood the talks were not to frustrate or delay Malaysia.

The Barwick–Subandrio discussions were less fruitful. Indeed, the Indonesian Ambassador to Australia, General Suadi, disclosed that their countries had agreed to differ over Malaysia.[45] While optimistic about a diplomatic settlement, Australia was nevertheless worried by a restive Indonesia. The Australian Cabinet meeting of 5 March had examined the security situation and called for progress reports on defence measures. Although it was widely believed that Hull and Selkirk both discounted the likelihood of open war between Malaysia and Indonesia, the consequences of Indonesian opposition were difficult to predict.

This uncertainty, coupled with the impending occupation of West Irian by Indonesia, encouraged Australian restraint. Moreover, Australia's defence capability was deficient. As the *Sydney Morning Herald* observed, the existing defence programme took no account of Indonesia's military power or of Australia's need for a self-contained military capacity. The RAN had been relegated to an anti-submarine force, while the army could maintain in the field, apart from the battalion in Malaya, only one battle group of 3,000 men.[46] The air force, like the fleet air arm, had no strike capacity against sophisticated air defences and was no match for the Soviet fighters of the Indonesian air force.[47] The growing sense of vulnerability subsequently became an issue in the October 1963 Federal elections, culminating in Menzies' decision to purchase two squadrons of American F-111 aircraft. Already Australia had, in February 1963, announced the decision to acquire another 40 Mirage fighters, thus bringing the total on order to 100. These long-range measures, however, could not be expected to produce 'instant security'.

Circumstances underlined Australia's reliance on 'great and powerful friends'. Yet, as T. B. Millar argued, 'we must *produce* security if we are to *consume* it'[48] (Millar's emphases) and, given Confrontation, that involved a demonstration of solidarity with Britain. But an unequivocal definition of the Australian military role in Malaya (Canberra's 'club fees' for regional security) risked great instability in Australia's immediate locality. In such an event, Australia would require reassurance and protection from its other 'great and powerful friend', the United States. The Tange mission in February 1963 reflected an Australian desire for some expression of shared political attitudes, if not policies, between itself and its two major allies prior to its open declaration of support for Malaysia. However, despite President Kennedy's blessing, the US posture remained one of 'non-involved cordiality', with Malaysia seen primarily as Britain's responsibility. The US feared that antagonising Indonesia or the Philippines could only benefit the PKI. American readiness, publicly expressed in June 1963, to define ANZUS to include Papua New Guinea, left at this period a persisting ambiguity over the question of a similar guarantee to Australian forces in the Malaysia area.[49] This uncertainty involved the Australian Government in endless controversy with the ALP and constrained Australian military support for Malaysia. On the other hand, Britain's firm commitment to Malaysian defence necessitated some Australian response if ANZAM co-operation were to look credible. Hence the decision (announced on 5 March) to dispatch half the RAN's combat fleet of six warships, including its flagship, to Southeast Asian waters for a two-months' exercise with other CSR components.[50]

That announcement, together with Barwick's declared approval of Malaysia and Menzies' decision to give 'prompt considerations' to security and defence measures, was interpreted by the *Sydney Morning Herald* as evidence of a 'firm attitude' towards Indonesia.[51] It might have been what prompted the Tunku to inform a rally at Malacca on 10 March that AMDA obliged Britain and Australia to support Malaya in the event of a war resulting from Confrontation. The CRO in London concurred with the Tunku's interpretation of Britain's obligations, but the Australian Government maintained an embarrassed silence. The following day the Tunku was obliged to explain to Parliament that what he actually said at Malacca was that Australia, a Commonwealth member, had openly supported Malaysia. Australia, too, 'would surely rally to our help'. If his statement had been misconstrued to read that Australia had committed itself to fight alongside Malaya, then he would apologise for the embarrassment caused.[52] To Australia, the Tunku's Malacca speech, which coincided with Barwick's Manila trip, was ill timed, although the Tunku might have viewed it as opportune for Malaya to signal its unease. Indeed, the Tunku referred in Parliament to Indonesian attempts to 'isolate' Malaya from its allies. Sukarno was due on a state visit to Australia and Subandrio was now trying to impress Australia with his country's peaceful intentions. 'Once they achieved this split, Indonesia would walk in with all the forces at her command.'[53]

This episode reflected the difficulty facing Australia as both consumer and provider of alliance security. Australia's AMDA association entrenched a certain expectation in Kuala Lumpur which drew increasing attention to the nature of Australia's military deployments in Malaya. Barwick's reticence on his return from Manila merely fuelled speculation about the role of Australian forces in Malaya. He declined to define Australia's military position in the 'hypothetical' event of Indonesian aggression against Malaya and would only restate the obvious fact of Australia's association with the CSR, adding, 'we have no commitment in any formal sense'.[54] Further probings when Parliament reconvened in late March (following a recess which coincided with the Brunei revolt and the exchange of invective between Malaya and Indonesia) elicited little. Barwick's promised statement on 28 March was 'little more than a recapitulation of previous benedictions, together with a useful précis of the Cobbold and Lansdowne Reports',[55] which respectively assessed Bornean opinion and devised constitutional arrangements for the new Federation. Reference to this statement was Menzies' standard reply to all persistent parliamentary queries during the following month.

Given Indonesia's Confrontation policy, Canberra sought to keep its options open. One common feature in all of Barwick's statements on the Australian 'commitment' during the early stages of Confrontation was the emphasis on the absence of a formal 'military alliance with Malaya, although its security is of direct significance and importance to us'. On 26 March he reiterated Australia's right of control over the use of its forces in the CSR 'in assisting the performance of the British obligation'[56] although, as he subsequently explained, the fact that Malayan security was a direct concern of Australia would undoubtedly influence its decision on the employment of these forces.[57] The position with respect to the Borneo territories on their incorporation in Malaysia was even more ambiguous.

The status of Australian forces in Malaya was indirectly defined in the 1959 Exchange of Letters which associated Australia with AMDA. Barwick produced these Letters for the first time in parliament on 27 March. As T. B. Millar argued, Australia had not formally associated itself with Article I of AMDA, which defined Britain's commitment to Malayan defence, but rather with those parts of AMDA granting Britain the 'right to maintain in the Federation' the CSR with its unspecified role.[58] This technical interpretation, read against Barwick's equivocation over the use of Australian forces, underlined an important distinction between the Australian military presence *in* Malaya and the British defence guarantee *to* Malaya.

Yet, since its formation, the CSR had had three implicit roles – regional defence, external defence and counter-insurgency. It was politically inconceivable in Malayan eyes that the CSR, which could be construed to have a regional role (this being the primary Australian interest), could not be called upon to meet what Malaya defined (and British support acknowledged) as an immediate external threat. Kuala Lumpur, which had reacted as the *de facto* Central Government of Malaysia since Confrontation began, derived little comfort from Barwick's reservation of the Australian position *vis-à-vis* the Borneo territories when the extension of AMDA had already been negotiated with Britain.

Thus AMDA's fine print did not illuminate the Australian position. Indeed, if AMDA's deliberate ambiguity was intended to accommodate an overlapping of interests, Australia's attempts to avoid defining its interests publicly enhanced that ambiguity. The diplomatic moves in late March and early April gave hope to a Malaya–Philippines–Indonesia solution and reinforced Canberra's reluctance to prejudice this by undue publicity about its defence relations with Britain and Malaya.

Yet developments, such as the imminent Indonesian occupation of West Irian and increasing Peking–Jakarta cordiality (capped by Liu Shao-Chi's visit to Indonesia and the subsequent joint communiqué of 20 April declaring their determination to destroy Malaysia), which might have more immediate bearing on Australian security, could not be ignored. Following Barwick's consultations in London and Kuala Lumpur in April, the much-anticipated increases in Australian defence expenditure were announced on 22 May. The Defence Review projected an annual increase of A£41 million in the defence vote for the five-year period beginning in 1963/4.[59] All three services, but especially the army, received increases which, it was hoped, would support an overseas capability. With obvious concern for the 'Australian backyard', Menzies emphasised that Papua New Guinea would be defended 'as if they were part of our mainland'.[60]

Australia's extreme cautiousness towards Indonesia at the outset of Confrontation had no parallel in New Zealand. Separated by 4,800 km of the Tasman Sea from the Australian land-mass, New Zealand did not share Australia's sense of vulnerability. Nor did Barwick's concern for, and efforts at, cultivating long-term good relations with Indonesia find an advocate of similar zeal and stature in Wellington. However, although New Zealand had welcomed the Malaysia proposal in forthright language, Holyoake's initial comment on New Zealand's 'commitment' to Malaya reflected a cautiousness similar to Barwick's. On 19 March Holyoake corrected the Commander of the New Zealand cruiser *Royalist*, who had reportedly said in Kuala Lumpur that his country would be duty-bound to help defend Malaya if it were attacked. Holyoake reaffirmed New Zealand's associate status *vis-à-vis* AMDA, disclaiming any 'treaty commitments between New Zealand and Malaya'. In Holyoake's view, the main purpose of the New Zealand battalion in Malaya was to provide an available force for SEATO commitments. Should external aggression threaten Malaya, any request for assistance would be considered not only on its merits, but also in the circumstances surrounding the particular incidents.[61]

Yet this reaffirmation of the right of national control over the components of the CSR was simply a strict interpretation of an established ANZAM practice. In declaratory policies, however, New Zealand was not restrained to the same extent as Australia during the first phase of Confrontation. By early May 1963, even as intra-Maphilindo diplomacy was under way, the New Zealand Defence Minister, Dean Eyre, was saying in Kuala Lumpur that New Zealand would 'deal promptly with any request for assistance in the event of aggression against the area'. He did not expect any significant change in his country's position after the formation of Malaysia. Nor was New Zealand too worried over the massing of Indonesian troops in West Irian.[62]

By way of new positive measures towards Malayan defence, New Zealand had actually kept in step with Australia's non-committed position although, like Australia, plans were being considered to provide for a logistically self-supporting overseas force in an emergency.[63] Although New Zealand indicated readiness to respond promptly to Malaya's request for military aid, the would-be recipient was expected to make a public request only if it had received private indications that, if asked for, aid would be forthcoming. This convention was particularly important to relations between Malaya and the antipodes, whose 'commitments' depended on a continuous evaluation of their interests against the volatile background of Confrontation. For Kuala Lumpur to make a public request and then see it refused would have damaged the façade of alliance unity. The embarrassment caused by the Tunku's Malacca speech could hardly have been forgotten. That no public request was made, even when anxiety was growing in Kuala Lumpur, attested to a certain reserve in both Canberra and Wellington. But Wellington was less restrained in its declaratory policies.

It was unlikely that New Zealand, the 'junior partner' (in terms of national power), would have departed radically from Australia on the issue of Malayan defence. On the other hand, it was equally true that if Australia could be pressured into a less ambiguous position, New Zealand would very likely keep in step. This realisation, and the greater Australian ambiguity, could well have made Canberra rather than Wellington the main target of British and Malayan pressure.

Strategic and economic vulnerability led Singapore to qualify its support for Kuala Lumpur's vigorous response to Confrontation. As Lee Kuan Yew indicated, there were 'local issues', apart from defence and internal security, on which 'Singapore might differ from Malaya'.[64] Among the 'local issues' was the likely economic consequences of sudden disruption to Singapore's entrepôt trade. Malaya, whose economic dependence on this trade was very much less, was not as concerned.[65] In February 1963 Lee Kuan Yew twice remarked that, because of Singapore's 'correct policy' towards Indonesia, 'there has been no incident between us'.[66] This 'correct' relationship did not preclude repair work on Indonesian patrol boats undertaken by private dockyards, one of which had provided this service as recently as early February. The Singapore Harbour Board provided similar services, although no Indonesian patrol boats had arrived since October 1962.[67] Singapore's low-key response reflected a wariness not to upset Indonesia. As Dr Toh Chin Chye commented in May 1963, the less said about Confrontation, the better.[68]

During the first phase of Confrontation, attempts by certain of the AMDA partners and associates to differentiate their separate interests were linked to hopes of a diplomatic solution. A full analysis of Confrontation diplomacy is beyond this work, but it is worth noting that a clean break between negotiations and Confrontational acts did not occur until mid-1964. Only temporary agreement emerged from the various diplomatic encounters and none produced the promise of Indonesian military withdrawal from Malaysian territory which Kuala Lumpur regarded as a prior condition to any settlement. Border incursions and 'incidents' occurred with varying intensity throughout the negotiations.

The dynamics of early Confrontation, as will be shown subsequently, put into much sharper focus both the shared and the separate interests of the allies. As the anchor power, Britain tended to concentrate its responses on the military, the arena of Confrontation diplomacy being left largely to Malaya. In upholding Malaysian independence, Britain avoided an unduly overt direction of Malaysian diplomacy. Even the military responses were later institutionalised, through a Joint Defence Council under the Tunku's chairmanship, to underline that Confrontation was Malaysia's war. Yet there was unconcealed British discomfiture when Malaysian anxiety to resolve the crisis appeared to result in undue Malaysian concessions. Malaysia, in turn, attempted to extract the maximum security cover from Britain and was equally keen for more tangible demonstrations of solidarity from the AMDA associates. Malaysia remained apprehensive of being isolated by Indonesia from New Zealand and, especially, from Australia.

Although Singapore had, on joining Malaysia, accepted the transfer of foreign policy and defence responsibilities from London to Kuala Lumpur, it nevertheless sought to influence foreign policy and 'hotly debated international problems which seemed to impinge on the island's political future'.[69] In this respect, Confrontation also presented issues over which Singapore was obliged to register its distinct interests so as to minimise the risks to itself.

The British response throughout the stepping-up of Confrontation demonstrated a continuing interest in upholding its anchor role. In early May 1963, after a full alert was ordered on the Sarawak–

Indonesia border, the new British Commander, Far East, Admiral Sir Varyl Begg, promised that Britain would 'meet any reasonable eventualities in the formation of Malaysia'.[70]

Meanwhile increasing attention was drawn to the diplomatic arena following an initiative by Macapagal in Manila during a meeting of the Association of Southeast Asia (ASA). The attendant joint statement announced the willingness of Malaya and the Philippines to hold tripartite summit talks with Indonesia. Sub-ministerial discussions followed that same month and an agenda for a Foreign Ministers' conference was worked out. Approval for this conference was given in separate meetings between Macapagal and Sukarno in Manila on 23 May, and between Sukarno and the Tunku in Tokyo at the end of May. Ministerial-level discussions were held between 7 and 11 June. The Philippines and Indonesia agreed, *inter alia*, to welcome the new Federation provided Bornean opinion was ascertained under UN auspices. The conference also endorsed Macapagal's proposal for a confederation of nations of Malay origin (Maphilindo). But before the three-nation summit (scheduled for the end of July) could take place, the agreement providing for the establishment of Malaysia was signed in London.

Sukarno construed the Malaysia Agreement signed on 8 July (which provided for the birth of Malaysia on 31 August 1963)[71] as a breach of the Manila Accord and therefore renewed his opposition to the establishment of the Federation. Sukarno reaffirmed his Confrontation policy and Indonesian raids spread into Sabah on the day the Malaysia Agreement was signed. In mid-July, the Indonesian Navy announced the formation of an 'attack fleet' to further Confrontation.

Canberra viewed the renewal of Confrontation with dismay. On 14 July, on returning from the US and Britain, Menzies strongly regretted Sukarno's renewal of public criticism of the Malaysia idea, which 'has been actively supported by us as a matter of principle quite clearly'.[72] Menzies had apparently discussed the future role and status of antipodean forces in relation to an extended AMDA (now formally enshrined in Article VI of the Malaysia Agreement) with Macmillan and his Foreign Secretary, Lord Home. Menzies indicated in London that, if and when Malaysia was established, Australia would have to consider making some form of agreement with her on such matters as defence and trade.[73]

With the Malaysia Agreement signed, a declaration by Australia and New Zealand on the future of their forces in Malaya became necessary. Menzies' trip to the US and to Britain in June 1963 was reminiscent of trips in 1955 prior to the dispatch of Australian forces to Malaya. As in 1955, too, there was no complete convergence of British and American interests over the defence of Malaysia. As Menzies admitted on 14 July, the US, while supporting the Malaysia idea, considered Malaysia's defence at that stage to be essentially a Commonwealth matter.[74]

This uncertainty of the American response, *inter alia*, continued to restrain Canberra's posture. New Zealand's declaratory policy, however, was increasingly firm. By the end of July Holyoake had informed Parliament that, with AMDA's extension, New Zealand expected to retain forces in the Federation and be associated with the modified agreement just as before.[75] It is unlikely that this expectation was not shared by Canberra at this time. Significantly, Australia, despite press speculation at the end of August, did not feel free to make a similar declaration until 17 September 1963. Britain's reaction towards Indonesia was also hardening. July saw the expulsion of two Indonesian Consular officials from Jesselton (now Kota Kinabalu) and the arrest of some twenty Indonesians throughout Sabah. Jakarta reciprocated by expelling two British Vice-Consuls from Medan and Surabaya and later announced naval and air manoeuvres in the South China Sea and Straits of Malacca.

The anxiously awaited three-nation summit materialised on 30 July, but not before Sukarno had promised to 'crush Malaysia' and carry Confrontation to Manila. Sukarno found a useful bone of contention in Article VI of the Malaysia Agreement, which defined the role of the British bases in Singapore as being 'the preservation of peace in Southeast Asia'. Indonesia took this to be a violation of the Manila Accord of 11 June, which made 'the maintenance of the stability and security of the area from subversion in any form' a Malaya–Philippines–Indonesia responsibility.[76] Indonesia's interests were strongly reflected in the 5 August joint declaration that 'foreign bases – temporary in nature – should not be allowed to be used directly or indirectly to subvert the National Independence of any of the three countries' and that 'the three countries will abstain from the use of arrangements of collective defence to serve the particular interests of any of the big powers'.[77]

The Tunku made it clear that Malaya considered AMDA necessary, although the defence arrangements were not permanent.

Britain, however, apparently not consulted on this issue, announced that Malaya had given assurances that nothing agreed to at the Manila summit in any way affected the validity of the extended AMDA. It affirmed that these arrangements could only be amended or revoked by mutual consent.[78] The Tunku, too, attempted to avoid an apparent sacrifice of British defence interests (which the Manila Agreement might otherwise have succeeded in conveying) by explaining to Parliament that allies were needed for the preservation of peace. When Malaya was sure it could live peacefully it might not require British help.[79]

While Britain and Malaya sought to square the circle of the *fait accompli* of the declaration at Manila and the existing AMDA, Singapore was impelled to register its separate interests. Its Government was discomforted by a possible loss of identity within a Malay-dominated Maphilindo at a time of impending elections in the predominantly Chinese island. There was also evident dismay in Whitehall over the Tunku's acquiescence to the demand for a UN assessment of opinion in the then British territories, an exercise which postponed the birth of Malaysia.[80] The Philippines claim to Sabah still remained unresolved.

Malaysia's postponement precipitated a unilateral declaration of *de facto* independence by Lee Kuan Yew on 1 September 1963. Although partly intended to assure the electorate that independence or merger was not dependent on the UN enquiry, and partly to bolster Singapore's bargaining position in some still outstanding issues in the merger negotiations with Kuala Lumpur,[81] the gesture spawned further mutual resentment in Malaya–Singapore relations. Britain was caught in the cross-fire of accusations between its two defence clients. Duncan Sandys' presence in Singapore just prior to Lee's proclamation added to Malaysia's suspicion that Britain had, by remaining silent, condoned an unconstitutional act.[82] This intra-alliance discord, eventually resolved through Sandys' intervention, did not, however, damage AMDA's fabric. Indeed, Lee was careful to emphasise the continuity of the existing defence provisions.

But while the UN enquiry was still under way, the Tunku announced on 29 August that 16 September would be the new date for Malaysia, i.e. two days after the expected publication of the UN findings. Although the findings subsequently confirmed that a sizeable Bornean majority favoured Malaysia, Indonesia and the Philippines protested that the unilateral establishment of a new date for

Malaysia was a breach of the Manila Agreement. They refused to recognise the new Federation on its inauguration, whereupon Malaysia severed diplomatic relations with both states. Confrontation then entered a new and more dangerous phase.

6. TOWARDS A CLOSING OF RANKS

Malaysia's severing of diplomatic relations with Indonesia and the Philippines opened a new phase in Confrontation marked by heightened physical and political conflict between the antagonists. Intensification of the threat led to a corresponding change in the nature and speed of intra-AMDA responses culminating in the closing of ranks among the allies.

With the evident failure of a political settlement, Jakarta began to shift the emphasis of its tactics in a military direction. In August, Indonesian-based terrorists appeared for the first time in Sarawak's Fifth Division, while encounters in Sarawak resulted in the first fatal casualty (of British officer rank) in Borneo. In mid-September the Indonesian army announced that 'special battle units' had been dispatched to territories bordering Sarawak. And, when the Federation was proclaimed, anti-Malaysia riots erupted in Jakarta and Medan. In Jakarta, the Malayan and British embassies, as well as British homes and property, were attacked (the British embassy being set on fire) and British firms progressively nationalised.

The day after Malaysia's inauguration, Kuala Lumpur proclaimed a 'state of preparedness' and established a Joint Defence Council under the Tunku's chairmanship. The council decided to call up the reserves, increase the armed forces (especially the territorials) and revive the special constabulary. Singapore's reaction, however, was decidedly low-key. Lee Kuan Yew described the Indonesian demonstrations as a contemporary 'ritual of showing disapproval'. As far as Singapore was concerned, it was 'business as usual'.[1] And indeed, Jakarta continued to tolerate the representative of the Singapore trade and cultural office until mid-October 1963, i.e. two months after Indonesia's trade embargo and one month after it had refused Malaysia diplomatic recognition. During the first half of October, when anti-Sukarno rallies were being held throughout the peninsula, a similar rally, scheduled in Singapore the following month, was cancelled. Lee Kuan Yew later explained that Singapore's restraint did not detract from its loyalty to Malaysia, but that Singapore's trading interests necessitated a certain respect for Indonesian susceptibilities.[2] However, the intensification of Confrontation, by the enforcement of trade embargoes, and mounting acts of violence, increasingly directed at Singapore from early 1964, left its leadership with little alternative but to close ranks with Kuala Lumpur and openly condemn Indonesian policy.

British military preparedness was manifested in the dispatch, in mid-September 1963, of a third aircraft carrier to the area, while the commando carrier HMS *Albion* was held in readiness in Hong Kong. Duncan Sandys expected Confrontation to be a long-drawn-out affair and stressed the need for 'a joint co-operative effort' to meet it.[3] Thus, although anti-Malaysia demonstrations in Indonesia had left the Australian and New Zealand communities relatively untouched, and although public denunciations were confined to Britain, Malaya and the US, the escalating crisis and the birth of Malaysia necessitated further responses from the antipodes. Barwick, who stopped over in Jakarta *en route* to the Malaysia celebrations, had already been left with no illusions about the seriousness of the situation.

In meetings with Sukarno, Subandrio and Nasution on 13 and 14 September, Barwick (as he later disclosed) made clear that Australia was likely to stand with Britain if Malaysia's security was violated. He had hoped such a restatement of position might influence the Indonesian leaders.[4] However his objective was not fulfilled. On reaching Kuala Lumpur, Barwick was beginning to sound tougher. He ruled out any possibility of Australian mediation because it had already made its pro-Malaysia stand 'bluntly' clear, particularly to Indonesia.[5] The worsening crisis made it awkward, domestically and externally, for Canberra to differentiate its position,[6] while the birth of Malaysia required some formal definition of the status and role of antipodean forces in the new Federation.

On 18 September Australia and New Zealand, following discussions in the previous weeks between Britain and Malaya, formally extended their association with AMDA (which now applied to Malaysia) by an Exchange of Letters with Kuala Lumpur.[7] This Exchange of Letters, while allowing for the new political geography, also reflected the continuity of Australian–New Zealand defence interests and embodied the existing ambiguity over the role of their forces in Malaysia. As Holyoake put it on 20 September, the new documents 'impose no legal obligation on New Zealand to maintain forces in Malaysia, or to follow specific courses of action for its external defence'.

The seriousness of Confrontation meant that some indication of Australian–New Zealand intent was nevertheless necessary. Holyoake emphasised the importance of Malaysian security to New Zealand which, he said, 'would not stand idly aside in the event of an armed attack on Malaysia'. If this occurred, New Zealand would 'promptly consult with the Malaysian and other Commonwealth Governments concerned on the measures to be taken'.[8] While on 25 September Menzies, following close consultation with the Cabinet, issued a parliamentary statement whose most significant passage ran:

> if in the circumstances that now exist, and which may continue for a long time, there occurs, in relation to Malaysia or any of its constituent states, armed invasion or subversive activity – supported or directed or inspired from outside Malaysia – we shall to the best of our powers and by such means as shall be agreed upon with the Government of Malaysia, add our military assistance to the efforts of Malaysia and the United Kingdom in the defence of Malaysia's territorial integrity and political independence.[9]

In a letter to Menzies, the Tunku described the statement as 'immensely reassuring' and 'timely'.[10] The CRO in London 'warmly welcomed' it, while Malaysia's *Straits Times* carried the buoyant headline: 'Aussies will fight for Malaysia – Menzies'.[11]

Menzies' statement certainly caught the public mood and raised hopes in Malaysia and Britain over the imminent entry of Australia into the Borneo campaign. Yet nowhere did it explicitly refer to the dispatch of Australian forces to Borneo. It remained essentially a declaration of intent. As J. D. B. Miller observed, it left undefined the circumstances in which Australia might commit troops to Borneo. Its reference to 'the circumstances that now exist, and which may continue for a long time' could mean either that Australia ought already to be committing troops to Borneo or that the situation would have to further deteriorate before anything was done.[12] Equally perplexing was the promise to render assistance in the event of 'armed invasion or subversive activities – supported or directed or inspired from outside Malaysia'.[13] Should Australia consider Confrontation as constituting 'armed invasion' or 'subversive activities'? If not (though Kuala Lumpur's charges of Indonesian 'aggression' and 'subversion' were frequent enough), upon whose definition would Australia act?

Nevertheless, one point did emerge clearly: Menzies carefully stated that the Australian contribution would come, if needed, by addition of 'our military assistance to the efforts of Malaysia and the United Kingdom'. This underlined the prevailing assumption that Australia's contribution depended upon British readiness to defend Malaysia and reflected the peculiar Australian position as both consumer and sub-provider of alliance security. Australia had preferred to associate with an AMDA in which Britain's role as guarantor had been formalised rather than enter into a separate treaty with Malaysia. As Menzies later explained, 'a simple . . . declaration of intention on our part . . . in its very nature, preserves our own judgement, as to the nature, extent and disposition of Australian forces to be deployed'.[14]

From Malaysia's perspective, although AMDA might have associated Malaysia indirectly with SEATO, the treaty was sufficiently fluid for Kuala Lumpur to express its separate interests. Britain's role of guarantor was crucial and sufficient for Malaysian security in the context of external defence. A further treaty, say with Australia, might have involved it in an even more formal way with SEATO. Nor was Malaysia, like Australia, by entering into additional defence treaties, prepared to make it any easier for Britain to contemplate an eventual withdrawal of its defence guarantee. Thus, although the issue of specific Australian–New Zealand action was left undefined, the way was now open for responses of a military nature if required. The question remained: how and when would those responses be activated?

The Borneo situation worsened following the Menzies–Holyoake declarations of intent. Coinciding with Menzies' statement, Indonesia announced the dispatch of parachute troops to the Borneo border, while Indonesian mortar shells landed for the first time within Sarawak's First Division, marking a new phase in the Indonesian army's involvement in Confrontation. On 5 October Sukarno declared that Indonesia would oppose Malaysia 'at all costs'. Indonesian troop movements to the border were reported from Jakarta in early October. One column indeed penetrated 56 km into Sarawak before being halted by Gurkhas and Home Guards. While Malaysian forces were being rushed to Borneo in mid-October, security measures in Sarawak for the first time envisaged the possibility of 'open aggression' by Indonesia. On 24 October a special alert was imposed on the peninsula's west coast. Three days later the 1960 Internal Security Act was extended over the whole of Malaysia. Expectations that mediation might materialise on the occasion of the meeting of the Colombo Plan Consultative Committee in Bangkok during mid-November were short-lived. Rather, tension rose with reports of Indonesian jet bombers flying over Singapore and other Malaysian territory. Indeed, earlier, on 17 October, one such bomber was intercepted as it approached Singapore.

Indonesia's brinkmanship was straining Anglo-Malaysian resources. Already the manpower of the British Far East Fleet had been increased from 8,500 to 13,000 over the past three years and further increases in British naval strength were announced in late October. Malaysia, too, sought to bolster its military manpower by invoking, on 18 November, the National Service Ordinance of 1952 requiring all male Federal citizens between the ages of 21 and 28 to register for national service.[15] It was considered that Confrontation would be a protracted conflict – with all that that implied for a hard-pressed anchor power. Although reserves could be drawn from Britain and the Middle East, other commitments would necessarily be weakened, while much of the twelve-battalion-strong Malaysian army was then still in training.

Attention again switched to Australia and New Zealand, each of which had a battalion in the peninsula. Although both Menzies and Holyoake reaffirmed their support for Malaysia during their respective election campaigns in late November, nothing more was said about specific defence contributions to meet Confrontation after their electoral victories. The cautious prediction was that Australia might render limited air support in Borneo or deploy its forces elsewhere in the peninsula to release British forces for Bornean engagements. Razak himself had, on 6 December, stated in London that Malaysia needed military assistance from its US and Commonwealth allies. Holyoake commented that discussions among the Commonwealth allies had been held over many months, particularly in recent weeks, without 'any concrete proposals or results'.[16] On 13 December Razak indicated that Malaysia would shortly initiate discussions with New Zealand for greater military assistance.[17] But, following press speculation that Australian forces would soon be deployed in Borneo, Razak maintained that there were sufficient troops in Borneo, although he admitted that the involvement of Australian troops there was under review.[18] The Tunku disclosed on 3 January 1964 that further aid had been offered by Australia in the event of an Indonesian attack.[19] The precise nature and timing of this aid remained speculative. Yet, following discussions with the British Defence Minister, Thorneycroft, who had arrived in early January, the Tunku curiously disclosed in Jesselton that Malaysia had not requested assistance from anyone. There were enough troops in Borneo. Malaysia did not intend asking Australia and New Zealand for help, although he carefully added, 'not at the moment, anyway'. Thorneycroft merely remarked that it was for Malaysia to request that Australian–New Zealand forces be sent to Borneo. As for Britain, reinforcements could be detached from the Rhine army if necessary.[20]

A few illuminating points stand out from this confusion. Clearly, British resources were strained, as Thorneycroft himself implied, and unrest in Cyprus and East Africa in early January imposed further demands on the British. Britain and Malaysia had consistently sought more tangible support from Australia and New Zealand, and the widespread suspicion at this point that Australia especially had come under British pressure for a commitment was never officially denied in Canberra even when the Opposition leader, Calwell, later repeated it in Parliament.[21] Discussions on the issues of Australian–New Zealand military assistance to Malaysia had reached a peak towards the end of 1963, albeit without concrete results. Given the September 1963 declarations of intent by Menzies and Holyoake, Malaysia alone would have to trigger their responses by a formal request. There was no a priori reason why Malaysia (with or without British advice) should not have made a formal request at this juncture, but there was a valid reason (as will be explained below) why the antipodes, especially Australia, should hold out against a military commitment in Borneo. The evidence strongly suggests that an informal approach had indeed been made, but which had been unfavourably met. Hence, the confusing public statements of the Tunku and Thorneycroft in early January: the AMDA associates continued to keep their options open.

Canberra especially sought to maintain a dialogue with Jakarta. An exchange of diplomatic notes led to a meeting in Jakarta in early January between Subandrio and the Australian Ambassador. Canberra's hopes were raised by a subsequent shift in Confrontation diplomacy. A meeting between Sukarno and Macapagal in Manila between 7 and 11 January reopened an avenue towards negotiation with Malaysia. Washington seized the diplomatic initiative by announcing on 13 January that Attorney-General Robert Kennedy would meet Sukarno, then holidaying in Tokyo. Kennedy's mission, which also took him to Manila and Kuala Lumpur, resulted in an Indonesian cease-fire announced on 23 January. This was to be a prelude to tripartite ministerial meetings followed by a tripartite summit.

Concurrent with these developments, Malaysia's defence needs were being considered by the AMDA associates. On 7 January the Defence Ministers of Australia and New Zealand met informally in Canberra. Comments expressed by the New Zealand Defence Minister, Dean Eyre, on returning to Wellington indicated that he, at least, favoured more concrete support for Malaysia. He criticised New Zealand for being myopic about Indonesian threats and suggested that Malaysia could be helped considerably by way of training or equipment.[22]

It was soon apparent that Australia and New Zealand would respond, short of committing ground forces to Borneo. In January both Holyoake and Menzies confirmed that discussions were under way with Malaysia. But the thrust of Menzies' statement on 16 January was directed at deterring Indonesia rather than at reassuring Malaysia. On the surface it would seem that assurance to Malaysia would be a logical consequence of successful deterrence against Indonesia. But for Australian deterrence to succeed it was first necessary to withhold the striking hand and *that* was not seen as reassuring by Kuala Lumpur. Nevertheless, there was a link in the statement between the ambiguity of Australian intent in Borneo and the express belief in a diplomatic solution to Confrontation. In the latter context, Robert Kennedy's forthcoming meeting with Sukarno was particularly welcomed. Menzies hoped that Sukarno would obtain 'a clearer understanding ... of the seriousness with which the United States and her allies regard present developments on the Indonesia–Malaysia border in Borneo'.[23]

Clearly, Australian reluctance to intervene in Borneo at this point was influenced by hopes of a diplomatic settlement. Equally, the obvious reference to 'the United States and her allies' could be a veiled warning to Indonesia that escalation in Borneo might involve Australia and perhaps the US. Whether the US had given a private assurance to extend ANZUS to Australian and New Zealand 'armed forces, public vessels or aircraft in the Pacific'[24] (including the Borneo area), should these come under Indonesian attack, was a different issue.[25] The fact remained that 'the prospect of eventual American help ... could presumably be used in diplomatic negotiation with Indonesia, so long as Australia held its hand while emphasising that it would strike hard, and strike with the help of a powerful friend, if it decided that the need to strike was urgent'.[26]

Menzies' statement on 16 January reflected the peculiar position occupied by Australia and New Zealand between the overlapping circles of strategic interests represented by AMDA and ANZUS. The statement was not wholly AMDA-orientated. It took account of associations with the US, although Menzies admitted that Washington saw Malaysian defence as primarily a Commonwealth responsibility.[27] Menzies' reference to ANZUS also reflected Australia's position as both a provider and a consumer of alliance security. Attention was drawn to American protection should 'in the course of this defence of Malaysia we face a genuine (i.e. full-scale) attack on ... Malaysia – a matter which invokes our promise'.[28] Australia's motive was to protect itself while helping to protect Malaysia and underlying it was the uncertainty whether British power alone was sufficient to handle all-out Confrontation. Quite possibly, too, underlying the attempts to deter Indonesia, was a belief that Indonesia was bluffing with its policy of Confrontation. According to General Walker, Frank Hasset, Commander of the 28th Commonwealth Brigade, had indicated (possibly in early 1964) that this belief was held by some Australian officials. General Walker hoped that Hasset would see that the attack on Malaysian troops by Indonesian regulars at Kalabakan (Sabah) was no less than war and would report to Canberra accordingly.[29]

Although New Zealand did not share Australia's vulnerability, it had to act in concert with the latter on the question of dispatching troops to Borneo to sustain the deterrent effect of Menzies' 16 January statement. New Zealand could not make a virtue out of a given US ambiguity if its forces came under attack in Borneo at this stage. By action or inaction the American position would be much clearer. In this sense, a consideration of the aims of ANZUS policy exerted some constraints on New Zealand's AMDA-orientated decision.[30] Nevertheless, the option of the deployment of New Zealand troops in Borneo was kept alive precisely to deter Indonesia from escalation.

This intent was reflected in a formal note to Subandrio in January. In it Holyoake expressed New Zealand's reluctance to commit forces to Borneo. But, he added, New Zealand would not shrink from such a move if the Borneo situation deteriorated seriously.[31] To prepare the way for a response that would fall short of committing ground forces to Borneo, Menzies announced, on 28 January, the dispatch of a defence mission to assess Malaysia's material and training requirements. The AMDA associates also acceded to a Malaysian request for the employment of their ground forces in the CSR in anti-insurgency operations in northern Malaya, thus freeing Malaysian forces for deployment in Borneo.[32]

By early March the tripartite ministerial negotiations, which began in Bangkok on 5 February and reconvened on 3 March at Malaysia's request, had reached an impasse: Malaysia had failed to obtain a withdrawal of Indonesian forces from its territory, Indonesia had failed to tie a military withdrawal to some general political settlement and, by late February, the Indonesian cease-fire had all but broken down. Following the collapse of the March talks, Malaysia declared that it no longer considered the cease-fire operative. On 10 March the Malaysian Cabinet decided on an immediate call-up under the previously arranged National Service scheme which was now extended to Singapore, Sabah and Sarawak. The increasing threat to Malaysia also resulted in Kuala Lumpur and Singapore closing ranks. The Central Government's decision to extend National Service to Singapore was firmly endorsed by Lee Kuan Yew. In mid-April, as Indonesian-directed violence in Singapore increased, Dr Toh Chin Chye called on the people of Singapore to rise up to meet Confrontation. As he put it, 'now we have no more cheeks to offer'.[33]

The breakdown of the Indonesian cease-fire was openly condemned by Barwick, who warned Indonesia that, while Australia would continue to promote friendly relations, it would not sacrifice its vital interests, which included 'the performance of its commitment to other nations and the maintenance of its own territorial sovereignty'.[34] The Defence Minister, Paul Hasluck, in turn, affirmed Australia's readiness 'to honour [its] commitments on request, either with those forces [already in Malaysia] or with other forces at our disposition'.[35] Australia's general policy, announced in Menzies' statement of 16 January, took concrete form on 17 March when details of training and material aid (the latter amounting to

M$20 million) to Malaysia were announced. Coming within a week of Barwick's condemnation of Indonesia, this contribution was readily seen in Malaysia as a clearer demonstration that a greater emergency would bring further military responses. In April New Zealand followed with an offer of aid to Malaysia worth M$4.5 million in personnel training and military equipment. In announcing the offer, Holyoake again hinted at the possibility of direct New Zealand participation in Borneo should the situation deteriorate.[36]

Within a month of the first Australian offer of military aid, Hasluck announced the processing of another Malaysian request. Australia had meanwhile alerted its fighter squadrons at Butterworth for air defence and committed two RAN ships attached to the CSR to duties off the Malaysia–Borneo coast. The second programme of aid included the dispatch of an army engineer squadron to Borneo.[37] Although the 180-strong engineer squadron was essentially non-combative and deployed in an area relatively free of Indonesian infiltration, the introduction of Australian military personnel into Borneo inevitably risked direct contact with Indonesian forces. Indeed, the army directive to the squadron to shoot back if fired on by guerrillas[38] implied an official acknowledgement of such a risk.

That such a risk should be taken characterised the qualitative change in the Australian 'commitment' and signalled another graduated response. Its deterrent value rested with the fact that it carried Australia nearer to an actual commitment of fighting units in Borneo. In this sense it was a reassurance to Malaysia and an intended deterrent to Indonesia. Thus it was necessary to impress upon Indonesia the onus of not triggering further antipodean responses and hence, perhaps, American responses. Indeed the prospect of greater Australian involvement in Borneo led to an increasingly open Australian emphasis on the American connection. Thus, while in Manila for a SEATO conference in mid-April 1964, Barwick disclosed that he had warned Subandrio that escalating Confrontation would eventually involve Australia because of AMDA and that the US would be involved in large-scale hostilities over Malaysia because of ANZUS.[39] Barwick explained that the policy of 'graduated response' involved his maintaining diplomatic relations with Jakarta and pointing out to the Indonesians 'where all this might [progressively] end up'.[40]

Holyoake was equally involved in the exercise of dissuasion. After the SEATO conference he proceeded to Jakarta to meet Sukarno, Subandrio and Nasution. Reacting to progress suggestions that his visit (and his invitation to Sukarno to visit New Zealand) represented a softening of policy, Holyoake twice explained that he had gone to reiterate that any further deterioration of the situation in Borneo would result in New Zealand forces being made 'available alongside those of Malaysia, Great Britain and Australia to protect the territorial integrity of Malaysia'.[41]

Indonesia was not dissuaded. By early May Sukarno had issued an 'action command' to Indonesians to topple Malaysia. On 6 May it was officially announced that a combat brigade of Indonesian 'volunteers' was ready to enter Malaysian territory. Reflecting the seriousness of the situation in Borneo, the Malaysian Defence Council met in Kuching on 15 May – the first time it had been convened outside Kuala Lumpur. ANZAM's scenario of a possible clash with Indonesia was played out in a large exercise in central Pahang during June designed to test the CSR's capabilities in operations against forces from an imaginary hostile neighbouring country.

Although the Tunku, Macapagal and Sukarno eventually met in Tokyo on 20 June 1964, the summit ended inconclusively. Hostilities, temporarily suspended in Borneo, were resumed with even greater intensity. In General Walker's assessment, Indonesian regulars were thenceforth beginning to fight as units rather than as 'advisers'.[42] The Tunku commented, shortly before departing for the Commonwealth Prime Ministers' Conference in London (scheduled for early July), that it would be up to the external allies to decide on what they could offer after they had heard his appraisal.

In Britain, Duncan Sandys expressed both disappointment at the failure of the Tokyo summit and determination to defend Malaysia. In the February 1964 Defence White Paper the Conservative Government had reaffirmed its intention to maintain the East of Suez role 'for as long as circumstances in the areas, and the vital interests of our friends and allies, demand'.[43] Confrontation created an added interest in the peace-keeping role which the Opposition supported 'with an enthusiasm that even the Government could not equal'.[44] Yet that peace-keeping responsibility, particularly in the case of Malaysia, had placed increasing demands on British resources. Confrontation had, according to Thorneycroft, cost Britain an additional £3.5 million up to 31 March 1964.[45] But he was saved by the Speaker from commenting on the *Times* report that the

Borneo operations were costing Britain an estimated £1 million per week. That report, when read against General Walker's remarks that, in the absence of a political solution, Confrontation could continue for ten years, was scarcely comforting. To a parliamentary question seeking elucidation on the reduction of British strength in Borneo as a result of recent antipodean offers of aid, Thorneycroft had curtly replied: 'None'.[46]

It was hardly surprising that, even as the Tunku called for more Commonwealth assistance, the British military in the area was asking what Malaysia was doing for itself.[47] Razak, in turn, justified the need for external defence support by claiming that national and rural economic development might otherwise be disrupted.[48] The Finance Minister, Tan Siew Sin, deployed a moral argument: the CCO in Sarawak was a British legacy; Britain, therefore, had a moral obligation to assist.[49] While Britain and Malaysia expected a greater defence contribution from each other, their common sights were trained on the AMDA associates. Following the failure of the Tokyo summit, Holyoake firmly declared that if the renewal of guerrilla warfare in Borneo led to a serious deterioration in the military situation: 'New Zealand forces would be made available to support ... [Malaysia].'[50]

The next stage of the Australian–New Zealand response was not triggered by a serious deterioration of the situation in Borneo, nor by the sudden departure from office of Sir Garfield Barwick (who had been most closely associated with Australia's 'good neighbour' policy towards Indonesia), nor even by the combined pressure of Britain and Malaysia, but by a sudden change in the nature of Indonesia's territorial threat. On 17 August, 96 raiders (three-quarters of them Indonesian marines and paratroopers) landed by boat at Pontian on the south-west coast of Johore. A second attack followed within a fortnight when 108 paratroopers were dropped near Labis, again in Johore State.[51]

These were the first incursions into the Malayan peninsula and represented a dramatic escalation from the cross-border incursions and subversion in Borneo. Previously, Australia and New Zealand, by withholding their combat troops from Borneo and thus avoiding direct contact with Indonesian troops, had implied a *de facto* differentiation between the defence of Malaya and that of Malaysian Borneo. Precisely because they had had no troops in Borneo, the threat of introducing them into Borneo, and hence the prospect of direct contact, could, it was hoped, be used to deter Indonesian escalation. The air- and seaborne invasion of Malaya thus transformed the conflict in that it both proved the failure of deterrence and made contact between antipodean and Indonesian forces inevitable.

It would have been untenable to refuse deployment of the Australian and New Zealand components of the CSR (which had a SEATO-orientated regional role and were in part actually employed in anti-insurgent activities in North Malaya) to meet this external threat. As Razak commented, Indonesia had originally recognised Malaya as a sovereign state although it had not recognised Malaysia. The attack on the peninsula was thus 'a clear case of aggression'.[52] Holyoake agreed that the use of Indonesian air transport, as contrasted with guerrilla infiltration, made this 'aggression' even more easily definable.[53] Menzies himself described the new attacks as 'a clear case of military aggression'.[54] The following day Senator Paltridge, who had succeeded Paul Hasluck as Defence Minister (the latter having replaced Barwick), disclosed that his Government would agree to any Malaysian request to use Australian troops against the Indonesian forces which had landed in Malaya.[55] His statement was the clearest indication that this time Australia would respond positively if requested. The Labis attack coincided with the meeting in Kuala Lumpur of the ANZAM Finance Ministers who promptly agreed to render further financial assistance to the expansion of Malaysia's military capability. The New Zealand Cabinet, too, 'specifically confirmed' its general agreement to make its forces available to combat the Indonesian infiltrators.

Malaysia's need for external assistance at this stage was acute. Malaysia's resources were already stretched by the need to send two of its Royal Malay Regiment battalions to Singapore on 4 September to quell a second outbreak of Sino-Malay rioting. Britain responded by committing Gurkha forces against the infiltrators, but the Australian battalion, partly deployed on the Thai border, was not immediately available although preparations for its eventual deployment against Indonesian infiltrators were being made. A squadron of RAAF Sabre jet fighters was ordered to Darwin on 8 September and on 11 September plans were completed for an air and sea invasion exercise on the southern coast of New South Wales. Finally, on 29 October, it was announced that a company of the 3rd Battalion

Royal Australian Regiment had been moved from Terendak to nearby Kuala Kesang where further Indonesian infiltrators had landed. This was the first contact between Australian and Indonesian troops.[56]

The escalation of Confrontation also triggered certain Malaysian demands for retaliation. Sarawak's Chief Minister, Kalong Ningkan, had, in late June, suggested counter-attacking guerrilla bases within Indonesia and the Tunku had indicated that it would be discussed when the AMDA partners gathered for the Commonwealth Prime Ministers' Conference in London, although he admitted that such action was contrary to the UN Charter.[57] Some senior British officers involved in the campaign had also favoured a sharp, combined offensive against certain Indonesian strategic targets, but were opposed by the Foreign Office and by Field Marshal Hull.[58]

There was, nevertheless, considerable 'sabre-rattling' by the British immediately following the Pontian–Labis landings. On 9 September Britain announced the transfer of an anti-aircraft regiment from Germany to Malaysia. Later, a British naval force *en route* to Australia from Singapore was ordered to return, leading to speculation that it might pass through the Sunda Strait in defiance of Jakarta.[59] British naval and air manoeuvres from Singapore (the presence of British V bombers in Singapore was quite deliberately disclosed) were conducted amidst reports of the dispatch of Australian Sabre jets to Darwin and the arrival in Singapore of Canberra bombers from New Zealand. The British Foreign Office hinted at the possibility of following the precedent, set by President Johnson in the Gulf of Tonkin, of adopting retaliatory measures.[60]

The period of high tension and British brinkmanship during the first half of September somewhat disconcerted the Malaysians, who wished to avoid any undermining of their political strategy at the UN Security Council to which an appeal was being made. Razak denied Malaysia's complicity in any retaliatory measures and asked to see the British High Commissioner, Lord Head, about such reports.[61]

The Commonwealth Prime Ministers' Conference of July 1964 provided an opportunity for a meeting between Menzies, Holyoake, the Tunku and the British Prime Minister, Sir Alec Douglas-Home. The participants at the meeting on 14 July, who also included Thorneycroft, Sandys, Lord Carrington (the Deputy Foreign Secretary) and Lord Mountbatten (Chief of Defence Staff), reflected the strategic bias of the discussion. The Tunku expressed satisfaction over the allies' appreciation of the serious situation in Malaysia.[62] However, the advocates of a massive, co-ordinated retaliation against Indonesia did not hold sway. The final plan which emerged provided for cross-border operations initially limited in depth to 4.6 km, but later extended to 9 km and then to 18 km. Strict controls were to be exercised over the conduct of these raids and maximum secrecy was to be maintained.[63]

The guiding principle behind this plan contained an element of deterrence which was qualitatively different from the deterrence attempted by AMDA's associates prior to the Pontian–Labis landings: as the anchor power, Britain had had to maintain a strong and consistent support of Malaysia; now deterrence of Indonesia was to be attempted tactically. The aim was to keep the enemy under pressure and off balance, and to impress upon it the possible consequences of further escalation.[64] On the other hand, any response by AMDA should not be overwhelming since Indonesia would then find it difficult to disengage without excessive loss of face.

This aim was reflected in the dropping of leaflets (warning Indonesia to cease its raids against peninsular Malaysia) over Indonesian forward bases in early November. To demonstrate a certain retaliatory capability, the leaflets were dropped from a RMAF plane escorted by RAF jet fighters. The Tunku underlined the message by saying that the exercise exposed Jakarta's empty boasts of having strong aerial defences: the Indonesian forward bases could easily have been destroyed.[65] In anticipation of a retaliatory Indonesian air attack, air defence exercises were conducted over Singapore and Kuala Lumpur.

The AMDA associates did not seem enthusiastic about a dramatic response to Confrontation. A *Guardian* report on 29 September suggested that they had refused to support the idea of an air strike against an Indonesian naval base. When questioned, Holyoake neither affirmed nor denied the report. Instead, his emphasis, that New Zealand troops with the CSR could not be committed to any action Britain might take, reflected a certain cautiousness.[66] Hasluck was similarly questioned in Parliament but refused to comment except to say that consultation between Australia and its partners had been 'close, constant and effective and has served Australia's interest'.[67]

Australia could not discount the likelihood of further escalation of Confrontation since, in Menzies' view, Sukarno had now 'gone past the point of reason'.[68] Thus, Menzies' Defence Review of 10 November spelt out actual preparations 'for all eventualities'. The immediate strategic interest to be protected was the West Irian/ Papua New Guinea border. But the most socially significant measure (though not one that could produce immediate results) was the first peacetime introduction of selective conscription for overseas service. The new military build-up was to result in an increase in defence expenditure of A£404 million over the next three years, bringing the final total to A£1,220 million. This increase, however, did not represent a large material contribution considering that Australia had, during most of Menzies' 15-year Government, spent as little as 3% of its GNP on defence. But politically, the Defence Review served not least to reassure Malaysia and to demonstrate good faith to both Britain and the US, the latter now increasingly drawn into the Vietnam conflict since the Gulf of Tonkin incident.

In Malaysia the source of external instability towards the end of 1964 continued to be Confrontation. In early December General Walker reported that, in the latest five-month period, 1,340 Indonesian infiltrators had participated in nearly one hundred aggressive actions in Borneo.[69] In the Malayan peninsula, the sixth Indonesian landing occurred on 23 December. And if Sukarno neither meant, nor had the capability, to 'crush Malaysia by cock-crow on 1 January 1965', there was every possibility of more frequent and larger-scale attacks.

Although there was a lull in Confrontation towards the end of 1964 and in early 1965, the continuing Indonesian build-up in Borneo was worrying Malaysia. General Walker believed that the lull reflected the busy reorganisation then under way on the Indonesian side.[70] Understandably, Malaysia reacted with sensitivity to the comments made on 22 January 1965 (after touring Malaysia) by Fred Mulley, the Army Minister of the new British Labour Government, that reports of the massing of Indonesian troops for an attack across the Borneo border were 'a gross exaggeration'. Indeed, he doubted whether Sukarno wanted to intensify Confrontation at all.[71] The *Straits Times* sharply criticised this 'apparent complete change of official view in London, and the gift to Sukarno of a high-value propaganda card'.[72] Mulley later clarified the 'misunderstanding' by saying his remarks referred to Indonesian forward positions and not to the continuing Indonesian build-up in the area. However, a massive co-ordinated attack was unlikely 'as of today'.[73]

Razak, though, did not underplay the Indonesian threat lest the

British themselves underplay their response. To him, the Indonesian build-up, 'even at this stage, proves a grave threat to the security of Malaysia'. Consequently, AMDA had been invoked and reinforcements had begun to arrive.[74] But Razak was nevertheless emphatic that responsibility for Malaysian defence 'is purely ours', i.e. that all defence measures including the deployment of troops – both Malaysian and Commonwealth – were subject to the direction of Malaysia's National Defence Council.[75] Underlying Razak's elaboration was a reluctance to concede to any unilateral redefinition of the Indonesian threat which Britain might be tempted to make.

Despite the burdens of Confrontation, the new Labour Government in Britain (which assumed office in October 1964) was equally resolved to uphold the anchor role notwithstanding Fred Mulley's earlier sanguine view of Indonesian intentions. By early 1965 Britain had committed to Malaysia nearly 50,000 servicemen, of whom 10,000 were in Borneo. Its naval strength in the area had grown to 80 warships – the largest naval concentration in the Far East since the Korean war. In mid-January the dispatch of further reinforcements from the Strategic Reserve in Britain was announced. By Harold Wilson's account, the weekend meeting at Chequers (attended by all the leading Ministers, their Permanent Secretaries, the Chiefs of Staff and their advisers) held in late 1964 to review defence had confirmed that Britain's defence forces were seriously overstretched. Wilson himself had feared that the following year's Trooping the Colour ceremony might be cancelled if an emergency placed further demands on British troops.[76]

Malaysia's own military build-up had been progressing. By January 1965 Malaysian armed forces numbered 30,000 regulars, 15,000 reserves and 32,000 policemen. Defence spending (inclusive of internal security expenditure) had risen from 16% of ordinary expenditure in 1962 to 24% by 1965.[77] With the continuing strain on British and Malaysian resources and the diminishing prospects of a political settlement, the stage was set for a deeper Australian–New Zealand involvement in the campaign.

From the moment that Australian–New Zealand forces were committed against Indonesian infiltrators in Malaya, the pressures from London and Kuala Lumpur for an extension of their contributions to Borneo had become increasingly difficult to resist. While touring Malaysia, Fred Mulley had said he would welcome more from the AMDA associates.[78] Mulley was closely followed by the Australian

Defence Minister, Paltridge, who arrived in Malaysia on 19 January. Razak subsequently confirmed that Malaysia had requested further Australian assistance in Borneo during Paltridge's visit – a similar request having also been made to New Zealand. By Paltridge's account, Razak had 'explained comprehensively and forcefully the need for reinforcements'.[79] An opportunity for final consultations with Harold Wilson was presented by the presence of Menzies and Holyoake in London during Sir Winston Churchill's funeral in late January.

On 3 and 5 February respectively, Australia and New Zealand officially announced that their forces attached to the CSR, together with Special Air Service detachments, would be sent to Borneo for combat duty in rotation with British and Malaysian troops. Holyoake later revealed that the New Zealand decision had already been made at a Cabinet meeting on 26 January, prior to his departure for London.[80] Thus the London meeting between Wilson, Menzies and Holyoake did not precipitate the Australian–New Zealand decisions, but rather formally approved them. This was corroborated by Menzies who disclosed that the Australian decision had been taken after consultation with Malaysia and only then conveyed to Wilson who had received it with great pleasure.

But Menzies also admitted that while in London he had discussed 'means of reconciling views ... and [of] getting some order of priorities', because at times 'an actuality like fighting in Malaysia, would have to be balanced with a SEATO contingency'.[81] Australian–New Zealand priorities had resided primarily in the SEATO-orientated role of the CSR and, because no other antipodean troops were ready for immediate service in the region, their decision to commit forces to Borneo meant a shift of their first priority to Borneo. Menzies was in effect indicating to the US that Indonesia now posed a more direct threat to Australian interests. The main priority had returned to the AMDA framework, although the lingering interest in ANZUS cover motivated Menzies to extract Washington's permission to include a phrase in his 3 January statement that the US, as an ANZUS partner, had been 'consulted'. The State Department, however, refused publicly to 'express approval' for the Australian decision and merely indicated that the US had been 'informed'.[82] The commitment of Australian and New Zealand fighting units to Borneo marked a closer convergence of the associates' interests with the AMDA system and a culmination of their assistance to Malaysia. In so far as their initial withholding of this commitment had contained an element of deterrence directed at Indonesia, their January announcements reflected the failure of their attempted deterrence.

On the other hand, to the extent that Australia's graduated response had hinged on the hope of averting a serious deterioration in relations with Jakarta, it was a success – graduated assistance to Malaysia did not inhibit peaceful attempts by Indonesia and Australia to demarcate their common border in West Irian/Papua New Guinea, nor did it inhibit their continuing diplomatic dialogue. Hasluck himself declared on 24 March (the very day Australia sustained its first casualties in Borneo), that the determination to assist in Malaysia's defence did not diminish Australia's willingness to search for an 'enduring peaceful relationship with Indonesia'. In that spirit, Australia was continuing its limited programme of aid to Indonesia.[83]

Within six months of the commitment of Australian–New Zealand forces to Borneo, the process which led eventually to the termination of Confrontation was set in motion – not by the 'winning' efforts of concerted Commonwealth military action, but by a domestic Indonesian upheaval which resulted subsequently in Sukarno's displacement and the abandonment of Confrontation. But prior to that event, and even while Confrontation was still unresolved, developments within the framework of AMDA were to exert further stresses on the cohesiveness of the alliance.

The geographic extension of AMDA coincided with the emergence of three intra-regional challenges to the Malaysia plan. Of these, Confrontation fitted most clearly the *causus foederis* of the alliance. Confrontation tested not only the capability of the alliance (which remained essentially a British capability), but also the cohesion of the alliance. The first phase of Confrontation provided the greater incentive for a redefinition of interests within the alliance. The necessity for restraint, as perceived in Canberra and, to a certain extent, in Singapore, was not shared by Kuala Lumpur (which had to bear the brunt of Indonesian invective and political and military pressures) or London (whose peace-keeping role had created a special interest in Malayan defence) or Wellington (which lacked Canberra's sense of vulnerability). For Australian policymakers, especially, the problem of choosing between Kuala Lumpur and Jakarta was complicated by the fact that Confrontation was not presented by Jakarta as an open quarrel with Australia.

The lack of concerted military response to Confrontation during the first phase, and the need for repeated, albeit unsuccessful, Anglo-Malayan pressure on Canberra for a less equivocal policy, might seem to reflect poorly on the cohesion of the alliance. Yet it also attested to a certain flexibility of AMDA which made possible a reservation of position without unduly undermining the efficacy of the alliance. The flexibility accorded to the AMDA associates, though not necessarily welcome to Kuala Lumpur, made possible their attempt at a graduated response and at deterrence (which differed qualitatively from Britain's deterrent tactics) by withholding forces from Borneo. The escalation of Confrontation in August 1964 proved the failure of Australian–New Zealand deterrence and marked a closing of the ranks among the allies.

More importantly, Confrontation tested the basic assumption of AMDA, i.e. the continuation of Britain's anchor role. The alliance functioned effectively mainly because Britain's determination, as the anchor power, to sustain the peace-keeping role remained firm, even though the economic strain was openly acknowledged. Paradoxically, the extension of AMDA necessitated by the formation of Malaysia was part of the process of British disengagement from Southeast Asia, a process which Confrontation delayed. Indeed, the cost of Confrontation was to convince Britain of the wisdom of non-involvement in similar affairs in the future. In that sense, the crisis represented a significant milestone in the transformation of the alliance. The next phase in the transformation was marked by increasingly evident contradictions between Kuala Lumpur and Singapore. These internal contradictions, which represented a challenge of a different order, fractured the Kuala Lumpur–Singapore axis and, in a *de facto* sense, amended AMDA itself.

7. THE FRACTURED AXIS

In the previous chapter it was observed that the mounting pressures of Confrontation had forced a closing of ranks between Singapore and Malaysia. To both, Confrontation had some positive unifying effects. The Tunku himself viewed Confrontation as 'a blessing in disguise'.[1] Much later, S. Rajaratnam, then Singapore's Minister for Culture, was to say that 'in the early stages . . . [Confrontation had] helped to rally the diverse peoples of Malaysia together'.[2] By the time Rajaratnam made this comment, in March 1965, the external threat was proving insufficient to hold together the Kuala Lumpur–Singapore axis.

The existence of an immediate external threat was not the *raison d'être* for AMDA's extension. Indeed, Confrontation, which engendered the crisis during which Canberra and Wellington extended their association with AMDA, was quite unexpected. AMDA's extension was rather an adjustment to the geographical dimensions of Malaysia, whose own *raison d'être* was the containment of Singapore's internal instability. While the inclusion of Singapore was intended to solve an internal security problem, it also opened up new areas of competition and conflict ranging from economic and financial issues to the fundamental question of Malaysia's national identity. And just as the extension of AMDA resulted from political unification, so the crisis of partnership between Malaysia and Singapore also affected defence co-operation among the allies. This crisis, which erupted despite the existing external threat, altered in the eyes of both Malaysia and Singapore, the priorities of various perceived threats and partly affected their later responses to Indonesia's abandonment of Confrontation. The repercussions of the fracturing of the axis were also felt by the external powers. The anchor power, particularly, was embroiled; first, in the problem of the hiatus in defence which ensued; second, in post-separation squabbles between the local powers; and third, in the manner in which disengagement from

Borneo was effected. Such intra-mural problems constitute the central issues in this chapter.

The decision of 5 September 1964, to commit New Zealand forces against Indonesian infiltrators in the peninsula, was made partly in the light of the Malaysian resources which, owing to the concurrent unrest within Singapore, were then overstretched. The Singapore racial riots of 2 September 1964, following a more serious outbreak on the island on 21 July and an initial disturbance in Bukit Mertajam in northern Malaysia, marked a chain of reactions to the PAP's intervention in the April 1964 elections in the peninsula. The PAP's challenge led to a rapid deterioration in the already strained relations with the Alliance Party. By December 1964 Alliance ministers were seriously considering the possibility of excluding Singapore from the Federation.[3] Significantly, the height of Confrontation (from September 1964 to February 1965) overlapped with the communal riots and also with the vituperative exchanges between the Alliance Party and the PAP between January and April 1965. A developing internal threat soon overtook an existing external one. The ruling Alliance Party perceived the looming internal threat in terms of political agitation by the PAP, attendant inter-ethnic strains and the undermining of the Alliance's political power through a weakening of the MCA, which the PAP had sought to displace. Above all, the Alliance Party was concerned with the essential interests of UMNO and the established rights and privileges of the Malays.

The PAP leadership perceived the internal threat in terms of possible repressive action which might be taken against them and, equally, the consequences of such action on racial peace. An extremist resolution was proposed at the UMNO General Assembly on 15 May 1965 to 'detain' Lee Kuan Yew, although it was later toned down. Alarm over this threat had also spread to London. Harold Wilson was sufficiently concerned by the news (received some weeks before the Commonwealth Prime Ministers' Conference of June 1965) of a 'possible coup against Harry Lee and his colleagues' to warn the Tunku against such action.[4]

From Kuala Lumpur's perspective, the threat posed by Singapore's presence in the Federation had, by mid-1965, become qualitatively different from the earlier perceived threat which had caused the Tunku to favour merger through Malaysia. The Barisan Sosialis was by now debilitated by the detention (in February and October

1963) of its key leaders and by its leadership struggle. Confrontation also cost the Barisan dearly in electoral terms and the losses it suffered in September 1963 were compounded by the defeat of its candidate by the PAP in the (second) Hong Lim by-election in July 1965.

While the original *raison d'être* for union with Singapore had been overtaken by events, the political costs of incorporating Singapore were sufficiently high for the Tunku seriously to consider separation during his convalescence in London, where he had fallen ill after the Commonwealth Prime Ministers' Conference. The final decision to separate was probably taken on 6 August, the day after the Tunku flew into Singapore from Europe. On 7 August, the Separation Agreement was signed by Lee and the Tunku after a brief meeting in Kuala Lumpur, other ministers from Singapore adding their signatures the following day. The decision was conveyed to the Alliance National Council by the Tunku the following morning and on 9 August the Malaysian Parliament passed, by 126 votes to none, the Constitution and Malaysia (Singapore Amendment) Act 1965 which made the separation formal.

The Tunku has insisted that the only alternative to separation was repressive action against the PAP leaders and that this forced the latter to accept separation. M. N. Sopiee argues, however, that the Tunku was never in danger of being forced by extremist pressures within UMNO into taking repressive measures but, rather, that the Tunku was supremely confident when he confronted the PAP leaders with this unpleasant alternative.[5] Nevertheless, in accepting separation, the PAP leadership also accepted in effect the reality of this alternative, i.e. repressive action. It was this fear (reinforced by the knowledge that Malaysian troops had been put on the alert in Johore) which clouded the post-separation relations between Kuala Lumpur and Singapore, especially in the military sphere. If Singapore had become the unstable factor within Malaysia, it now began, having gained its independence, to view Malaysia as a source of its own insecurity. The assumption underlying the extended AMDA – that Malaya–Singapore defence was inseparable – was now being tested by the atmosphere of mutual suspicion between them.

The most significant aspect of separation, with regard to intra-alliance relations, was its speedy and secret execution. That none of the ANZAM partners was informed of the final decision was indicated by the futile last-minute attempts at intervention by Britain and Australia. Lord Head, the British High Commissioner, alerted by a Sabah delegate at the meeting of the Alliance National Council, unsuccessfully sought to contact the Tunku throughout 8 August. Although he succeeded eventually in seeing the Tunku – having 'gatecrashed' a party where the Tunku, Razak and Tan Siew Sin were present – whatever proposal he had to avert separation went unheeded. That same evening Lord Head radioed the CRO which promptly informed Harold Wilson, then holidaying in the Scilly Isles. Simultaneously, Arthur Bottomley, the Commonwealth Secretary, then in West Africa, received a similar message. Lord Head's final attempt to intervene was made just an hour and a quarter before the Amendment Bill was tabled. Armed with a letter from Harold Wilson expressing 'grave concern', he requested a 24-hour delay. The Tunku was not moved. Lord Head's efforts were repeated shortly after by the Australian High Commissioner, T. K. Critchley, known for his close association with the Tunku and Alliance Party leaders. He too was rebuffed.

If secrecy was essential for a smooth severance of Singapore, the timing was providential. The British Parliament was in summer recess with Wilson and Michael Stewart, the Foreign Secretary, holidaying in the Scillies, Arthur Bottomley in West Africa and his deputy, Cledwyn Hughes, in Anglesey. Even the Malaysian High Commissioner to Australia and New Zealand later admitted ignorance of the impending crisis. Thus, none of the diplomatic functionaries of the external powers were aware of the crisis until too late. Furthermore, neither Sabah nor Sarawak, which had accompanied Singapore into Malaysia, was consulted.

Liska comments that, 'like separate action itself, the consequences of failure to consult indicate the degree of an alliance's cohesion. They constitute a better index than does a successful consultation, since they occur in the more revealing conditions of risk'.[6] The 'risk' in AMDA's case stemmed from the Tunku's ready assumption that the external partners (especially Britain) would, because of Confrontation, remain as committed to the defence of territories which politically no longer coincided with the geographical boundaries of the extended AMDA. However, if the Australian decision to commit forces against Confrontation had been reached only with great difficulty, would separation not provide Canberra with an excuse to review its whole position? And if Britain initially could not entrust its bases to an independent Singapore, how would it now react to this *fait accompli*? As will be indicated below, parts of the Separation

Agreement anticipated this risk by bridging the gap between the British commitment enshrined in AMDA and the revised Federation.

In the event, the 'risk' proved well taken. First, Britain did not at this stage think in terms of abandoning its East of Suez role, which required local bases and facilities. Second, although Denis Healey was 'very tempted' to consider withdrawal, it just could not be done 'as long as Sukarno was there'.[7] In this sense, the external threat both sustained and strained the cohesiveness of the alliance. The inherent risk of non-consultation was outweighed by the Tunku's perception of the risk of consultation. He felt that if news of the prospect of separation had leaked out, the external allies would have tried to prevent it.[8] Britain, as the most important provider of Malaysian security at a time of continuing external threat, might well have exercised a decisive leverage.

Moreover, a general suspicion existed in Kuala Lumpur that Britain had become the advocate of Lee Kuan Yew's interests. Kuala Lumpur's suspicion had been aroused during the pre-Malaysian wrangling over the establishment of a Malaysian common market and Singapore's subsequent unilateral declaration of independence. And when the Kuala Lumpur–Singapore rift widened, the British attempt to play counsellor appeared to advance a Singapore claim. Similarly, Wilson's warning to the Tunku prior to the 1965 Commonwealth Prime Ministers' Conference must have compounded the latter's irritation with the anchor power's protectiveness (augmented by a substantial military presence in Singapore) towards Lee. Intangibly, but significantly, cohesion within the alliance was being strained as Britain became entangled in the quarrels of its two defence clients. But, while Confrontation continued and Malaysia remained heavily dependent on British assistance, Malaysian irritation with the British had to be contained. In this sense, the external threat exaggerated the cohesion of the alliance, which in reality was being eroded by internal friction.

The AMDA associates likewise felt the reverberations of the growing rift between Malaysia and Singapore. Lee Kuan Yew had used a visit to New Zealand and Australia in March 1965 to highlight the growing danger of Malay communalism and the shortcomings of the Alliance Government in the hope that the associates would restrain Kuala Lumpur. Following separation, Holyoake was obliged to state that while Lee's views were taken 'most seriously', it was felt that Malaysia–Singapore differences could best be settled between themselves.[9] Lee had also lobbied Menzies during discussions in Canberra on 18 March. At Menzies' request, Lee put his thoughts on paper three weeks after returning to Singapore.[10] Lee's basic argument was that Australia should support the Malaysia concept rather than a particular regime.[11] Menzies was probably more sympathetic towards the Alliance Government (on account of the long and personal connections of Critchley in Kuala Lumpur) although, with the stationing of a Deputy High Commissioner in Singapore after Federation, Canberra had, in effect, two windows on the Malaysian scene.[12] Lee openly claimed later that separation need never have happened had Canberra taken his analysis more seriously.[13] It appeared that the British, in warning the Tunku against repressive action, were preparing for the worst, but that they had neglected the possibility of separation. As Lee indicated: 'I did not believe that, unless I had Arthur Bottomley in Kuala Lumpur with me, and I could tell him face to face, I could ever convince him.'[14]

When news of the separation broke upon the capitals of the ANZAM partners, they were at one in expressing regret and disappointment. In his first post-separation statement, Menzies stressed that no prior consultation with Canberra had taken place. Accepting the reality of separation, he maintained that the most important matter was 'the continued and combined defence of the region'.[15] In this connection, Hasluck had earlier stated that 'any adjustments in the machinery for defence and co-operation with other countries such as Australia would form the subject of consultations'.[16]

The lack of prior consultation with the external powers and the continued dependence of the local powers on foreign assistance meant that Malaysia and Singapore had to retain the element of continuity in the 'central and most important matter' of 'the continued and combined defence of the region' while making adjustments to Singapore's new sovereign status. Where Kuala Lumpur had previously exercised exclusive control over the defence and foreign policies of a Federation which had included Singapore, the new situation placed Singapore in the position of *de jure* equality as a defence partner with full competence in foreign affairs. However, as will be shown below, the new distinguishing features were not so clear-cut.

The formal adjustments to Singapore's status as a defence partner were embodied in Article V of the Separation Agreement.[17] In paragraph 2 of the Article, Malaysia agreed to give 'reasonable and adequate' assistance for the external defence of Singapore on the basis of a 'reasonable and adequate' contribution by Singapore's own armed forces for the same purpose. Paragraph 3 allowed Malaysia to retain bases and other facilities used by its military forces within Singapore and to use such bases and facilities for the purpose of external defence. These two paragraphs made formal the concept of the indivisibility of Malaysia–Singapore defence, and this was reinforced by paragraph 4 in which both Governments pledged to refrain from entering into any treaty or agreement with a foreign country detrimental to the independence and defence of either Government. The mutuality of their defence interests was to be institutionalised by a Joint Defence Council (JDC) for the purposes of external defence and mutual assistance (paragraph 1).

Article V preserved, as far as possible, the defence status quo between Malaysia and Singapore which had provided the original strategic basis for the military assistance rendered by the ANZAM partners within the extended AMDA while nevertheless adjusting to Singapore's new status. In yet another sense the status quo was being preserved *vis-à-vis* the external powers. Singapore's independence necessitated a restatement of the terms under which Britain maintained its bases, facilities and troops within the island. Until a treaty was concluded between Britain and Singapore, the status quo was maintained by Annex B of the Separation Agreement. This stipulated that 'any treaty, agreement, or convention' entered into before Malaysia Day between Malaysia and another country or countries would, where it applied to Singapore, be deemed 'a treaty, agreement or convention between Singapore and that country or countries'. With AMDA in mind, Annex B further stated that Singapore would continue to grant Britain the right to continue maintaining the bases and facilities occupied by British service authorities and would permit Britain use of these bases and facilities for 'the purpose of assisting in the defence of Singapore and Malaysia and for Commonwealth defence and for the preservation of peace in Southeast Asia'.[18] This appeared to preserve a British interest in the use of the Singapore bases within the SEATO context.

Preservation of the British military position in Singapore and *de facto* acknowledgement of an indivisibility in Malaysia–Singapore defence helped reassure the anchor power, whose initial response to separation had taken the form of 'very strong messages to both leaders' from Harold Wilson 'to avoid any action that could lead to an outbreak of hostilities'.[19] Although Lord Head felt that AMDA would have to be rewritten, he also implied that Article V and Annex B would provide the basis for that rewriting.[20]

Britain's position was expressed in a statement issued after discussions on 15 August at Culdrose, where Wilson and Michael Stewart had flown from the Scillies for a special meeting with Healey, Cledwyn Hughes and senior officials including Field Marshal Sir Richard Hull and Lord Head, who provided an assessment of the situation. The statement acknowledged that the Malaysia–Singapore declaration that 'facilities accorded to British forces will be unchanged . . . [provided] an assurance that we shall be able to continue to assist both countries in their external defence'. Britain would continue to assist Malaysia and Singapore in repelling outside attacks so long as both countries desired such assistance.[21] The change in Singapore's status, however, necessitated a review of AMDA. This was authorised by the meeting, and since Singapore was not a high contracting party to AMDA, Lord Head believed that Singapore would have to renegotiate with Britain for its defence needs.

Article V and Annex B were equally important to the AMDA associates. Indeed, Hasluck indicated in Parliament on 18 August 1965 that the terms of the Separation Agreement which were 'of particular interest to us' were those in Article V. He said that the essential features of the situation which provided the context to Australia's association with the extended AMDA still existed, i.e. Confrontation continued; Britain's commitment remained as before; both Malaysia and Singapore, though separate, faced the same defence problems; and the facilities and resources of both were involved in their common defence. Although separation had come about, it was felt that the strategic rationale behind the Australian contribution to the defence of the area remained. In Hasluck's opinion, this constant factor was reinforced by 'the existing system of combined defence' which had stood up well against Confrontation. It was this system, turning the Malaysia area into 'one theatre, operating under one operational system and governed by a common purpose', that facilitated the collective effort by which Australia and New Zealand were able to *add* their contributions to 'the total defence structure'. Hasluck saw considerable difficulties arising if the unscrambling of such a structure meant that Australia would have to enter into 'separate and possibly differing commitments with a variety of authorities'.[22]

The significance of the concept of combined defence for the Malaysia–Singapore region was highlighted when secessionist alarm was engendered over Sabah and Sarawak following Singapore's separation. The surreptitious ejection of Singapore had caused unease in the two Borneo states which had entered Malaysia together with Singapore. The attempts by Donald Stephens, the Federal Minister for Sabah Affairs and previously Sabah's Chief Minister, to obtain a review of the Malaysia arrangements disturbed the Tunku. Although Stephens soon resigned from the Federal Cabinet, the Tunku found it expedient to tour Sabah and Sarawak to explain Singapore's separation and to assert his authority. At Sandakan (in Sabah) on 21 August, the Tunku disclosed that the external powers had made clear that Sabah would not be defended if it tried to secede. Ironically, the Tunku, who feared that the defence leverage available to the external powers might frustrate his plan to eject Singapore, now used precisely that lever to pre-empt any secessionist movement in eastern Malaysia. The fact remained that while a real defence problem existed, that leverage was effective.

Hasluck denied that Sabah and Sarawak had been thus cautioned by Australia but rejoined that Australia would 'undoubtedly find it much easier if combined defence arrangements were made as envisaged in the Separation Agreement between Singapore and Malaysia'.[23] Holyoake issued a similar denial but cautiously added that if Sabah did secede, New Zealand would have to reconsider its position.[24] There was no reason, on *a priori* grounds, why Australia, which had lamented Singapore's separation, had emphasised the virtues of combined defence in the Malaysian area, and had cautiously renewed its commitment to Malaysian defence, should not be dismayed by a further disintegration of the Federation. Indeed, the Tunku was surprised by Hasluck's and Holyoake's denials. While warning 'those secessionist people' not to be encouraged by such denials, the Tunku, prior to his visit to Borneo, reiterated that it was understood that the Commonwealth allies would withdraw support if Sabah seceded. He was, however, not perturbed and would not seek clarification from them. In any case, the fear of East Malaysian secession appeared to have passed.

The doctrine of the indivisibility of Malaysia–Singapore defence embodied in Article V of the Separation Agreement was soon given substantive form. On 17 August Malaysia and Singapore announced the establishment of a Combined Defence Council (also known as the Joint Defence Council) for their common defence as provided for in paragraph 1 of Article V.[25] Dr Goh Keng Swee, then Singapore's Defence Minister, also committed the 2nd Battalion of the Singapore Infantry Regiment (renamed the Malaysian Infantry Regiment on the formation of Malaysia but reverting to Singapore's control after separation) to action along the Borneo border.

The *Straits Times* remarked that the gesture 'firmly removes solidarity in defence matters from the list of bargainable issues'.[26] The doctrine of indivisibility had not been affirmed merely for the consumption of the external powers. Apart from the fact that Malaysia's external defence was still heavily dependent on the British presence which was centred on Singapore, neither Malaysia's nor Singapore's defence could be conceived of in complete isolation from the other. If Singapore became a party to action that jeopardised Malaysian security, it would be placed in a position where its own security would be threatened. In this sense, Malaysia could no more be defended without Singapore than Singapore could be defended without Malaysia.

The doctrine of indivisibility was most relevant in the context of an external threat from a third power. It was, however, not inconsistent with the observation that, in a narrower Malaysia–Singapore context, the two local powers could well view each other as possible unstable factors in each other's security. Indeed, their close interdependence accentuated precisely that state of mutual apprehension which became acute immediately after separation. But strategic interdependence (a more accurate term than 'indivisibility') did not mean an indivisibility of political interests. And, since their political interests were indeed divisible, the vicissitudes of their post-separation relations were to have disturbing repercussions on matters of their common defence.

Paragraph 4 of Article V, which precluded Malaysia and Singapore from entering into any treaty or other arrangements with a third country which might be detrimental to the defence and independence of the other, stemmed from the concept of indivisibility and certainly had relevance to Confrontation. Indeed, the Tunku stated that 'we have seen to it that . . . Singapore would be denied the opportunity of establishing diplomatic relations with

Indonesia'.²⁷ But the introduction of such a constraint (more heavily felt by Singapore) into their foreign policies, at a juncture when Singapore could now exercise *de jure* and *de facto* competence in such areas, provided new grounds for dispute.

The test soon emerged when Indonesia, temptingly, offered to recognise Singapore. Lee Kuan Yew, who said that Singapore would trade 'even with the devil' in order to survive, indicated (on 9 August) Singapore's readiness to establish consular relations with Indonesia. He cautiously added that any relations with Indonesia must not prejudice the conditions of Singapore's survival which included co-operation with Malaysia and the ability to summon friends to its defence. The Tunku promptly remarked that, if Singapore normalised relations with Indonesia, 'their obvious intention would be to harm our interests'.²⁸ He subsequently declared that under no circumstances would he be disposed to let Singapore enter into diplomatic relations with any country hostile to Malaysia. Any dealings such as a trade agreement or the reopening of the Indonesian consulate in Singapore could be 'nothing but double-crossing'.²⁹ Having affirmed that Singapore's embargo on Indonesian traders remained and would only be reviewed after Indonesia had finally called off Confrontation, Rajaratnam, Singapore's Foreign Minister, appealed to the Tunku to consider sympathetically the problems of Singapore's survival and economic stability.³⁰ The Tunku remained adamant.

At the end of September Lee Kuan Yew revealed that Indonesia had made several attempts to negotiate with Singapore. The Tunku was aware of these developments but hoped that Lee would consider Malaysia's position, namely, that Indonesia must suspend operations against, and normalise relations with, Malaysia.³¹ Singapore took the view that there were certain relations into which it could enter with Indonesia without jeopardising Malaysian security. As Rajaratnam argued, Australia too was fighting Indonesia in Borneo but yet maintained trade and other relations with Jakarta. More fundamentally, the controversy reflected the process of adjustment to a new relationship. The Tunku's refusal to 'allow' Singapore this initiative in foreign policy showed a lingering desire to exert a determining influence on Singapore. Equally, Singapore's attitude underlined an intention to demonstrate its sovereignty. Malaysia, in Rajaratnam's view, 'must regard us and treat us as a sovereign and independent nation [with] the right to establish relationships with any other country'. He reiterated, however, that Singapore would not pursue its self-interest to the point where it became detrimental to Malaysia.³²

Singapore's assertion of independence had other repercussions on intra-alliance relations. The AMDA negotiations in 1956, it may be recalled, represented an adjustment of strategic continuity to political change in Malaya at a time when Singapore still remained a British responsibility. The extension of AMDA incorporated, with respect to Singapore, an ANZAM strategic interest in the regional function of the bases within AMDA, a function later recognised in Annex B of the Separation Agreement. Yet Singapore's independence had altered the political context of that defence relationship in that Singapore now became a *de facto* and a *de jure* host to an ANZAM presence. The necessity for strategic continuity made it even more important to emphasise the political change at a juncture when Singapore, whose avowed policy was one of 'non-alignment', was particularly keen to gain recognition by the Afro-Asian bloc.

Singapore also had to respond to reports from Jakarta suggesting that the British bases would be tolerated if they were solely for defensive purposes. Rajaratnam assured Jakarta that Singapore would disallow the use of the bases for hostilities against Indonesia or any friendly country.³³ Singapore's principal interest was defined by Lee Kuan Yew on 11 August when he warned that if the British removed their bases, then not only would Singapore be destroyed by Indonesia, but Malaysia also.³⁴ However, a clearer expression of Singapore's attitude towards the regional role of the bases emerged on 12 August when Rajaratnam declared that Singapore would only allow Britain to use its bases on the island for SEATO purposes if the interests of Singapore and SEATO coincided. Singapore's attitude towards SEATO was 'not one of understanding or sympathy'.³⁵

Rajaratnam subsequently agreed that British prerogatives in Annex B were certainly wide ranging. However, permission for the use of the bases would be considered at each specific occasion on the grounds of whether such use fitted 'our definition', the primary consideration being whether any such use was in Singapore's interests. He conceded that in some instances Singapore's defence could depend on the 'preservation of peace in Southeast Asia', in which case there would be no objection to the bases being so used. But Britain's rights as defined in Annex B were not dependent on mutual consultation. This would be demanded when the time came for renegotiation.[36]

It is debatable whether the Malaysian Government had had hitherto the *de facto* right to decide what uses of the Singapore bases should be regarded as being for the preservation of peace in Southeast Asia. However, Singapore's independence meant that it, Singapore, was now constitutionally placed to insist on the right even if Malaysia did not. Lee Kuan Yew strongly asserted Singapore's sovereign status on 31 August when he declared that he could give Britain 24 hours' notice to quit the bases. Appealing to Afro-Asian sentiments, Lee declared, on the eve of Singapore's application for UN membership, that the bases would not be used to blackmail Indonesia, nor would they be used for attacks on China. But far from wanting Britain to quit, Lee was in fact more concerned with Britain's growing disillusion with its East of Suez role. He said that if Britain withdrew, he would ally himself with Australia and New Zealand but not with the Americans. He proceeded to reveal a sensational Central Intelligence Agency intrigue in Singapore and to criticise maladroit American involvement in his personal affairs, thus underlining America's lack of understanding of Asia. Hence the need for a British presence.[37]

Britain denied any contemplation of a withdrawal from Singapore. The CRO statement also pointed out provisions in the Separation Agreement which allowed Britain use of the bases for Malaysia–Singapore defence and the preservation of peace in Southeast Asia. It acknowledged, however, the need for adjustments to be made to the treaty to allow for Singapore's independence and expected Lee to make proposals.[38] While the strategic arguments rested with Britain, the political arguments remained with Singapore, and Michael Stewart conceded that Lee's 31 August remark pointed out 'that we have no sovereignty ... in Singapore or Malaysia'.[39] However, the overriding local interest in the British presence meant that Singapore would not impose unreasonable constraints on the exercise of Britain's wider strategic role.

But Lee's remarks also revealed another facet of the continuing strains with Kuala Lumpur. His anti-American tirades could have been triggered partly by fears of American involvement in ethnic conflicts in the area. As Lee stated on another occasion, if Britain withdrew, he was certain, on account of America's record of supporting the most vocal anti-communists in Southeast Asia, that the

Malay leadership in Malaysia would use the Americans to preserve their status quo.[40] The Tunku dismissed this apprehension and affirmed instead the absolute necessity of the Singapore bases for their common defence. It was not simply a matter of Singapore telling Britain to quit. Following a Combined Defence Council (CDC) meeting on 2 September, the Tunku announced agreement to maintain the status quo of the Singapore bases until AMDA had been renegotiated. But he seemed to view renegotiation as a mere adjustment to Singapore's sovereign status, for he did not anticipate substantive changes in a new treaty.[41]

There was a consensus on the need for some adjustment to be made to allow for Singapore's independence. Malaysia, especially, wanted Singapore's general undertakings to be placed on a more concrete basis. Yet the other parties were not anxious for AMDA to be renegotiated. The Tunku disclosed that Singapore did not seem in any hurry. Goh Keng Swee conceded the initiative to Britain. While the British High Commission in Kuala Lumpur suggested that Malaysia and Singapore should first discuss their defence requirements. In October, the Foreign Secretary, George Brown, confirmed speculations that any British review of the Singapore bases would not be made merely to adjust to Singapore's independence, but would be subsumed under a wider reconsideration of Britain's East of Suez policy.[42] Paul Hasluck, for his part, saw no necessity for a separate Australian–Malaysian treaty. Indeed, to insist (as the ALP did) that defence support could not be achieved without such an agreement would, he said, complicate Australian–Malaysian relations.[43] Thus, although a new treaty was desirable, the existing arrangements adequately preserved the status quo pending a review of British policy. However, maintenance of the status quo was to prove a highly contentious issue between Malaysia and Singapore.

A portent of the difficulties ahead emerged on 18 August when Rajaratnam firmly rejected the view (attributed to the Tunku) that Malaysian forces in Singapore could intervene without Singapore's approval should any threat develop there. The Malaysian claim to an interest in the Singapore base was reflected in Razak's conception of a revised AMDA, embracing a bilateral treaty between the local powers and a trilateral treaty to include Britain.[44] Unhappy with Singapore's preference for a separate treaty with Britain, the Tunku, on the eve of Denis Healey's visit to the region in February 1966, again canvassed support for a trilateral treaty.⁴⁵ The central premise of Britain's defence arrangements with Malaysia and Singapore was the indivisibility of their defence bases. However, the British Defence White Paper published on 22 February did not refer to any new defence treaty with Malaysia and/or Singapore, despite Healey's fuelling of such an expectation while in Kuala Lumpur earlier that month.

Singapore was acutely concerned about its economic survival, especially after the rescinding of common market arrangements with Malaysia. The evident Malaysian interest in the Singapore bases provided a tempting opportunity for a trade-off. A satisfactory defence arrangement could be a *quid pro quo* for improved economic relations, in particular for greater access for Singapore goods to the Malaysian market. But linking defence problems to other, wider issues necessarily made it difficult to insulate defence co-operation from the complexities of these other issues. Malaysia and Singapore, against a background of unsettled British policy, were soon embroiled in further controversy.

A dispute arose over the return of the 2nd Battalion of the Singapore Infantry Regiment from Sabah to Camp Temasek, in Singapore, which had been occupied in its absence by a Malaysian battalion. Units of the Malaysian battalion had begun returning to the peninsula when, on 4 February, the Malaysian Defence Ministry asked that the Singapore battalion (whose advance units had already arrived at Camp Temasek) be sent to the mainland instead, while the Malaysians remained at Temasek. This request was refused on 9 February.⁴⁶ The Tunku responded to Singapore's refusal of the Malaysian request by declaring that Article V of the Separation Agreement provided Malaysia with a base in Singapore. The Malaysian Defence Ministry read into Article V, paragraph 3, a Singapore obligation to allow Malaysian troops to remain in Singapore. It further stated that the exercise of that right to station forces in Singapore depended solely on Malaysian judgement.⁴⁷

Singapore, for its part, pointed out that the two Governments had not yet entered into a defence treaty, that Camp Temasek was not being 'used' by Malaysia either on the date of separation or on the date of the Separation Agreement and hence did not fall within paragraph 3, which permitted Malaysia the continued use of bases and facilities previously occupied, and that all Singapore properties had reverted to Singapore after separation. Singapore then offered to submit Article V for arbitration to a Commonwealth or international tribunal.[48]

Whatever the merits of the opposing interpretations, the apprehensions of the two sides were obvious. Malaysia remained alarmed that its security might be jeopardised by the latter's independent foreign and trade policies. The concept of 'indivisibility' led the Tunku, Tun Razak and Razak's Parliamentary Secretary to elevate the presence of Malaysian forces in Singapore to that of 'a right'. Singapore's view was influenced by the fear that Malaysia might seek a permanent and controlling presence on the island. As Rajaratnam indicated, the impression could be conveyed that 'this so-called right' would be exercised regardless of Singapore's consent.[49] Singapore also feared that Malaysia would subsequently claim a precedent to establish new bases and that it would occupy them with new troops. Dr Goh saw the controversy as 'symptomatic of a deeper malaise in the relations between the two Governments on defence matters'.[50] Although the issue was eventually defused (after official talks and two meetings in early March between Razak and Dr Goh) by a *modus vivendi* which permitted Malaysian forces temporary accommodation in Singapore, that 'deeper malaise' was not expunged. A mutual defence treaty upon which Malaysia's rights under Article V, paragraph 3, would depend failed to materialise.

Another manifestation of the 'deeper malaise' appeared when Singapore officially withdrew from the CDC. A Singapore statement on 30 March referred to the increasingly anomalous position of the Singapore representative (i.e. Dr Goh) on the Council which dealt mainly with matters of exclusively Malaysian interest. On the other hand, a Singapore proposal to resume barter trade with Indonesia, using Pulau Senang to minimise security risks, was apparently vetoed.[51] Thus, the status quo, both in institutional form and as reflected in the general undertakings of Article V, failed to meet the conflicting interests of Malaysia and Singapore. Neither a new defence treaty nor a more representative CDC emerged. Henceforth, security matters common to both were dealt with on an *ad hoc* basis.

By the time Singapore withdrew from the CDC, Confrontation had entered a desultory phase as Indonesia struggled to regain its internal political equilibrium following the abortive coup of 30 September 1965 and the ensuing anti-communist purge. Sukarno's power was progressively reduced until by March 1966 the moderate triumvirate of General Suharto (who assumed Sukarno's executive power), Dr Adam Malik (Foreign Minister) and the Sultan of Jogjakarta (Economic Minister), whose clear priority was economic recovery, appeared reasonably established. Prospects for an end to Confrontation were improving.

The controversy in September 1965 over the possible Indonesian recognition of Singapore and resumption of Indonesia–Singapore relations had revealed the deep Malaysian fear of a separate peace and the lack of a co-ordinated response to Indonesia. By the end of 1965, when conditions for a peaceful settlement appeared even better, Malaysian concern shifted to Britain when Michael Stewart publicly indicated, on 27 November, Britain's readiness to consider, in concert with Indonesia, ways of ending Confrontation.[52] Kuala Lumpur now insisted that negotiations to end Confrontation be a Malaysian prerogative and promptly sought clarification from London. Britain's duty, said the Tunku, was to honour AMDA as long as Confrontation lasted. The CRO denied any intention to act unilaterally.[53] Responding to Michael Stewart's overtures, Subandrio offered an exchange of views. But his subsequent offer to hold bilateral talks with Singapore and with the separate components of Malaysia was curtly dismissed by the Tunku.

By April 1966 Suharto had assumed full executive power, banned the PKI and arrested many of Sukarno's old Cabinet favourites including Subandrio who was closely associated with Confrontation. Circumstances favoured a more overt initiative towards terminating Confrontation. Yet the new leadership, faced with a populace long nurtured on Confrontation, had to move cautiously. Moreover, Sukarno was still Head of State and the new leaders, wishing to avoid a showdown, would rather work through him if possible. However, the manner in which Indonesia publicly signalled its desire for a dialogue precipitated further Malaysia–Singapore differences.

The Tunku had barely declared that Singapore should be a party to any peace talks when Adam Malik said, on 10 April, that Sukarno had instructed him to speed up the recognition of Singapore so as to intensify Confrontation. Malik was suggesting (possibly for domestic consumption) that the recognition of Singapore was not inconsistent with Confrontation – indeed, that it might intensify Confrontation since Malaysia considered a separate peace between Indonesia and Singapore to be injurious to Malaysian interests. Privately, Malik saw the recognition of Singapore in a different light – that such a recognition was the beginning of diplomatic moves which would culminate in the ending of Confrontation.[54]

But this move, coming within a week of Singapore's withdrawal from the CDC, was construed differently in Kuala Lumpur. The *Indonesian Herald*'s remark, that recognition of Singapore was intended to isolate Kuala Lumpur, was hardly helpful.[55] Rajaratnam welcomed Indonesia's approach and assured Malaysia of consultations. The Tunku's reaction was furious. After an emergency Cabinet meeting, he said Singapore would have to choose between Malaysia and Indonesia.[56] On 14 April Lee Kuan Yew, then on an overseas tour, cabled the Tunku from Bangkok and denied any knowledge of negotiations in Bangkok as alleged by Malik and pledged not to jeopardise Malaysian interests. But he also pointed to the absurdity of publicly declining recognition by Indonesia.[57] Malaysia's suspicion was not allayed. During the weekend of 16–17 April Malaysia imposed security checks at the causeway. On 19 April the first build-up of travel restrictions against Singapore citizens was announced and an agreement on common visas allowed to lapse. After Singapore (responding to the Tunku's challenge) had published on 25 April 1966 Lee's Bangkok cable of 14 April and letter of 25 March written to the Tunku,[58] Kuala Lumpur expressed some satisfaction. However, the restrictions on travel remained.

Despite the open rancour between Malaysia and Indonesia, unofficial contacts had been maintained. In late April 'Kogam' (the Indonesian 'Crush Malaysia Command') clarified that Indonesia did not want a breach between Malaysia and Singapore over the recognition issue. Events accelerated after a discussion on Confrontation in Bangkok at the end of April between Adam Malik and the Philippine Foreign Secretary, Narcisso Ramos. Malik indicated that recognition of Singapore would be unconditional.

At this point Malaysian suspicion over separate Anglo-Indonesian contacts resurfaced. Michael Stewart had, on 25 April 1966, signalled British willingness to offer Indonesia emergency economic aid as an inducement to end Confrontation.[59] After the £1 million offer was made public and contacts via the British embassy in Jakarta stepped up in May, the Tunku declared that Britain had no authority to speak on Malaysia's behalf. The British High Commissioner to Malaysia denied any settlement behind Malaysia's back, but affirmed that Britain had 'very close and deep interests' in the dispute.[60]

Although official Indonesian statements during May showed little departure from Confrontation, secret Malaysia–Indonesia contacts were increased. Six secret meetings (four in Bangkok and two in

Hong Kong) culminated in a dramatic goodwill visit by 'Kogam' officers to Malaysia on 27 May. The euphoric *rapprochement* during the Indonesian visit revived strong sentiments of blood-brotherhood with Indonesia, much to Singapore's discomfort. Although Razak had earlier emphasised the desirability of a simultaneous recognition of Singapore and ending of Confrontation, Singapore was omitted from the meeting of Malaysian and Indonesian Ministers held at Bangkok at the end of May.

The Razak–Malik Bangkok Accord provided a face-saving way to end Confrontation while satisfying an Indonesian insistence on a testing of Bornean opinion by promising democratic elections in Sabah and Sarawak. Although internal Indonesian difficulties (particularly Sukarno's continued resistance) delayed ratification of the Accord until 11 August, Confrontation was, in effect, over. With the Bangkok Accord made final on 1 June, Razak indicated that Indonesia's attitude towards Singapore no longer worried Malaysia. Indonesia recognised Singapore soon after (the Philippines, too, re-established relations with Kuala Lumpur and recognised Singapore before the end of June) and on 3 June an Indonesian goodwill mission arrived in Singapore.

As with the dispute over sovereign rights, the failure to devise a Malaysia–Singapore defence treaty and the controversy over Camp Temasek resulting in Singapore's withdrawal from the CDC, the resolution of Confrontation provided yet another example of the difficulty in maintaining the cohesion of the alliance. Eight months after their separation, Malaysia and Singapore had failed to evolve a united response to Indonesia's overtures of peace. The open diplomacy and public acrimony between them contrasted with their respective secret exchanges with their erstwhile adversary. Before the 'Kogam' visit Singapore's response to Indonesia was seen as a security threat by Malaysia; after the 'Kogam' visit it was Singapore that needed assurance in the afterglow of the Malaysia–Indonesia *rapprochement*. It was ironic that the meeting between Lee Kuan Yew and the Tunku in Kuala Lumpur on 8 June was held *after* the unofficial ending of Confrontation and Indonesia's recognition of Singapore – both issues of contention between Malaysia and Singapore. Following their meeting, the Tunku publicly disclaimed the policy of Maphilindo, the racial undertones of which had long disturbed Singapore. Lee, in turn, indicated that their two countries would normalise relations with Indonesia simultaneously. The meeting, however, did not resolve the hiatus in their defence. Moreover, the anchor power was soon drawn again into these unresolved differences.

The hiatus in defence between Malaysia and Singapore must have been irksome to the suppliers of alliance security. Healey had, during his February 1966 visit, stipulated that British commitments must be based on a joint Malaysia–Singapore effort. Similar attitudes were reflected by the other ANZAM partners. As the anchor power, Britain possessed a certain leverage for extracting speedier progress in defence co-operation between its two clients. That this leverage was attempted soon became public.

Tan Siew Sin, Malaysia's Finance Minister, had, in late May 1966, visited London to discuss economic assistance, especially in connection with Malaysia's defence needs. These talks ended inconclusively. Britain's financial difficulties were London's explanation for the stalled discussions. According to Tan Siew Sin, assurances of British military aid were given during Healey's February visit and when he met James Callaghan, the Chancellor of the Exchequer, earlier in the year. The other external partners gave similar assurances in early 1966. Tan Siew Sin suggested another reason why Britain had reneged on promises of additional defence aid. On 17 June he disclosed that, just prior to his departure for Europe, the British Deputy High Commissioner in Kuala Lumpur, Mr J. R. A. Bottomley, had informed him that further British aid would not be forthcoming as long as there were no defence treaties between Malaysia and Singapore and between Britain and Singapore. In Tan's view, should Singapore choose to delay the conclusion of these treaties, Malaysia would suffer; and J. R. A. Bottomley agreed as much. Tan's impression, that a financial squeeze was being applied to force Malaysia to come to terms with Singapore (over common market arrangements), was confirmed during his subsequent encounter with Arthur Bottomley.[61]

Lee Kuan Yew's presence in London in the month before Tan's abortive mission reinforced Malaysia's suspicion. Commenting on Malaysia's reactions, Harold Wilson admitted that difficulties began when Singapore was evicted from Malaysia without consultations with Britain. He felt that once such a situation arose 'there is always a suspicion on the part of one party that we are leaning over in support of the other party'.[62] Tension with Kuala Lumpur could also have been exacerbated by Wilson's attempt (as a result of left-wing opposition within his own party) to get the East of Suez commitment accepted partly in terms of socialist fraternity for Lee Kuan Yew. Certainly, the 'socialist affinity' was mentioned by a Malaysian minister, Senu bin Abdul Rahman, as a reason why the Wilson Government might be attempting 'to force on Malaysia an attitude [that suited] Singapore'.[63]

The disclosure of British attempts to put pressure on Malaysia was made against a background of growing Malaysian confidence, feelings of fraternity with Indonesia and a national assertiveness evidenced by the number of anti-British speeches made from the Alliance back-benches during the June Parliamentary session. Alliance leaders, including Tun Razak, Tun Ismail, Tan Siew Sin and Senu bin Abdul Rahman, all expressed disappointment and disillusionment and called for a reassessment of relations with Britain.[64] This was not only a reaction to the issue of British aid, but was also influenced by uncertainty over Britain's East of Suez posture. Tan Siew Sin was most biting in describing Britain as 'a tired and dispirited nation which perhaps has lost even the will to govern itself'.[65]

In this strained atmosphere Britain's Air Minister, Lord Shackleton, arrived in Kuala Lumpur in June 1966. Without committing himself to further defence aid, Lord Shackleton hoped publicly that Malaysia would understand Britain's economic difficulties. But it was his reference to military withdrawal from Borneo which revealed even more serious Anglo-Malaysian differences. Lord Shackleton had said in Kuala Lumpur that he expected some reduction, after careful consultations, of British troops in Malaysia when Confrontation ended. He did not, however, think the number involved would be large.[66] Read in isolation, Lord Shackleton appeared to give a reassurance of a future British presence. But Malaysia, following the Bangkok Accord, was in fact now more anxious for a speedy British withdrawal from Borneo.

Malaysia was in evident haste for a *rapprochement* with Indonesia. But there was also an underlying desire to counter British influence in Borneo. This influence was manifested in the comparative performance of British troops and administrators as well as in what Kuala Lumpur took to be British support for dissident local politicians, as, for example, in the case of Sarawak's Chief Minister, Stephen Kalong Ningkan. Among the allegations made by the Central Government, prior to Ningkan's dismissal, was one which suggested that British officials had interfered in the internal politics of Sarawak.

Razak said, just after the Bangkok meeting, that he did not expect to have to ask Britain to withdraw from Borneo. He was sure the Labour Government would jump at the opportunity. During the Shackleton visit, Razak openly stated that 'obviously with the end of Confrontation, British troops will have to leave the two [Borneo] states'.[67] The following day three British newspapers carried headlines suggesting that Britain was being compelled to leave Borneo.[68] Lord Shackleton reiterated that British troops could be reduced once Confrontation ended, but stressed that, until this really was the case, the military problem remained. There was a British concern over a precipitate withdrawal from Borneo. Healey's military advisers tended to discount the value of the Bangkok Accord as long as Sukarno was still nominally in power, an attitude not shared by the Malaysians.[69]

Healey arrived in Malaysia in early July, shortly after the departure of Michael Stewart who had also visited Jakarta, and while there said that British forces in Borneo would be 'greatly reduced' as soon as the Bangkok Accord was ratified. This condition was repeated in all Healey's public references to the question of British withdrawal from Borneo. In Singapore he reiterated that withdrawal from Borneo would not be rapid because: 'We are not all that certain about the Bangkok agreement between Indonesia and Malaysia.'[70]

One disconcerting aspect of the security situation was the continued probing of Malaysian territory by Indonesian raiders in spite of the Bangkok Accord, a fact which the Malaysian Government attempted to keep secret. Indeed, the fortnight before Healey's arrival saw the heaviest fighting along the Sarawak border in four and a half months.[71] The situation was further complicated by CCO activities in Sarawak, prompting British fears of exploitation by intransigent political leaders in Indonesia.

It was not until early October, after Britain had already begun withdrawing from Borneo, that the Tunku confirmed earlier press reports on security in East Malaysia. Nevertheless he discounted the need 'for the British to stay on and help us'.[72] In fact, by Healey's account, the Tunku had begun pressing Britain to withdraw from Borneo much earlier. Healey admits that these pressures and the countervailing arguments from the British military had given him 'an awful period in July 1966'.[73] In the event, he took a gamble. On 5 July he announced that British forces would definitely be withdrawn from Borneo in accordance with Malaysian wishes. Privately, both Healey and Michael Stewart warned 'that once we had taken our troops out it was unlikely that we would agree to send them back'.[74]

Back in London, Healey announced that the signal for the ending of Confrontation (the condition for British withdrawal from Borneo) must be the ratification of the Bangkok Accord. Ratification came on 11 August. The next day Britain began withdrawing its air units. Other units would follow during the next few months. Australia and New Zealand similarly announced the phased return of their battalions to a garrison role in the peninsula. The British Director of Operations in East Malaysia was immediately replaced by a Malaysian. Razak also stressed that the Commander-in-Chief, FARELF, had ceased to sit on the Malaysian Defence Council.[75] According to Harvey Stockwin, the abrupt manner in which the external powers were 'read out' of the Defence Council gave 'unpublished offence'.[76] Australia and New Zealand, during the interval between the drawing up of the Bangkok Accord and its ratification, were concerned over the future of their forces as part of the CSR. To allay such apprehensions, Razak affirmed Malaysia's continued interest in AMDA and in the CSR's presence in the peninsula; withdrawal of Commonwealth forces from West Malaysia had not been requested.[77]

By the end of October 1966 Terendak Camp (the CSR's base) had returned to full strength. Within eight months of the announcement of Britain's phased withdrawal from Borneo, over 10,000 servicemen were returned to Britain. The stage was set for a wider reconsideration of the whole British posture in the region, but the next step in the process towards phasing out AMDA was not triggered by any local development but by a fundamental revaluation of British policy.

8. BRITAIN WEIGHS ANCHOR

AMDA's viability had depended heavily upon the British anchor role. Major shifts in Britain's East of Suez policy during the second half of the sixties had profound repercussions on this defence system. The different responses of the allies to the unfolding of British developments and their endeavours to influence the course of British policy constitute the substance of the ensuing analysis.

Continuity was emphasised in that part of the Separation Agreement extending British commitments to Singapore after 9 August 1965. Separation left intact AMDA's pre-existing structure. The defence status quo satisfied temporarily a variety of interests but, above all, reflected a continuing acceptance by Britain of its anchor role. Within the alliance, increasing discord, up to and following Singapore's separation from Malaysia, obstructed local defence collaboration. Malaysia and Singapore failed to work towards a satisfactory joint defence pact or concerted approach towards Britain over the review of AMDA. Britain's failure to influence the direction of political relations between Kuala Lumpur and Singapore engendered a certain disillusionment in the utility of its anchor role. Yet the opportunity which separation provided for a British withdrawal was not taken. The reason was not (as Denis Healey seemed to suggest) wholly because of Confrontation. Britain's military presence was also dictated by a wider East of Suez role which it was still determined to play. This necessitated overseas bases, of which Singapore was the most important.

Yet the cost of that role[1] had troubled the Labour Government ever since it had assumed office. Indeed, Labour, in its 1964 Election Manifesto, had promised to put British defence 'on a sound basis' that gave 'value for money'. Although the possibility of reducing commitments was considered initially, the preoccupation over 'cost-effectiveness' became increasingly a preoccupation over the means of policy. A provisional decision, taken in November 1964, to reduce planned defence expenditure in the 1969–70 period from £2,400 million to £2,000 million at 1964 prices became, over the months, an absolute target, while the revision of commitments receded into the background.[2] By late 1964 Wilson himself was, irrespective of cost-effectiveness, emphatic about retaining 'our world role ... which, for shorthand purposes, is sometimes called our "East of Suez" role'.

To Wilson, upholding that role was Britain's membership fee to 'the top table'. But there was also a sense of moral 'power' in his conception of Britain's position as a world peace-keeper. Britain's maritime tradition and reputation, the mere fact of the existence of its present-day navy and the mobility which this gave to its forces, together with Britain's Commonwealth history and connections all added weight to that role.[3] Years later Wilson admitted his mistake of clinging tenaciously to the East of Suez role when facts were dictating a recession: he was among the last to be converted by the hard economic facts.[4] In AMDA's context, that peace-keeping determination was reflected in a firm stand against Confrontation throughout early 1965. The February 1965 Defence White Paper still claimed a major interest in world, and not merely European, stability. In so far as British bases in these areas were still needed for peace-keeping purposes, abandoning them would be 'politically irresponsible and economically wasteful'.[5]

An awareness of the economic constraints was clearly evident beneath the steadfast posture. Healey's 1965 Defence White Paper intended to take stock of 'not only the economic position but also new or reaffirmed political objectives'. Conforming to the views he expressed while in opposition, Healey disclaimed any possibility of Britain being 'the permanent policeman for the whole of Africa and Asia'.[6] However, despite the strong opposition to the East of Suez role which the 1965 Defence White Paper provoked, there was no official indication that those commitments would be cut in the near future. Even the opponents of the East of Suez role could not openly advocate withdrawal while Confrontation lasted. But Singapore's separation from Malaysia, closely followed by the internal upheaval in Indonesia and the subsequent easing of Confrontation facilitated a questioning of the East of Suez presence. This sense of public questioning in Britain and the uncertainty over long-term British policy had prompted Lee Kuan Yew's outburst against the Americans in August 1965. Any major defence cuts were bound to affect the Malaysia–Singapore region which, including the Far East Fleet, accounted for an annual budgetary cost of £255 million, of which over a third was paid for in foreign exchange. If Confrontation ceased but no major British withdrawals followed, the net annual saving would be only £5 million. For most of 1965 the defence review concentrated on force structure rather than on commitments. Despite Healey's warning in August that the £2,000 million ceiling on defence spending could not possibly be achieved without revising commitments, it was only towards the end of 1965 and early in 1966 that the Cabinet began to reassess the scale of commitments East of Suez. The possibilities considered included withdrawal from the Singapore base in the mid-seventies and the development of alternative facilities in Australia.[7] It was the impression of a British Cabinet Minister at that time that the Defence Committee favoured withdrawal from Singapore in 1970 and that an alternative British presence in Australia was not seriously considered.[8] Recording events between January and March 1966, Harold Wilson recalls that the Labour left wing and a minority in the Cabinet favoured total withdrawal, while a majority, including himself, preferred retaining a minimum force in Singapore. Again, the international peace-keeping argument prevailed.[9]

Britain's East of Suez policy also provoked immense interest among Britain's friends involved in Southeast Asian security. The United States, deeply immersed in South Vietnam, appreciated an ally with a global peace-keeping role. The importance which the Johnson administration attached to Britain's East of Suez role had already been impressed upon Wilson and Healey during their US visit in December 1964. The British presence was central to Australian and New Zealand contributions to, and special associate status within, AMDA. Healey freely admitted that it was only because Britain succeeded in persuading them of Britain's long-term intention to play a role East of Suez that they agreed to make very substantial new contributions (in early February 1965) towards Malaysia's defence.[10] But as the 1965 Defence White Paper indicated, Britain was equally intent upon using its anchor role to extract greater contributions from its allies.[11]

Discussions were held, first in Washington and then in Canberra, Singapore and Kuala Lumpur during early 1966, prior to the publication of the 1966 British Defence White Paper. In Washington both Denis Healey and the Foreign Secretary, Michael Stewart, came under considerable pressure to postpone the East of Suez decision.

The Washington discussions were indeterminate on the issue of defence sharing East of Suez. Both sides expressed satisfaction that economies could be achieved without impairing the British defence effort. Healey and Stewart assured Washington that Britain would maintain its existing level of support to Malaysia and Singapore as long as Confrontation persisted. Stewart, however, stressed, on returning to London, that his Government was still 'in the stage of provisional conclusions'.[12]

British efforts to seek increased co-operation and cost sharing was most evident with respect to Australia and New Zealand. Australia, on the other hand, was most reluctant to allow Britain the merest possibility of withdrawal from the Singapore base and to assume, itself, any increase in defence costs. Harold Holt had given a preview of Australia's position when on 18 January 1966 (shortly before assuming the Prime Ministership from Menzies) he spoke of the doubling of Australia's defence expenditure since 1962–3 and stated that any further increases would be at the expense of the nation's industrial development and associated policies such as immigration.[13] A concerted antipodean response was attempted when Holt invited his New Zealand counterpart to participate in the Canberra discussions with Britain. Holyoake, however, declined the invitation and sent instead his Defence Minister, the Secretary of External Affairs and the Chief of Defence Staff. In a statement on 27 January Holyoake appended the reservation that no final decisions would be taken at Canberra.[14]

The Canberra discussions began on 1 February 1966. Australia and New Zealand were equally ready to acknowledge the economic restraints on defence spending. An official statement noted that all three partners had problems of economic and financial resources 'which, though different in nature, must influence the planning of their defence programmes'.[15] Healey's main task was to outline the preliminary ideas of the British defence review which, according to Holt, ranged over the period from the 1970s to the 1990s. One assumption behind Healey's projected economies was the ending of Confrontation by 1970. This would enable him to justify defence reductions in terms of the additional effort which would no longer be necessary after 1970, while reassuring the antipodes that the remaining forces, though smaller, would be better equipped. Australia and New Zealand were more concerned to extract assurances that, in spite of the significant reductions proposed, Britain would continue to uphold the global role. Healey's reaffirmation of Britain's Southeast Asian commitments was thus noted with satisfaction by the AMDA associates, although they also accepted the need for greater defence spending in the future.[16]

Neither Australia nor New Zealand enthused when Healey raised the possibility of establishing a base in Australia to replace that in Singapore. If British resolve to defend Malaysia and Singapore was instrumental to gain further defence contributions to the area from the AMDA associates, the associates were now reluctant to contemplate an alternative to the Singapore base lest Britain find it easier to withdraw from that area and in the process undermine the very basis of their commitments there.[17] Addressing the National Press Club in Canberra on 2 February, Healey reaffirmed Britain's defence commitments but also added, cautiously, that Britain's tenure in Singapore depended on local consent. If it were withdrawn and Britain had nowhere else to go, 'we shall have to go home'.[18] What appeared to be a statement of the obvious (but more readily interpreted in Australia as a threatening hint) was also, as Holt disclosed, expressed 'in direct but friendly fashion' during the official talks.

Australia, for its part, 'emphasised very strongly the need for a continued British presence in Southeast Asia'. Healey was told that the Malaysia–Singapore bases 'in which we share and to which we have made substantial contribution, should be retained for as long as possible'. Holt argued for the British presence on the grounds of its 'essential stability and moderating influence, and aid to morale'.[19] Indeed, Holt reportedly refused to explore the possibility of an alternative base in Australia and only agreed to Britain–Australia–New Zealand joint staff talks just in time for their inclusion in the British Defence White Paper of February 1966.[20] But the reference made in the White Paper and in all official references since has been to 'military facilities' rather than to a base in Australia.[21] No substantive results emerged from these talks to which Australia had given lip service.

By June 1966 the parties, according to Healey, were 'still discussing' the issues.[22] Apart from the fact that a 'fall-back' base in Australia would militate against the 'forward defence' posture, the working party was stalled by questions of economies, labour scarcity and, from Australia's viewpoint, the sensitive prospect of having British forces in Australia while Australian troops served in

Vietnam.[23] Significantly, the British themselves were largely unenthusiastic. As early as mid-February 1966 the Defence Committee seemed to hope that Australia 'will turn us down when we ask for a British presence there'.[24] But the suggestion of an alternative base in Australia had a positive effect in getting a dialogue started over the British future in Singapore and (since the Singapore base had become symbolic of Britain's commitment to that region) indirectly about the effects of this on AMDA.

The question of an alternative base was significant in terms of the changing debate over Britain's East of Suez presence. An added element in this debate was Britain's reference to local consent and 'acceptable conditions' as a precondition for the retention of bases in Malaysia and Singapore. Lee Kuan Yew claimed that in a meeting with Healey (following the Canberra talks) an impression had been given that Britain was thinking in terms of remaining in Singapore up to 1979 or 1980.[25] The British High Commissioner in Malaysia promptly explained that Britain wanted to keep its bases 'just as long as we are wanted by the Malaysian and Singapore Governments'.[26] In effect, Britain was 'passing the buck' by continuing the debate. That this was so was reinforced by the second qualification (written into the 1966 Defence White Paper) that Britain would retain its presence 'on acceptable conditions'.[27]

However, the British proviso could also be an insurance against an open commitment to stay in Malaysia and Singapore. The insurance was strengthened by two parameters of the peace-keeping role which the 1966 White Paper set out. Firstly, Britain eschewed undertaking any major operations of war 'except in co-operation with allies'. Secondly, Britain would not accept obligations to defend another country unless Britain had been assured, sufficiently far in advance of any actual necessity, of the use of the facilities required to effect such assistance.[28] Uncertainty over future British policy was heightened by the decision to phase out the aircraft-carrier, to abandon the Aden base by 1968 and to begin exploratory discussions on an alternative base to Singapore. These were ominous portents for Singapore, where the livelihood of 150,000 people depended directly or indirectly on the bases.

From the point of view of Britain's allies, more disturbing indicators soon appeared when disagreement erupted within the British Labour Party over East of Suez following Labour's re-election. In late May (when an end to Confrontation seemed likely) a private meeting of the Parliamentary Labour Party was faced with a motion, sponsored by a cross-section of Labour back-benchers, calling for a decisive reduction in commitments East of Suez by 1969–70, including withdrawal from Malaysia, Singapore and the Persian Gulf. Although the motion was rejected on technical grounds, the meeting's chairman allowed general discussion. Michael Stewart reportedly delivered a conciliatory speech indicating the Government's broad agreement with most of the speakers, i.e. that Britain should withdraw from East of Suez and reduce defence expenditure. The only disagreement lay with the timing of the withdrawal and the implementation of the defence cuts. A similar line was taken by Healey.[29]

To these reports of an apparent shift in British thinking, Canberra reacted sharply. On 27 May Holt sent a highly publicised message to his High Commissioner in London instructing him to seek clarification from the British Government.[30] Britain officially denied any change in policy, while Whitehall officials suggested that the press had been misleading. However, Australian suspicions were confirmed by Christopher Mayhew, one of the co-sponsors of the motion calling for British withdrawal. In a statement issued in London, Mayhew (the former Navy Minister who had resigned in protest against the decision to abandon aircraft-carriers as the main strike force for the 1970s) on 22 February accused the Government of telling the Australians one thing and the PLP another.[31]

Dissatisfied with the bland British assurance, Holt further instructed his High Commissioner in London to seek clarification of British intentions and to register Australia's opposition to a British withdrawal. Among other things, Australia was possibly concerned over changing Anglo-Malaysian relations following the *de facto* ending of Confrontation and the prospect of a precipitate reduction of British forces in the area. Indeed, the urgent meeting arranged on 1 June between Australia's High Commissioner, Sir Alexander Downer, and Harold Wilson coincided with news of the Bangkok Accord. The next day Holt expressed satisfaction with Wilson's re-affirmation of continuity in British policy following Healey's visit to Canberra. While welcoming the ending of Confrontation, he also reminded Britain that the Malaysia–Singapore bases should be maintained in the interests of regional stability.[32]

The British domestic controversy over the East of Suez policy soon attracted further attention. On 4 June the *Guardian* reported mounting Labour back-bench annoyance at the foreign exchange costs of the British presence in Malaysia–Singapore, which had increased by 23.4% since Labour came to power. Only a fraction of that increase (4 pence in the pound) was attributable to Confrontation. Clearly, savings from the ending of Confrontation were negligible; the cost of the whole British presence itself (running to £235 million annually) would need re-examination.

This report was a prelude to two significant events in the Commons. On 14 June Wilson was due to answer three parliamentary questions seeking information on the ANZAM communications, specifically the nature of the assurances Britain was able to convey. A full meeting of the PLP was scheduled the following day when the withdrawal motion would be voted upon. A gathering of antipodean Ministers in London since the preceding week indicated the anxiety about the Labour back-bench revolt. The Deputy Prime Ministers of both Australia and New Zealand arrived in London well ahead of a scheduled meeting of Commonwealth Trade Ministers. The Australian presence was later reinforced by the Defence Minister, David Fairbairn, and capped by the news that Harold Holt was due the following month.

Although he refused to disclose the exchanges with Holt, Wilson indicated in his parliamentary statement on 14 June that it was still the Government's policy to remain a world military power until the 1980s.[33] This was repeated the following day before the PLP. The unusual step was taken of publishing Wilson's speech in full.[34] To placate his critics, Wilson promised 'a massive reduction' in the number of troops stationed in Malaysia when the Bangkok Accord was ratified. But an implicit distinction was drawn between force reductions in Malaysia (specifically Borneo) and the British presence in Singapore, which was far more important and central to the whole British posture East of Suez. Wilson conceded that Singapore was 'an extremely difficult problem'. He justified the British presence there in terms of the views and interests of not only Singapore but also Australia and New Zealand, all of which wanted a British presence.[35]

Although Australia and New Zealand reacted favourably to Wilson's speech, scepticism over Britain's long-term role lingered. The defeat of the PLP motion calling for British withdrawal gave scant comfort. The strength of back-bench opinion could not be disguised as the Government, with over 100 abstentions, had to pack the meeting with Ministers and Peers to ensure a comfortable victory. A meeting between Holt and Holyoake in Canberra at the end of June affirmed the importance of Britain's Southeast Asian presence 'not only in terms of its defence significance but [also] in terms of the advantages which it will have for long-term world stability and for Britain's own world role'.[36] This was reiterated by Holt during his London visit in mid-July. Britain meanwhile continued to pledge support for the East of Suez role and Michael Stewart's visit to Australia (for the meeting of the SEATO Council) in late June and Healey's tour of Malaysia, Singapore and Hong Kong in early July were used to press home the message.

Darby's contention, that the allies' scepticism of long-term British policy was based mainly on an inkling of the political and economic drift in Britain rather than on conclusive evidence,[37] can be supported by the generalities in which the intra-alliance dialogue (until mid-July 1966) was couched and the repetitiousness with which bland assurances followed expressions of anxiety. However, the issue of the Singapore base (an abbreviation for Britain's East of Suez policy) had become part of the changing debate between Britain and its allies. Talk of an alternative to Singapore contributed to that general inkling of political and economic drift in Britain.

If Singapore's separation and Anglo-Malaysian friction over defence aid in June 1966 had sown disillusionment in Britain concerning its presence in the Malaysia–Singapore area, its growing economic difficulties accelerated the reappraisal of interests. On 20 July 1966, within a week of Harold Holt's London visit, another sterling crisis forced deflationary measures upon Britain. The end of Confrontation, now within sight, provided the opportunity for major savings and Wilson announced that economies would include cuts in overseas military and civil expenditures of at least £100 million,[38] even though Healey, only three days before, had played down the possibility of reviewing the entire East of Suez policy.

Healey had, during his Far East visit in July 1966, already 'mentally programmed the extent and pace of withdrawal in the post-Confrontation period – a withdrawal which foreshadowed an even bigger decision to pull out altogether'.[39] With the formal termination of Confrontation on 11 August, redeployment of forces in the Indonesia–Pacific region could be completed well ahead of the 1969–70 target set by the 1966 Defence Review. As the British withdrawal from East Malaysia continued into September, Healey was privately informing Wilson that 'an approximate terminal date for our deployment East of Suez' was ready for proposal, although its ramifications had not been worked out.[40] In October Healey announced that most of the 10,000 British troops in Borneo would be home by April 1967. Further withdrawals after that were also being considered.[41]

Outside the Cabinet, advocates of withdrawal were encouraged by a vote on withdrawal at the Labour Party Conference in early October. Despite pleas by the new Foreign Secretary, George Brown, the resolution calling for withdrawal from East of Suez by 1969–70 was passed with a sizeable majority. Within the Cabinet, the picture was less clear-cut. According to Wilson, a private meeting of senior ministers at Chequers on 22 October had agreed generally with Healey's proposals, including an approximate terminal date for East of Suez commitments.[42] Crossman's account, however, showed Healey still maintaining, against George Brown's scepticism, that the defence cuts proposed (something below £1,850 million the following year) required no change in East of Suez commitments.[43]

In Malaysian eyes, the British withdrawal from Borneo could have been faster. But a sudden rundown of British forces to below the pre-Confrontation level would create difficult gaps on account of Britain's refusal of additional defence aid. Nevertheless, Anglo-Malaysian friction over defence aid and the easing of the external threat did affect general Malaysian attitudes towards the British presence. Not surprisingly, when Razak (*en route* to the US in October 1966 to purchase helicopters) was invited by the new Commonwealth Secretary, Herbert Bowden, for discussions, he said afterwards that it was not Malaysia's habit 'to go begging'. He saw the British presence in Southeast Asia as an entirely British matter. There was of course AMDA which, however, could be reviewed at any time.[44] Britain did agree to assist Malaysian troops in Borneo with logistical and air support during the interim period. It soon transpired that Britain, prompted by needs to economise, would charge Malaysia for these services. News that Anglo-Malaysian negotiations over the £2 million per annum bill had progressed little emerged in the wake of reports in November of further friction over the transfer of military equipment in Borneo.[45] In the light of strained Anglo-Malaysian relations, a measure that seemed an economy to one party, was seen quite differently by the other.

By the end of November one half of the British servicemen had been withdrawn from Borneo. Although the British economic measures of

20 July 1966 telescoped the withdrawal rate (as envisaged in the 1966 Defence White Paper) by eighteen months, Harold Wilson doubted whether an approximate terminal date for East of Suez deployments could be announced before the 1967 Defence Estimates.[46] The 1967 White Paper was vague about terminating these commitments which, in addition, were less emphasised. More importantly, it declared an aversion to any further Confrontation-size operations outside Europe.[47] Healey argued against fixing a firm date for the termination of commitments: diplomacy must be allowed to construct 'a different basis for the security of the countries' which Britain was leaving. While conceding the inevitability of withdrawal in the long run, he refused to commit the Government to withdrawal from Singapore, the Persian Gulf and Malaysia.[48] Indeed, the 1967 White Paper called for 'a proper regard to the interests of our allies',[49] and its publication went with conscious effort to allay intra-alliance fears — evidenced by Herbert Bowden's visit to Wellington and Canberra later in February.

Bowden's arrival was preceded by a meeting in Wellington between Harold Holt and the New Zealand Cabinet. Their joint statement on 3 February spelled out the importance to them of Britain's decision to continue its Southeast Asian role. It expressed equally their determination 'to play their part in maintaining an adequate Commonwealth presence in the area'.[50] But, in consideration of the British determination to reduce forces East of Suez, Holt told Bowden that the fact of a British presence mattered more than its size.[51]

On 27 February Healey announced the intention of withdrawing between 5,000 and 10,000 men from the Far East in addition to the 13,000 already planned. This second stage of withdrawal would reduce the base facilities in Singapore. Foreign exchange savings would be greater since local redundancies were involved and consequently would present bigger economic and political problems.[52]

Faced with alarming signals of impending change in British policy, Malaysia turned first to the AMDA associates for confirmation of their continued, if not additional, support. In April, Tun Razak visited New Zealand and Australia to register the Malaysian expectation of antipodean assistance in the event of British withdrawal. For good measure, he reminded Australia that Malaysia was its front line. Australia and New Zealand agreed in general to extend their defence aid programmes to Malaysia. In Australia's case, the aid was extended specifically until 1970 – a date not unrelated to the questionable future of British policy in the area.[53] New Zealand's affirmation of continuing support for the CSR was made in return for Razak's acknowledgement that it was a 'positive contribution' not just to Malaysia, but to Southeast Asia as a whole.[54]

Renewed speculation about the imminence of a major change in British policy came just before George Brown's Washington visit for the SEATO annual conference held between 18 and 20 April. Indeed, a week before the conference, a meeting of the British Cabinet found only six members who were against drastic cuts East of Suez or withdrawal from mainland Malaysia, while the rest wanted even more radical measures by the following July. This led George Brown to wonder plaintively how he was to negotiate with Britain's allies for a slow, orderly withdrawal.[55]

A measure of the alarm of Britain's allies can be glimpsed in Hasluck's urgent dispatch from Washington (where he was attending the annual SEATO conference) which precipitated a special meeting of the Australian Cabinet on 21 April. Hurried diplomatic exchanges with London extracted an assurance from Harold Wilson that no announcement on withdrawal would be made until his scheduled meeting with Holt in June.[56] But Australian feelings had been strongly expressed at Washington when Hasluck admonished Britain for its 'lack of interest in Asia today' which amounted to 'isolationism in its most feckless form'.[57]

Shortly after the SEATO conference, Healey began discussions in Kuala Lumpur and Singapore with the host governments, British service chiefs and trade unionists over a further reduction to 30,000 servicemen in the area by April 1968. Since this phase involved local retrenchments, significant aid to cushion the effects was promised. The host countries' major concern was the impact of these changes on the ends of British policy. Malaysia told Healey that his proposals would be considered sympathetically as long as AMDA commitments were not affected.[58] But his assurances of continuing British interest in the area were undermined by the disturbing priorities revealed by the withdrawal plans, their first consideration being not what could be retained, but rather what could be withdrawn. In parrying a suggestion that complete withdrawal could take ten years, Healey hinted darkly, 'certainly not in the next two or three years'.[59]

On returning to London, Healey came under increasing pressure from the Treasury and left-wing Cabinet colleagues to announce a date for complete withdrawal. His stand during the internal debate 'brought him close to the political wilderness'.[60] However, the way was paved on 10 May when Healey addressed the Royal Commonwealth Society. He acknowledged that base facilities in Malaysia and Singapore exceeded British requirements due to Britain's growing air-deployment capability. The local powers, too, saw their basic requirements in terms of the provision of sophisticated weapons systems by the external allies. Britain's difficulty rested with the AMDA associates, with whom Britain was co-operating in providing the CSR. Healey did not underplay the impact on the allies of the British decisions that would be taken during the rest of the decade.[61]

In June and July, with the announcement of a final withdrawal date imminent, John Marshal (New Zealand's Deputy Prime Minister), Harold Holt, Lee Kuan Yew and the Tunku arrived in succession in London to be told of the British decision. In a memorandum left with Wilson after their meeting, Holt pointed to the damaging effects a premature British withdrawal would have, on account of the existing regional uncertainties.[62] Lee Kuan Yew himself admitted, following discussions on 27 June, that Singapore could only hope to influence the British decision marginally.[63] Indeed, the day before, the British Cabinet had considered a position paper arguing for phased withdrawal up to 1975–6 and a cut-back of forces in exchange for a general military capability.[64] Although Lee Kuan Yew and the Tunku were both in London, there was no co-ordinated approach between them towards the anchor power. The Tunku, in fact, complained about the absence of information regarding Singapore's demands.[65] The fact remained that Malaysia–Singapore interests were not wholly congruent. Nor were those of their problems which British withdrawal created, identical.

In Singapore, the build-up of the local military and the discreet tailoring of the structure of the forces by Israeli advisers were already initiated. The National Service (Amendment) Bill, establishing a two-year call-up system for all reaching the age of 18, was passed in March 1967. Although British withdrawal presented the security of both countries with uncertainties rather than immediate threats, the economic impact would be instantaneous and, for Singapore (with 12% unemployment), severe if withdrawal was not gradually implemented. Malaysia was not as economically vulnerable, although the Tunku was anxious over the future of those Malaysian citizens who accounted for half of the 30,000 civilian workers employed at the Singapore base.[66]

Malaysia's emerging self-assertiveness led to a de-emphasis of the foreign military presence. It was, nevertheless, concerned about Britain's ability to fulfil AMDA commitments. It still depended heavily on British arms and equipment and, although the continuing insurgency was one best left to local forces, it still preferred an option to re-activate foreign assistance should the security problem change in dimension. Notwithstanding Britain's aversion to future Confrontation-like engagements, the Tunku indicated that a small British nucleus would be acceptable if it could be reinforced rapidly in a Confrontation-type emergency. Doubting the usefulness of bilateral talks with Britain, the Tunku (the last to arrive in London) proposed a five-nation conference which Malaysia would willingly host. Two important questions requiring clarification were whether Britain would honour AMDA and how British withdrawal would affect the CSR.[67] It was equally necessary to sound out the opinions of the AMDA associates, especially since neither of them had a defence treaty with Malaysia.

As a high contracting party to AMDA, Malaysia was concerned about the fundamental change in the role of the anchor power. Malaysia did lay claim, during the July discussions in London, to a say (this right being provided for under Article IX of AMDA) in the question of British military strength in the treaty area.[68] These discussions did not fully satisfy Malaysia, although the Tunku's proposal of a multilateral conference was favourably received and, in preparation for this, ANZAM staff talks were initiated. Britain itself suggested an integrated Commonwealth force, reflecting the collective undertaking of all five allies, as a possible solution to the defence gap.[69]

The Supplementary Statement on Defence Policy, published on 18 July 1967 at the height of the sterling crisis, confirmed the reduction of British forces by half in the Malaysia–Singapore area during 1970–1 and their complete withdrawal by the mid-70s.[70] It reaffirmed Britain's AMDA obligations and its continuing contribution to the CSR. However, the period beyond 1970–1 was couched in uncertain terms. The precise timing for a complete withdrawal in the mid-70s was linked to progress in achieving a new basis for stability in Southeast Asia. But Wilson soon conceded that the final withdrawal might be effected, even without regional stability, in 1977.[71] The White Paper spoke vaguely of 'a military capability' in the area after the withdrawal of permanently based forces. It left undefined the precise nature of this capability. Several questions remained unanswered. They concerned the ability of British-based 'fire brigade' forces to withstand acclimatisation problems, the extent to which sustaining the 'military capability' might involve even greater expenditure in specialised transports, the scope of Australian participation in the provision of facilities, and the development of a new staging post in the British Indian Ocean Territory.

These uncertainties provoked considerable unease in Australia and New Zealand. Both Holt and Holyoake publicly regretted the British decision. Holt argued against planning so far ahead at a time of great unpredictability in Southeast Asia and attached special importance to Britain's recognition of the need to relate decisions beyond 1970–1 to progress in achieving regional stability.[72] Holyoake was deeply concerned over the CSR since British logistical support and facilities had been central to New Zealand's own contribution, which was not designed to operate independently.[73]

Hasluck warned that changes in British policy would in turn change the assumptions of Australia's own policy. The likely impact of these changes on Australia's military presence in Malaysia, the legal basis for which had been Australian–New Zealand association with those provisions of AMDA which related to the CSR, required special attention.[74] But he emphatically ruled out any assumption of Britain's role, although the Australian Defence Report of September 1967 continued to reflect a forward posture.

By October, when Lee Kuan Yew arrived for further discussions in London, he was still hoping for a token British force in Singapore by 1975. He envisaged some British personnel remaining to operate the early warning system, and the amphibious forces (vaguely mentioned in the July 1967 Defence White Paper) being based closer to Singapore than, say, Australia.[75] While Singapore looked to its distinct requirements, the Tunku assured Singapore of its co-operation and pledged non-interference with Singapore's sovereignty after Britain's departure. Malaysia's own concern was the legal position of Australian–New Zealand forces, since these were in Malaysia essentially because of their association with Britain. However, he discounted the likelihood of a treaty with Australia and New Zealand.[76] These problems soon acquired new urgency with the devaluation of sterling on 18 November 1967, which automatically added £50 million per year to defence costs. Immediate cuts were necessary.

Among the economies announced on 20 November was a cut in defence spending of over £100 million in 1968–9, although the Chancellor still maintained that the reduction could be made within the framework of defence policies announced in July.[77] However, the decision to abandon the Aldabra project (one of the proposed staging posts in the Indian Ocean), reduce the number of Buccaneer aircraft on order and phase out prematurely the carrier HMS *Victorious* now put the existence of that 'special military capability' beyond the mid-70s in doubt.[78] Economic stringency also forced upon Britain yet another defence review (announced on 18 December), despite the July White Paper's assertion that the process had been concluded. This time no area would be sacrosanct.

There was now little hope of retaining a military capability after complete withdrawal, the date for which was soon advanced to 31 March 1971. Healey himself admitted that cuts in capability meant in effect cuts in commitments.[79] The task of informing the AMDA partners fell upon the Commonwealth Secretary, George Thomson, who toured all four capitals in early January 1968. The swiftness of his visit, the short working schedules in each capital and Healey's absence all pointed to a crisp private pronouncement rather than 'negotiations'.

The joint communiqué, issued in Kuala Lumpur on 8 January, expressed Malaysia's 'grave concern' over the latest proposals and stressed AMDA's importance to Malaysia.[80] The Tunku made only one request: that Britain stand by AMDA. However, he also told Thomson that Malaysia did not expect British intervention in the event of an 'overwhelming' attack – Malaysia would simply capitulate.[81] George Thomson's promise was economic aid to help with the transition.

Thomson's visit provoked a sharp response from Lee Kuan Yew, who threatened retaliation including the removal of Singapore's sterling reserves if British forces were withdrawn by 1970. Lee said that he regarded the withdrawal timetable agreed to in June as 'final' and that Singapore had since geared all its economic (and, one might add, military) planning to cope with the rundown terminating in the mid-70s.[82] According to Lee Kuan Yew, Healey had said, just ten days after devaluation, that there could be no reversal of the July announcement on withdrawal by the mid-70s. Nor did Wilson mention any changes when they met at Harold Holt's funeral in December 1967.[83] But when Thomson confirmed on 8

January that the new plans would be announced in the Commons the following week, Lee realised he had to act swiftly. He bluntly refused to accept Thomson's proposals and, in an attempt to reverse the British decision, decided to see Wilson personally. Lee counter-proposed a 'NATO-type' arrangement whereby Malaysia and Singapore would provide the ground elements, Australia and New Zealand the support units and the British, perhaps, the commander-in-chief.[84]

For his last-minute mission, Lee Kuan Yew solicited joint action from the other three partners. The sense of drama was enhanced in the Australian case where Lee's telephone call was received only a bare 90 minutes after John Gorton was sworn in as Prime Minister in succession to the drowned Harold Holt. Gorton immediately convened the Cabinet and telephoned Holyoake, who had received a similar call from Lee.[85] The AMDA associates, however, decided against joining Lee. Holyoake saw little purpose in such a visit and, reflecting a belief in the finality of the Thomson proposals, merely agreed to participate in a five-power conference 'at the appropriate time'.[86] The Australian Government supported Lee's objectives in an official statement, but Gorton doubted the usefulness of sending a senior Australian Minister to London. The Tunku, whom Lee also contacted, felt it was too late and remarked that Lee should have taken him into his confidence when they were both in London the previous year. He further criticised Lee for not taking his five-power proposal seriously.[87] Singapore officially explained that Lee had indicated interest in the conference provided that the others also supported it.[88] In effect, the situation was one in which everybody's business became nobody's business.

Lee was left to confront Wilson alone. Such bilateral bargaining had invariably resulted in compromises which served essentially Singapore interests. In London Lee emphasised the need for adequate defence against 'a rapacious piratical attack' and sufficient time to 'develop muscles of my own' so as to assure investors of continuing security.[89] Singapore, which lacked an air force of its own, saw the continuance of an air defence system after 1971 as a top priority. Lee had earlier shown his preparedness to purchase the British Bloodhound missiles which were already in Singapore. Other essential requirements ranged from sophisticated weapons (including possibly the Hunter jets based in Singapore) to the training of local personnel and the expertise to command, *inter alia*, an early warning radar network.[90] Singapore also required missile-launching patrol boats to deter the type of Russian cruisers which Indonesia possessed. This was as near to naming a potential aggressor as Lee would go.[91] But Singapore's fear of a possible sneak attack from Indonesia was not necessarily linked to anticipation of an erratic change in the Indonesian leadership or to deliberate planning by Jakarta. As he explained to the British, it needed only a few irrational and uncontrollable 'hotheads' to blitz Singapore's exposed and vital installations. On the other hand, any ground attack would more likely come from the north and in such a contingency it was doubtful if Britain would intervene.[92] Hence air defence became a Singapore priority.

Lee Kuan Yew's London mission during mid-January was only partially successful. On 16 January Harold Wilson announced British preparedness to assist Malaysia and Singapore in establishing, and in training personnel to operate, a joint defence system. The final withdrawal from Singapore was postponed by nine months to December 1971. For Singapore, the postponement meant that British forces would be in Singapore until the last possible date for the next British general election and, hence, the possibility of a Conservative Government reversing the Labour decision.

The programme announced on 16 January left Britain with no special military capability East of Suez beyond 1971. The order for the F-111s was cancelled and the carrier force would be phased out after withdrawal. The most decisive change was reflected in the replacement of the already attenuated 'military capability' by 'a general capability' for deployment overseas, and even this was made operable only if, 'in our judgement, circumstances demand'.[93] Healey de-emphasised the momentous change contained in the January 1968 announcement by shifting attention to the moment in July 1967 when Europe became the focus of future foreign and defence policy.[94] But as Darby rightly points out, the debate had in the end centred on the timing of British withdrawal.[95] In this respect, the economic crisis of November 1967 and the resulting domestic political pressures were highly significant for an accelerated withdrawal. Emphasis on the earlier 1966 Defence White Paper and the subsequent July 1967 decisions merely obscured the latest intra-alliance dialogue (indicating the progressive back-tracking on British promises) and the reluctant British concessions to economic realities. In retrospect, the decision 'appears so reluctant as to have been unintended until almost the last moment. The Cabinet looks as if it were pushed and coerced by unforeseen events into an unwelcome conclusion.'[96]

Intra-alliance discussions (characterised by the quality of bilateralism within an ostensibly multilateral framework) were triggered by the British defence review which, by the beginning of 1966, appeared to include the scale of British commitments East of Suez. However, Britain's efforts to hold separate discussions in Washington and in Canberra, Singapore and Kuala Lumpur were incongruous in terms of the subsequent 1966 Defence White Paper. There was still no relinquishment of the East of Suez policy. Britain was still determined to sustain its world role. The effect of intra-alliance pressure was to reinforce that determination. On the other hand, Britain's allies also successfully resisted British attempts to shift the burden of East of Suez defence. But the intra-alliance dialogue, which covered such issues as an alternative to the Singapore base, did facilitate thinking about the unthinkable. As Darby noted: 'By March 1966 the main arguments for and against the East of Suez commitment have been developed and presented.'[97]

Within a year of the 1966 White Paper, Britain was forced to withdraw completely from the Malaysia–Singapore area by the mid-70s. With the loss of British determination, intra-alliance pressure proved ineffectual. This was most clearly demonstrated in the intra-alliance dialogue which preceded the accelerated withdrawal. The claim of consultation could not mask the real purpose of George Thomson's visit, which was to inform and to apologise. Lee Kuan Yew's subsequent lone mission to London was only marginally effective in delaying withdrawal by nine months. The result was nevertheless significant in terms of the later Tory amendment to Labour's plans.

For AMDA, the most immediate factor of change was the loss of Britain's capacity to sustain the anchor role. George Thomson had, *inter alia*, served notice on Kuala Lumpur to review AMDA.[98] The abandonment of Britain's anchor role gave new impetus to the changing perceptions and redefinition of the allies' interests, which had become increasingly apparent since Confrontation and Singapore's separation. The dynamics of these changing perceptions and interests (resulting in further intra-alliance discord over the resurgence of the Sabah problem later in 1968) overlapped with the termination of AMDA and influenced the next phase of the transformation of the alliance relationships.

9. FROM AMDA TO THE FIVE-POWER DEFENCE SYSTEM

The Tunku's proposal for a five-power conference, first made in July 1967, received increasing support once it was clear that Britain was no longer prepared to play the role of anchor power to AMDA. But the main obstacle to a revision of AMDA was the defence relationship between Malaysia and Singapore, whose interests, though close, were nevertheless differentiable. On account of their history of past difficulties in defence co-operation, the external allies were inclined to let them work out a basis for future collaboration.

The most immediate defence need of Singapore (following British withdrawal) was a close functional co-operation with Malaysia. Their geographical propinquity and the size of Singapore island meant that an effective air defence system for Singapore could not be provided without reference to the Malaysian hinterland. The short reaction time available to meet encroaching hostile aircraft meant that a continuing close identification of Malaysia–Singapore interests would have to be established, at least in matters of air defence. Moreover, maintaining separate defence systems with sophisticated weapons would be too expensive.

There were, nevertheless, certain differences in Malaysia–Singapore attitudes towards air defence. As was pointed out to Vishal Singh by a senior Malaysian official, Malaysia was less concerned with air defence *per se*, but instead desired a more collective air defence involvement among all the partners. But in those aspects of air defence which exclusively concerned Malaysia–Singapore (e.g. fixed installations), Malaysia would prefer joint ownership and administration.[1] In May 1968 the Tunku publicly advocated joint ownership in an apparent attempt to stake an interest in Singapore. A visit by Dr Goh Keng Swee to Kuala Lumpur on 21 January 1968 led to a Malaysian Foreign Ministry statement that the two countries had agreed that their defence was 'inseparable'. The Tunku himself remarked that it was Singapore's first concrete attempt to have mutual defence talks – a change of heart which he welcomed. Malaysia, for its part, had announced, in a letter to Dr Goh dated 14 November 1967,[2] the withdrawal of all Malaysian army units from Singapore by 31 December 1967, thus removing one contentious issue with Singapore.

Meanwhile, the Tunku revived his proposal of a multilateral conference. Dr Goh had explained that this move should be left to the Tunku since Singapore had no defence agreement with the external powers. While renegotiating AMDA could well mean its abrogation, the Tunku said that Malaysia itself would not do the abrogating.[3] But the British attitude was expressed unambiguously by Harold Wilson in a comment on John Gorton's openly held doubts about Britain's military capability in the region after 1971. There was 'no blank cheque on intervention', said Wilson.[4]

The imminent termination of the open-ended British commitment and the uncertainty over Britain's East of Suez policy had eroded one central pillar of Australia's defence policy, namely, the traditional reliance upon 'great and powerful friends'. Any hopes that the attenuation of the British connection could somehow be compensated by closer relations with the United States (*vis-à-vis* Southeast Asia) were dispelled following the North Vietnamese and Vietcong Tet offensive of January 1968, which prompted President Johnson's decision to restrict US bombing in North Vietnam (Australia having just publicly supported the American bombing of Vietnam) and to decline renomination for the forthcoming presidential elections. These developments questioned further Australia's forward defence posture. While New Zealand could, at least, play the role of 'junior partner' and wait to relate its position to the final Australian decision, Australia had to face the possibility of acting without great-power support. And since it was Australia (compared to New Zealand) which might need to increase its Malaysia–Singapore commitments substantially, it had to deliberate carefully on the extent of such contributions and the circumstances of their use. However, Australia and New Zealand had to deal equally with the central problem of British withdrawal from Malaysia and Singapore since it removed 'the framework in which our forces at present operate'. As Holyoake observed, the 28th Commonwealth Brigade (part of the CSR) was 'a fully integrated British–Australian–New Zealand formation'.[5]

Early 1968 was thus a period of reassessment and uncertainty for Australia and New Zealand. In early February Hasluck visited

Singapore, Malaysia and Indonesia for an exchange of views. In Singapore he reiterated that Australia would not assume Britain's role after 1971. Although Hasluck merely reaffirmed to the Malaysian Government that Australia was 'continuing to maintain its military presence in Malaysia',[6] he left the impression that it was only the size and role of the future Australian presence that was in question and not the fundamental issue of the very existence of that presence itself.[7] Indeed, the manner in which he later posed the 'nuts-and-bolts' aspects of post-British withdrawal problems for Australia reinforced this impression.[8]

Both Malaysia and Singapore had clearly indicated that they wished Australia to contribute to regional stability by maintaining some military presence. Australia and New Zealand in turn supported an early convening of the five-power conference. The New Zealand Defence Minister, David Thomson, retrod Hasluck's Southeast Asian route between late February and early March. Although some of his statements encouraged the Tunku to place a higher expectation on future New Zealand commitments, Holyoake quickly clarified that no decisions had been taken on future New Zealand forces in the area, although they would, meanwhile, remain.[9]

Australian–New Zealand discussions resumed when Gorton visited Wellington between 27 and 31 March. In contrast to Hasluck's statement in Kuala Lumpur that, to Australia, 1971 was 'not a point in a timetable',[10] Gorton was more guarded. In a joint interview with Holyoake on 28 March, he commented that it was premature to speculate beyond 1971.[11] It was widely accepted that Gorton was more inclined than either Hasluck or the Defence Minister, Allen Fairhall, to question the forward defence posture on account of the changing external environment. Indeed, Gorton identified himself with an Australian nationalistic spirit to the extent of viewing many of the established assumptions behind Australia's foreign policy, including the assumptions underlying Australia's military involvement in Malaysia, with a sceptical eye.

This scepticism, and the need to keep all options open, gave Australian policy an appearance of vacillation and even isolationism during the prolonged assessment. While favouring the second interpretation as being more accurate, van der Kroef suggests that the 'Gorton manner' could reflect either a 'mixture of caution and confusion or a new independent approach which, through deliberate "uncertainty", serves notice on allies and enemies alike that traditional Australian attitudes can no longer be taken for granted'.[12] Whichever interpretation one chooses, Gorton's approach was unsettling for intra-AMDA relations.

The approximate date for the five-power conference – first announced while David Thomson was in Kuala Lumpur – was endorsed when Razak visited Singapore in early March as a follow-up to the dialogue initiated by Dr Goh in January 1968. Razak stated, after meeting Lee Kuan Yew, Dr Goh (now the Finance Minister) and Lim Kim San (who had taken over the Defence Ministry from Dr Goh), that both countries had agreed on close co-operation in defence since the existing British military presence treated Malaysia and Singapore as one. But Razak ruled out any return to the old JDC arrangement with Singapore and spoke instead of the possibility of a 'collective defence organisation',[13] which implied an equal involvement and responsibility on the part of the external powers.

Both Malaysia and Singapore accepted the need for a joint air defence system. This, Lim Kim San subsequently confirmed, meant operating the installations (including airfields, radar and possibly ground-to-air missiles) which Britain was leaving behind. Lim's announcement of tentative defence plans (in late March, after the PAP's massive electoral victory) served, *inter alia*, to demonstrate Singapore's credibility in any collective defence effort.[14] The general elections in Singapore had been advanced by seven months to give the PAP a fresh mandate to meet the economic and military challenges of British withdrawal. The magnitude of Singapore's accelerated military expansion was reflected in Dr Goh's statement of 8 September 1968 announcing the increase of 1969 defence expenditures to S$300 million (compared with S$100 million the previous year), representing about 10% of Singapore's gross national product.[15]

The problems posed by the British withdrawal were not exclusive to Singapore in that they also involved the island in a relationship with Malaysia that was not only co-operative but also competitive. One problem which surfaced within days of Razak's Singapore visit in March was posed by the Singapore Government's plan to repatriate between 40,000 and 50,000 Malaysians threatened with redundancy by the rundown of British bases. Kuala Lumpur, in turn, threatened to 'return' some 60,000 Singaporeans employed in

Malaysia. The threat of massive mutual expulsions was averted after another meeting between Razak and Dr Goh.

A second problem emerged from competing Malaysia–Singapore demands on the limited aid provided by Britain to cushion the accelerated withdrawal. At the time of Razak's Singapore visit the British Deputy Secretary of the Ministry of Overseas Development, Sir Alan Dudley, was visiting Singapore and Malaysia for the second time to negotiate withdrawal aid. On returning to Kuala Lumpur, Razak revealed that Malaysia already knew the amount of British aid being offered to Singapore. When asked if Singapore's figure was very much higher than Malaysia's, Razak replied: 'Whatever aid Britain gives cannot ever be sufficient . . . all we can do is trust they will be fair to us.'[16] The lingering suspicion of unfair treatment was not dispelled by the separate aid negotiations which Kuala Lumpur and Singapore were conducting with London. The above two episodes appeared not to have adversely affected the process of renegotiation of AMDA. Nevertheless, they influenced the changing attitudes held between Malaysia and Singapore on the one hand and between Malaysia and Britain on the other.

Notable among the various bilateral discussions preparatory to the first five-power conference were efforts to seek Jakarta's views. Since the end of Confrontation, the Suharto Government had been involved in various aspects of regional co-operation, reflected above all in ASEAN (the Association of Southeast Asian Nations, formed in August 1967 in a climate of Malaysian–Indonesian *détente*) whose other members were Singapore, Thailand and the Philippines. British withdrawal lent momentum to defence re-thinking within AMDA and to reconsideration of a new regional order. The latter was reflected in the suggestion by Tun Ismail, Malaysia's ex-Home Affairs Minister, of a declaration of neutralisation by the regional states. Tun Ismail even suggested that soundings on neutralisation and pacts of non-aggression among these nations should precede the five-power conference.[17]

The Tunku was disinclined to allow hopes of neutralisation (which might prevent the emergence of other substantive results) to dominate the discussions of new defence arrangements. But he did show a certain sensitivity about the impact of new defence arrangements upon the interests of Indonesia, which had previously been seen as a threat and against which AMDA had once provided protection. Indonesia was now an active partner within ASEAN and a major influence within the region. Like Hasluck and David Thomson, who had sounded out Indonesian opinion during their recent Southeast Asian tours, the Tunku himself visited Indonesia on the very day (4 March 1968) that Razak left for defence talks in Singapore. It was the Tunku's first visit to Indonesia since Confrontation and Razak's first visit to Singapore since separation, and although the Tunku's hopes of a non-aggression pact with Indonesia were not fulfilled, Indonesia did not raise objections to the forthcoming talks to rearrange Malaysia–Singapore defence. Stronger approval of the rearranging of Malaysia–Singapore defence was given when Adam Malik declared in late April that Indonesia had no objections to New Zealand and Australia maintaining, or even increasing, their military commitments to the region after 1971.[18] The anti-communist Suharto Government was receptive to new Commonwealth defence arrangements which could conceivably contribute towards regional security against communist encroachments. While the way towards redrawing AMDA was cleared with Indonesia, Malaysia's problems with the Philippines over Sabah re-emerged in a way which subsequently affected the general progress towards the renegotiation of AMDA. It is necessary to digress at this stage to examine briefly a curious incident.

The Philippine claim to Sabah had lain dormant since the resumption of diplomatic relations between Kuala Lumpur and Manila in June 1966. President Marcos, who had assumed office in January 1966, did not seem inclined to jeopardise relations with Kuala Lumpur. Indeed, Marcos had paid an official visit to Malaysia in January 1968. However, during the first quarter of 1968, Malaysia–Philippines relations were shaken by revelations of the so-called 'Corregidor incident'. This and the consequent revival of the Sabah claim will be mentioned only briefly here, since the main focus is on their spill-over effects on the redefinition of intra-AMDA interests.

The Corregidor incident arose from the revelations of an apparently lone survivor of mutinous recruits from a training camp on Corregidor island in Manila Bay. According to him, the real objective of the Corregidor camp was to train Muslim recruits from the Southern Philippines for infiltration into Sabah. As Marcos ordered a Congressional enquiry, Malaysia formally protested to the Philippines on 23 March. It also revealed the arrest in Sabah of 26 Filipinos found in possession of arms and explosives. In response, the Philippines somewhat defensively revived the Sabah claim, suggesting that it be brought before the World Court, a move which Malaysia had consistently rejected.

While claims and counter-claims of witnesses at the Philippine Congressional enquiry raised even more questions about Marcos' role in the affair,[19] Malaysia began reassuring Sabah. In early April Tun Razak arrived in Sabah aboard the RMN flagship *Hang Tuah* for a review of the security situation. Defensive measures taken included the deployment of more troops in Sabah, the immediate formation of vigilante and local defence groups and the registration of all male citizens in Sabah within the 18–28 age group for a limited period of conscription.

Malaysia and the Philippines, meanwhile, agreed to meet officially in Bangkok to discuss the Sabah claim. These talks were later postponed to June at Malaysia's request because of the forthcoming five-power conference. Malaysia, being unsure of the outcome of the Bangkok talks, was not disposed to let any serious deterioration of relations affect adversely the early process of rearranging Malaysia–Singapore defence, especially when the extent of the external powers' commitments were still undefined. The period between April and early June was marked by increasing hostility between Malaysia and the Philippines, a hostility fanned by the press and voluble politicians from both sides. Against this background, the first of the conferences to rearrange Malaysia–Singapore defence began.

By the time ministers of the five powers gathered in Kuala Lumpur on 10 June, Singapore and Malaysia had already each separately settled with Britain the issue of financial and military assistance to alleviate the effects of the British military withdrawal. These settled issues thus became the 'given factors' before the five-power negotiators. Indeed, differences in the nature and magnitude of the problems of withdrawal confronting Malaysia and Singapore would only have complicated any attempt at tripartite discussions. Yet, disparity in the resulting financial settlements did not endear Britain to the Malaysians, who remained privately dissatisfied with the aid worth £25 million (spread over the next five years) offered by Britain – half of what Singapore had received.[20]

Anglo-Malaysian discussions on withdrawal aid had culminated in Razak's visit to London one month before the Kuala Lumpur conference. Razak sought a clearer picture of British intentions from

Wilson, Healey and George Thomson. While Britain reaffirmed its preparedness to help in the training of pilots and technicians for the air defence system earlier promised, little progress on the question of new arms purchases was made. Dissatisfaction with British credit terms was hinted at in Razak's later comment that he was prepared to discuss arms purchases with the Russians and the French.[21] Such purchases would have run counter to the standardisation and integration of equipment among the five Commonwealth partners.

Like Razak, who had made no reference during his European trip (which also included Paris and Moscow) to joint defence needs, standardisation of equipment or inclusion of Singapore in any deal, Lee Kuan Yew also visited London without further talks with Kuala Lumpur. Ironically, the Tunku appealed to Singapore to 'talk things over' while Lee was meeting the British. While Rajaratnam responded by visiting Kuala Lumpur in early June, it was to brief the Tunku and Razak on Lee's London trip.[22]

Compared to the Anglo-Malaysia discussions, the Anglo-Singapore ones (22–28 May) were more wide-ranging and yielded a more definable aid package. The S$367 million (£50 million) of British aid (in loans and grants), whose terms had hitherto met with repeated disagreement between the two sides, was finally agreed, although only about 25% of it was an outright grant.[23] In air defence, Singapore would take over from the RAF (subject to negotiation) the radar network and Bloodhound missiles. Plans for the creation of an air force were discussed and agreement reached on the training of Singapore fighter pilots in Britain while Singapore was establishing its own Air Force Training School. Within a year Singapore was to receive twelve jet trainer aircraft, with the result that at the first five-power conference Singapore could pledge a squadron of Hunter Mark 9 aircraft (operational by 1971) for the common air defence umbrella. On order were six fast patrol boats to constitute the nucleus of a navy. Conversion of the British naval dockyard in Singapore into commercial use was arranged, while efforts were made to attract new British investments to Singapore and to make available for commercial utilisation the workshop facilities soon to be vacated by Britain.

Each of the partners came to the conference with different expectations and priorities. For Britain, the conference was intended to facilitate disengagement. This overshadowed whatever promises it could make about the period after 1971. To Australia and New

Zealand, the conference represented a means of defining (indeed, of discovering) their own roles after the British withdrawal. To them, the important question was what to do with forces already in the area. Singapore, reconciled to the inevitability of British withdrawal, was concerned with securing an adequate air defence cover, while Malaysia was psychologically least prepared for any move which would bring Britain closer to an abrogation of AMDA. In its reluctance to accept the *fait accompli* as *accompli*, Malaysia was in a very similar position to New Zealand.

From the start the Tunku attempted to pin Britain down to some commitment after 1971. Refining his earlier advocacy, the Tunku declared that 'an essential prerequisite to an effective defence arrangement' was the placing under the joint control and maintenance of the five powers those defence installations to be vacated by Britain. Such equipment and installations could not be 'entrusted to one country only or one people' and, as a quid pro quo, he offered to allow the stationing of Singapore troops in Malaysia.[24] The Tunku's advocacy in Kuala Lumpur of five-power administration of British installations and base facilities was construed as an attempt to re-involve Britain. Healey quickly reiterated that Britain would not share such responsibilities.[25] Britain's contribution would be the free transfer of all fixed installations and non-operational equipment to Malaysia and Singapore. Healey also offered training assistance with the hitherto British-operated Jungle Warfare School (JWS) at Kota Tinggi. The conference agreed, in principle, to restructure the JWS on a 'multi-national basis'.[26]

The British offer to participate in future five-power exercises was intended to demonstrate a continuing interest in the area. But to Malaysia, in particular, the important question was how militarily capable Britain was likely to remain. The Tunku hoped that 'this general capability ... would not be more general than capable!'[27] To answer the sceptics, Healey announced a major reinforcement exercise from Britain to the Malay peninsula in 1970. The question remained – under what circumstances would that capability be exercised? If Britain was giving 'no blank cheque on intervention', how limited was the liability? Britain had already expressed its aversion towards Confrontation-type situations. The exact circumstances of any British intervention were not indicated, although involvement in matters of internal security was definitely ruled out. If there were general areas in which external intervention could not be counted on, what about the Sabah problem? Here Hasluck had already provided a partial answer when he stated on a previous visit to Manila that Australia would seek to avoid taking sides in any intra-regional disputes.[28] It remained unclear what external support Malaysia could expect should the Sabah dispute escalate into open conflict.

Thus, it seemed to be difficult to find a precise military *raison d'être* for the new defence arrangements.[29] Increasingly, these arrangements were justified on the less definable grounds of maintaining 'regional stability' and 'local and business confidence', while in an extra-military framework they could perhaps best be seen as the re-institutionalising of an area of Commonwealth interest. The powerful functional argument, that the external presence would act as a buffer between Malaysia and Singapore, was too delicate to be used publicly.[30]

The conference, however, upheld the indivisibility of Malaysia–Singapore defence as 'an indispensable basis for future defence co-operation'. Malaysia and Singapore agreed to co-operate effectively in coastal defence and the RMN was allowed to continue using the base at Woodlands. Singapore's commitment to the IADS was the squadron of jet fighters which they would be acquiring.[31] Malaysia, however, appeared less ready to be committed (specifically in terms of its own contribution) to collective defence beyond 1971. This reflected, in part, a lingering reluctance to let Britain 'off the hook' and a traditional preference for economic development over excessive military spending. Malaysia did not, at this stage, feel the same vulnerability as Singapore: the Corregidor affair was still a lot of 'sound and fury'. Malaysian reticence was reflected in paragraph 12 of the communiqué which declared that, '*in the light of the commitments and contributions by the other Governments*' (emphasis mine), Malaysia 'would be prepared to consider additional contributions . . . of their armed forces which were already a substantial contribution to joint defence'.

The commitments and contributions from Australia and New Zealand appeared most indefinite and represented mainly a reservation of positions: at the conference in Kuala Lumpur they would only convey their short-term decisions. New Zealand forces (half a battalion of infantry, four transport planes and one frigate) already in the area were small compared to Australia's. There was a limit to which New Zealand forces could be expanded in the future. Like Malaysia, New Zealand showed a continuing inability to come to terms with the *fait accompli* of British withdrawal. During the final session on 11 June, Holyoake hoped that, exercises apart, 'a more continuous and tangible demonstration of [British] concern might be possible even if on a reduced and even token scale'.[32] In response, George Thomson assured him that British policy would remain global in orientation, although the means of policy would change.

Australia, like New Zealand, continued to opt for a holding operation, thereby adding to the sense of fluidity. It did, however, contribute to the IADS by providing an 'RAAF component based on Butterworth with elements deployed to Tengah'. But Australia also added the proviso that operations beyond 1971 'would depend on a decision to be taken by the Australian Government on the part which Australia would play in the defence of the area after that date'.[33] Australian uncertainty was influenced by the doubtful value of Britain's general capability and by questions raised in the course of US presidential electioneering concerning America's Southeast Asian commitments and foreign policy emphasis. The statement in May by the Australian Defence Minister, Allen Fairhall, which effectively 'suspended' forward defence planning was a play for time in which to observe a new American Government in office.[34] To assess the likely future US role in Asia, Gorton himself visited the US between late May and early June 1968, during which time he met Johnson and some of the presidential candidates. The Australian delegation at Kuala Lumpur adhered to an 'all-options-open' approach.[35]

Although both Australia and New Zealand sought to keep their options open at Kuala Lumpur, a subtle difference existed between their positions. New Zealand was prepared to adopt, within constraints, a less ambiguous line. Australia would only state that its forces (with the exception of its air contributions) would 'meanwhile' remain in the Malaysia–Singapore area. Its position in the period up to 1971 was in fact not clarified. New Zealand, however, publicly stated that it would maintain the same shape and number of forces in the Malaysia–Singapore area up to 1971. This, admittedly, was not included in the final communiqué. It was made by Holyoake during a brief visit to Singapore after the five-power conference and repeated in the New Zealand Parliament on 17 June. Holyoake said that New Zealand's policy was 'not tied to that of Australia', although the two countries consulted each other closely and thought similarly on defence matters.[36]

The Australian position, spelled out by Fairhall on 2 May, was that its military presence in the area must be maintained 'in the context of a total co-operative effort, involving all the five powers'.[37] But Britain's attitude at the conference indicated clearly that the co-operative effort beyond 1971 would be less than total and reinforced Gorton's inclination to keep all his options open. These options ranged from total Australian withdrawal after 1971 to a relocation of forces with the retention of air elements in Butterworth and army units resited in Singapore.[38] This meant that no specific mention could be made of the future of Terendak Camp – HQ of the 28th Commonwealth Brigade, the land component of the CSR. Indeed, Australia had made it known at the conference that a decision to retain forces in the area after 1971 would inevitably question the continued occupancy of Terendak.[39] The Australian Defence and External Affairs Departments were, however, broadly inclined towards an Australian military status quo in the area after 1971, partly because of the positive psychological effect on the region and partly because, once withdrawn, it would be more difficult to accomplish the return of forces if unforeseen circumstances demanded it.[40]

Closely related to the CSR's future was the future of AMDA itself. At the conference, Malaysia indicated both its status as a high contracting party and its role as principal beneficiary of the alliance. The Tunku projected a continuing validity for AMDA by declaring that 'some fresh understanding and modifications' were needed, while Singapore's participation in the Agreement would need to be formalised. Abrogation of the treaty was not mentioned. On the contrary, he reminded Britain of Malaysia's responsibilities in AMDA and referred specifically to 'the commitments of *all of us* [emphasis mine] with regard to Brunei after 1971'.[41] The communiqué, however, said nothing about Brunei and the Sultanate itself had not enthused over the five-power deliberations. In its only reference to AMDA, the communiqué merely noted that a new understanding was necessary 'in due course'.[42]

The Kuala Lumpur conference provided a useful forum for multilateral discussion and the airing of individual attitudes. It sanctioned a collective endeavour to devise new defence arrangements for the Malaysia–Singapore area. The important sphere of air defence, to which new thinking and effort would have to be directed, was recognised. Acknowledging the desirability of joint exercises in the area after 1971, the conference agreed to establish joint exercise planning machinery. In the same connection, agreement in principle was obtained to organise the JWS on a multilateral basis. The most important basis for five-power collaboration, namely, the doctrine of the indivisibility of Malaysia–Singapore defence, was reaffirmed in paragraph 6 of the final communiqué. A distinction should be made, however, between the five-power discussions and a 'renegotiation' of AMDA. Strictly speaking, AMDA was never renegotiated. Nevertheless, the cumulative results of the five-power deliberations were to make it possible to abandon AMDA, which had already ceased to be an adequate frame of reference for defence co-operation.

The unresolved problem of Sabah (most recently highlighted by the Corregidor affair) was not discussed at the five-power conference in Kuala Lumpur. The external powers were reluctant to become involved in any crisis over Sabah. This was especially the case with Australia and New Zealand, both of which had serious doubts over Britain's future defence posture and commitments to AMDA. Their association with AMDA meant that their contributions to the defence of the area hinged on Britain's willingness, in the first place, to play its anchor role. The 'threat' posed by the Philippines was of an entirely different order compared to the Confrontation crisis and Malaysia itself did not seem to attach great significance to it *per se*, but rather to the reactions of the other defence partners. However, the fact that the attempt to draw up the arrangements for the future defence of the area was made against the background of the unfolding quasi-crisis over Sabah, which worsened after the failure of the Bangkok talks between Malaysia and the Philippines, increased the significance of this threat.

One week after the five-power conference ended, discussions over Sabah opened in Bangkok. However, these talks, which began on 17 June 1968, became bogged down in procedural matters. Malaysia insisted that the meeting was to enable the Philippines to clarify its claim, while the Philippines persisted in pressing for the submission of the claim before the International Court of Justice. The Malaysians were adamant in their refusal to consider a settlement by this court. On 16 June, after a month of protracted exchanges, the Bangkok talks broke down. An intensification of sabre-rattling ensued. Malaysia–Philippines relations deteriorated with the mutual recall of ambassadors in July. Diplomatic relations were not formally severed, but resembled the situation at the time of Malaysia's inauguration. While direct action was avoided, a 'verbal frenzy' arose in the Philippines, culminating in a 'paper mobilisation' of the Philippine Armed Forces at the beginning of August.[43]

The meeting of the ASEAN Ministers in Jakarta in early August provided an opportunity for Razak and the Philippine Foreign Secretary to reach agreement on a 'cooling off period', but this was breached within weeks when the Philippine House of Representatives passed, on 27 August, an amendment (to a Bill establishing the maritime baselines of the Republic) declaring Sabah to be part of the Philippines. The Bill drew immediate protests from the Tunku and from Razak, who charged the Philippines with attempting a verbal annexation of Sabah. Marcos signed the Bill on 18 September 1968 and fulfilled the 'territorial threat' about which Malaysia had warned. Marcos, probably, was only flowing with the Congressional tide, because he quickly explained that the Act did not 'contemplate the physical incorporation of Sabah'. But to Malaysia, Sabah had become an issue of national honour. Malaysia replied by suspending diplomatic relations and abrogating an anti-smuggling pact with the Philippines. Razak declared that Malaysia would now have to defend itself in the face of a 'flagrant annexation of Malaysian territory'.[44]

Having publicly identified a territorial threat, Malaysia began to solicit support from its ANZAM partners. Although the likelihood of military conflict was underplayed by the British military, they responded positively to a direct Malaysian request for a show of force. On 19 September six RAF Hunter jets were flown over Sabah's capital, Kota Kinabalu, while returning from Hong Kong to their base in Singapore. *En route*, they stopped over at the US Air Base at Clark Field near Manila. Complementing this show of force, the Commander-in-Chief Far East, General Sir Michael Carver, said that his Government fully supported Malaysia's view that Sabah was part of Malaysia and affirmed that Britain would honour its obligations under AMDA if fighting broke out.[45] Publicity was given also to a scheduled joint exercise along Australia's Queensland coast in which British and ANZUS forces would be participating. A large flotilla of British warships would sail through Philippine waters near Sabah *en route* from Singapore. Britain (and Australia) gave advance notice of the intended passage to which Manila promptly objected. The naval force nevertheless passed through the Sibutu Passage and the exercise was held in early October. Of the

Philippines' SEATO allies, the US refused to be drawn into the dispute while the reactions of Australia and (to a lesser extent) New Zealand showed the ambivalence of their position as both SEATO and Malaysian allies. In the Australian case, its stronger insistence on non-involvement, coupled with Gorton's independent style, was to have adverse consequences on relations with Kuala Lumpur.

Malaysia, remembering Australia's response during the first nine months of Confrontation, remained uncertain about the strength of Australian support. In the aftermath of the Philippine annexation by legislation of Sabah, press reports suggested that Canberra might withdraw its armed forces from Southeast Asia. The issue was revived during an interview with Hasluck in Singapore on 23 September. Hasluck denied that the dispute as it then stood would have any influence on Australian defence planning. As in the early stages of Confrontation, Hasluck was again exploiting the flexibility of Australia's associate status. Pressed hard to define Australia's stand in the event of hostilities breaking out, he replied, 'we would not wish to be involved, and there should be no expectation on the part of anyone that we would become involved'.[46]

On 25 September the Malaysian High Commissioner, Dato Donald Stephens, the former Sabah Chief Minister, sought an interview with Gorton. He was met instead the following day by Gordon Freeth, then a junior minister acting for Hasluck who was away. Dato Stephens departed dissatisfied with the Australian assessment, which discounted the seriousness of a Filipino military threat.[47] Unlike Australia, New Zealand did not indulge in the same sort of public reservation of its position. On the contrary, Holyoake reflected a mildly pro-Malaysian attitude when he stated in September that New Zealand would be deeply disturbed if it appeared that Marcos was rejecting the view – 'widely held internationally' – that Sabah was a constituent part of Malaysia.[48]

While support among the external powers was less than total, Singapore's response at least gave credence to the doctrine of the indivisibility of Malaysia–Singapore defence. Singapore had already declared on 21 September that any attempt to alter the status of Sabah by force would constitute aggression. Its message to the Malaysian Foreign Ministry said that Malaysia's security and integrity was of 'vital concern' to Singapore.[49] Support for Malaysia was reiterated when Lim Kim San visited Kuala Lumpur in October for further talks on the IADS. Although his comments in Kuala Lumpur underlined the existing constraints on the defence support which Singapore could render, a firmer statement came from Rajaratnam a fortnight later when he affirmed that Singapore would seriously consider offering military aid to Malaysia if armed conflict broke out.[50] There was, in fact, little difference between the Singapore and Australian assessments of the Philippine threat. Dr Goh himself viewed the Sabah issue as 'not very serious'.[51] Yet, whereas Australia regarded that as a reason for inaction, Singapore saw it as an acceptable opportunity for verbal involvement.

Since the end of 1968, the Australian Cabinet had possessed a Defence Committee report reviewing Australia's strategic environment and prospects up to the 1980s. This would provide the basis for long-term decisions. Although the report discounted the likelihood of a regional threat to Australia in the foreseeable future,[52] the Cabinet prevaricated for twelve weeks, during which time Malaysia–Philippine relations grew more turbulent following the passage in mid-October of a resolution in Malaysia's Parliament rejecting the Philippines' claim and 'annexation' of Sabah. It was only in the course of replying to a Labour censure motion criticising his inaction that Gorton finally announced the decision to retain the Australian battalion, two naval ships and two squadrons of Mirage jet fighters in the Malaysia–Singapore area until the end of 1971.[53] In the intra-alliance context, this announcement (the timing of which strongly suggested that it was motivated by domestic considerations) was not as significant as the emphatic qualification that it was a decision 'in principle' which depended, *inter alia*, on what 'assistance and support' Malaysia and Singapore themselves could provide. Moreover, as Gorton indicated, the decision had been taken in September and Malaysia and Singapore had already been informed privately. More important to Malaysia was the question of the Australian position after 1971, and that was still unclear.

Gorton's revelations led Holyoake to restate a similar New Zealand decision which had been publicised in June. The tone of Holyoake's statement on 20 November encouraged the inference that in the short term, at least, New Zealand had never quibbled about its intentions.[54] Holyoake appeared less circumspect in stating New Zealand's 'continuing interest in the stability, security and defence in the Southeast Asian area after 1971'. He saw sense in joining with Australia to form an ANZAC group and recognised the advantage of remaining at Terendak. Holyoake appeared to blame

Canberra for the delay when he endorsed the Opposition leader's comment that it was certainly not the New Zealand Government's fault that there had been even an apparent delay in making these decisions.[55]

The Australian Cabinet began to discuss the strategic reassessment in early December. Without revealing details, Gorton suggested, at a press conference on 11 December, the possibility of an option that involved neither a big permanent garrison abroad nor total withdrawal to national territories.[56] On 18 December Gorton disclosed that Malaysia and Singapore were being informed of arrangements for the period up to the end of 1971. On 3 January 1969 Gorton announced that Australian and New Zealand troops at Terendak would move to Singapore while a detachment would be deployed to Butterworth. Air and naval units would, however, remain as before. The move would begin at 'an appropriate stage during the British withdrawal from Terendak'.[57]

Holyoake issued a similar announcement on the same day, but hinted that the decision was mainly Gorton's.[58] New Zealand, indeed, would rather remain at Terendak, but could not possibly do so on its own. The New Zealand argument for 'not rocking the boat' was shared by those who hoped that the pronouncements by the Tory leader Edward Heath (made during his tour of the Far East and Australia in August 1968), which included his pledge of a continuing role in Southeast Asian defence, indicated some possibility of reversing the Labour Government's decision should the Conservatives return to power before the final withdrawal. Gorton's decision thus destroyed any hope of Terendak being still available should Heath revive the CSR.

Gorton's unilateral decision was underlined by its announcement just four days before his departure for the Commonwealth Prime Ministers' Conference in London, which would have provided an opportunity for consultation with the Tunku and other interested parties. Singapore, which had to host the redeployed forces, was, as Lee Kuan Yew admitted, fully consulted, although it too later argued strongly for retaining these forces in Malaysia. Indeed, Dr Goh was in Canberra when Gorton announced the decision. It could be argued that if Malaysia did not see Singapore as being excluded from Australian defence intentions when Australian forces were in Terendak, then there was no reason why Malaysia should feel abandoned when these forces were transferred to Singapore. The rationality of this argument was lost on account of Australia's equivocation over Sabah and the suddenness and brevity of Gorton's announcement, Gorton's subsequent clarification, that the redeployed ground forces would still be freely available to assist Malaysia, was insufficiently persuasive to prevent a rapid erosion of Malaysian confidence in Australia.

When the five defence partners gathered in London on the occasion of the Commonwealth Prime Ministers' Conference in January 1969, the Sabah issue had become for the Malaysians (who were faced with what, in their view, was Gorton's deliberate ambiguity) a test of Australian intentions. Although the Tunku had publicly restated in London his unhappiness at Britain's abdication of military responsibility, it was Gorton who became the principal target of Malaysian pressure. It was most unlikely that the Tunku, who on 21 January sought and obtained in London assurances from Michael Stewart (who had replaced George Brown as Foreign Secretary) that Britain would support Malaysia in the event of hostilities with the Philippines,[59] would not have broached the Sabah issue when, on 9 January, he met Healey, Holyoake, Lee Kuan Yew, Hasluck and Gorton in Gorton's Savoy Hotel suite. In fact, the Tunku failed to extract from Gorton any kind of verbal commitment over Sabah. Indeed, Gorton had pointedly refused to be involved in Sabah defence.[60] The one positive result of the Savoy encounter was Gorton's offer to host the next five-power conference in Canberra.

Gorton's offer hardly appeased Malaysia. It now publicly questioned the utility of Australia's association with AMDA. Whereas firm expressions of intent were once regarded as adequate substitutes for 'scraps of paper', Gorton's equivocation produced the opposite effect, making written commitment appear even more important to Malaysia. But if, as Hasluck had indicated on 22 January, a new agreement was unnecessary, then the existing AMDA had to be made to serve Malaysian needs. In the process, Malaysia was not disposed to interpret strictly Australia's associate status *vis-à-vis* AMDA. On returning to Kuala Lumpur, the Tunku commented that Australia was bound by AMDA to come to Malaysia's defence if Malaysia was attacked by the Philippines and that Hasluck's declared neutrality (publicised by his Singapore airport interview in September 1968) must represent a new attitude.[61]

The Australian and Malaysian press were generally aligned on opposite sides in the controversy, which reached a peak in February.

Surprised at the critical tone of the Australian press towards Malaysia, a Malaysian Foreign Ministry official argued defensively that the continuation of AMDA could be awkward if Australia were to say that the very threat which Malaysia then feared did not come within its scope.[62] To pin down a commitment, Razak highlighted a quid pro quo: 'if Australia wished to continue to station forces in Malaysia as part of a "forward defence" stance, then it must expect to become involved in intra-regional disputes such as Sabah'.[63] On the other hand, Gorton was adamant that the Australian Government should have ultimate control over the role of its forces in the area.

Malaysian unease over reported Australian neutrality was expressed in a Malaysian Foreign Ministry statement issued on 3 February. Although reference was also made to New Zealand, it was evidently directed at Australia. The statement declared: 'A threat of armed attack or an armed attack from any quarter on any part of Malaysia (be it East or West) naturally brings about a situation in which the provisions of the Defence Agreement come into play. Having that situation in mind, Malaysia is understandably anxious to have a clear cut idea of the commitments of her allies under the Agreement.' Comparing the recent 'satisfactory' discussions which the Tunku had had with Britain to the lack of detailed discussions with the Australian (or New Zealand) Government, the statement hoped that 'a clear and agreed understanding will be reached between Malaysia and Australia [and New Zealand] . . . at the coming five-power talks in Canberra'.[64] The intensification of Malaysian pressure on Canberra could have been partly in anticipation of Gorton's defence statement later in February. Furthermore, the Alliance Government (remembering the boost which Confrontation gave to their electoral campaign in 1964) was perhaps tempted to use the Philippine threat to mobilise mass support in the forthcoming general elections. And the more the Philippine threat was highlighted, the greater too was the public attention given to the issue of allied support for Malaysia.

Certainly, from late January to late March 1969, Kuala Lumpur greatly played up the Philippine threat and the reported violations of Malaysian air space. Malaysian vulnerability was underlined by the Philippines' American-supplied Sabre jets which were superior to anything in the small RMAF, whose role was mainly to support counter-insurgency operations. Malaysia's intention to acquire sophisticated fighter aircraft was discussed when the Tunku approached Michael Stewart on 22 January for firmer support over Sabah. Yet Malaysia had hitherto shown little enthusiasm for any substantial contribution of its own towards air defence. Indeed, the defence budget, announced as recently as 9 January, had not contained any extensive defence expenditure.[65] Certainly, the Tunku would have been willing to defer the purchase of such aircraft if only Britain would station an RAF contingent in Labuan (Sabah) till 1971.[66] Britain was not attracted to this suggestion. Its withdrawal programme was not to be interrupted by any reinvolvement in Sabah.

There was increasing confusion during February and March as Malaysia vacillated between buying French Mirages and British Lightnings. Such speculation was ended on 15 April 1969, when Gorton offered a gift of 10 Sabre jets (together with spares, ground equipment, a training simulator and a secondment of nearly 90 RAAF instructors and personnel) to Malaysia. Although Canberra cautiously explained to the Philippines that the gift should not be construed as anything other than a contribution to regional security, it was also made known to Malaysia that the gift was unconditional as regards its use.[67]

Following the announced withdrawal from Terendak, Singapore had refrained from making public demands or joining Malaysia in calling upon Australia to state clearly its position for the post-1971 period. A section of the Australian press commended Singapore for its shrewd observation of the 'ground rules' of the game, i.e. the greater the demand for a clear understanding on the use of Australian troops, the more equivocal Canberra was likely to be.[68] Singapore, of course, had neither a Sabah problem nor an impending general election.

New Zealand was equally successful in differentiating its position from Australia's and avoided much of Malaysia's ire. First, it did not disguise its dissatisfaction with a decision that was mainly Gorton's. As Holyoake put it, 'Malaysia's disappointment . . . is natural. We were disappointed ourselves. We have to withdraw [from Terendak] for compelling reasons.'[69] Second, it had been consistently less equivocal over Sabah, nor did it differentiate East from West Malaysia. While Holyoake and his colleagues had not promised military aid to Sabah, neither had they announced their refusal to help. Moreover, they had expressed their concern in a way that implied Malaysia was in the right. Malaysia, too, appreciated New Zealand's posture – adverse Malaysian comments on Australia sharply contrasted with Razak's description of New Zealand as 'one of our staunchest friends'.[70]

Malaysian unease and the need to check deteriorating relations with Malaysia could have provided an impetus to Gorton's parliamentary statement of 25 February, made in advance of his Washington visit, on the future Australian role in the Malaysia–Singapore area. On this day both Gorton and Holyoake declared without setting a terminal date, that their forces in the Malaysia–Singapore area would remain beyond 1971.[71] These decisions were significant in that they were taken 'in circumstances in which there is no assurance of great power backing, in a situation without a wider military framework in which an Australian and New Zealand military contribution might conveniently be fitted, and at a time when it is virtually impossible to foresee the conditions which will prevail in Vietnam, Laos and Cambodia, Malaysia's close neighbours, at the end of the Vietnam war'.[72]

The Tunku was satisfied with this 'levelling-up' of Australian and New Zealand responsibilities and with Gorton's expressed recognition of Malaysia's sovereignty over Sabah. Yet there were disturbing features in Gorton's statement which diminished politically Australia's military contributions. Both Gorton and Holyoake excluded the use of their forces in internal security, but Gorton went on to state that the Australian presence was 'not directed against any other country in the region'. Their prime function was to meet 'externally promoted and inspired Communist infiltration and subversion of the kind which became familiar during the Emergency'. To Malaysia, whose most immediate problem was Sabah, this appeared deliberately to skirt around an essential issue. Indeed, Gorton distinguished East from West Malaysia when he said that the Australian presence 'in *Malaya* [emphasis mine] and Singapore' would 'make it possible for Malaysian troops to be assigned to other parts of Malaysia'.[73] In an earlier passage, which dealt with the indivisibility of Malaya–Singapore defence, the exclusion of Sabah was equally clear. Gorton stated that 'no matter in what part of the *Peninsula* (including Singapore) our forces are stationed, we regard them as being there in order to assist the security and the stability of the whole of *that Peninsula*' (emphasis mine).

In defining New Zealand's military role, Holyoake adroitly

avoided controversy over Sabah by simply stating that New Zealand forces were designed as a 'contribution to the security of Southeast Asia as a whole, as they have been since they were first deployed'. Furthermore, Holyoake invoked 'the spirit and content' of his 20 September 1963 statement as a continuing and valid basis for the retention of New Zealand forces in the area after 1971. In recalling at length that statement (which extended New Zealand's association with AMDA during Confrontation), Holyoake underlined a certain continuity against the background of change. Holyoake said that New Zealand had 'always given cause to believe that she would not stand idly aside in the event of an armed attack on Malaysia'.[74] His reaffirmation of the September 1963 statement was welcomed by the Tunku who commented that 'in the case of Mr Holyoake he never altered his position at any time'.[75]

Yet Holyoake's reference to New Zealand's associate status was also a reminder that, despite its traditional support for Malaysia, there was 'no legal obligation . . . to maintain forces in Malaysia or to follow specific courses of action for its external defence'.[76] In extending New Zealand's defence contributions beyond 1971, Holyoake, like Gorton, had carefully avoided any allusion to an automatic commitment. More than ever, AMDA had become an anachronism. Gorton himself declared that, should AMDA lapse, Australia would prefer 'general understandings rather than specific treaty obligations'.[77] But before the next five-power meeting could be held, further clarifications on the use of external forces were necessitated by the outbreak of civil disorder in Malaysia.

On 13 May 1969, in the aftermath of the set-backs suffered by the Alliance Party in the general elections and the communal tensions aroused during the campaign, communal violence erupted in Kuala Lumpur. Minor outbreaks followed in other urban areas, spilling over to Singapore. The magnitude of the Kuala Lumpur riots resulted in the suspension of the Alliance Government on 15 May under Emergency Rule. Malaysia initially blamed the MCP for the riots – an explanation regarded sceptically by the external partners. Gorton promptly reiterated that Australian forces were 'not intended for use, and will not be used [to maintain] internal civil law and order'.[78] Britain and New Zealand also made similar clarifications. Whitehall added that the civil disturbance would not alter British withdrawal plans. The incident nevertheless showed the problems that could be caused by the differentiation of the function of counter-insurgency from the role of internal security, particularly when Kuala Lumpur itself had encouraged the existence of such an ambiguity.

Kuala Lumpur was reportedly impatient with the delays in receiving replies from Canberra and London to its appeal for arms and equipment. The circumstances (including the suspension of parliamentary democracy) in which the Malaysian request was made presented political problems since the external Governments would not wish to appear to be endorsing or supporting a 'status quo perceived to be in the primary interests of only one community'.[79] There was also concern about how any such assistance rendered at that juncture might appear to the Singapore Chinese. The Kuala Lumpur riots had greatly alarmed the Singapore Government which, in early June, had to deal with communal violence in Singapore itself. Present, too, were fears of a serious deterioration of Malaysia–Singapore relations, which had already come under strain when Malaysian ministers had earlier accused Singapore of interference in the general elections. The hurried appointment as High Commissioner in Malaysia of Maurice Baker from his New Delhi post (Baker had a good personal relationship with Razak and Ghazali Shafie) reflected the growing importance Singapore attached to improved relations with Kuala Lumpur. The incident also illuminated another facet of Malaysia–Singapore indivisibility – internal instability in one country had repercussions in the other. The episode unavoidably overshadowed the next five-power conference. And, while Malaysia's arms request was eventually met by both Britain and Australia, it had become even more important to Australia and New Zealand that their remaining forces should be under firm control of national decisions.

The main practical function of the Canberra conference held on 19 and 20 June was to approve the proposals of the advisory working groups based on general policy agreed at the Kuala Lumpur conference. Overshadowing that were the communal disturbances in Malaysia and Malaysia's preoccupation with external defence. Singapore's concern with Malaysia's internal unrest was reflected in Lee Kuan Yew's criticism of the Australian withdrawal from Terendak. In Australia he argued publicly that Australia's claim of favouring peace and security in the area would have been more credible if 'backed by a token of Australia's firm intention to maintain [in Malaysia] as far as she is able to, forces of sanity and stability'.[80] Malaysia emphasised that it was fully capable of handling its current internal problems. However, Razak, who led the Malaysian delegation, openly stated that Malaysia's primary concern at the Canberra talks would be to obtain assurances against external aggression.

In his opening speech, Gorton sought to reply strongly to the latest public comments by Lee and Razak.[81] With the Malaysian riots in mind, Gorton spoke of the requisites for regional stability, which depended both on the diminution of racial tensions and on the creation of equal economic and social opportunities. Replying to Lee's comments, Gorton justified the redeployment of forces to Singapore on military, logistical and financial grounds. Then, echoing an earlier passage, Gorton declared that Australian forces were based in Singapore under the concept that 'defence against external attack is, as far as Singapore and Malaya are concerned . . . indivisible'.[82] Gorton included a provision against external attack but, significantly, each reference to 'external attack' was made within the context of 'Malaya' (the term being used thrice) and not 'Malaysia'.

The Malaysians had thought that this issue had been clarified and resolved after 'a lot of diplomatic work' following Gorton's first official reference to the 'Peninsula' in his 25 February statement.[83] The visit of Gordon Freeth (who became External Affairs Minister in February 1969) to Kuala Lumpur in April and his public remark that Australia had not excluded the possibility of its forces being used in the event of aggression against Sabah had placated the Tunku. Malaysia's assumption, that the Australian Mirages could be involved under the same conditions in East and West Malaysia, was upset by Gorton's opening speech. Razak, in turn, declared at the conference that any distinction of commitment to East and West Malaysia – whatever the commitment – was unacceptable. As he angrily related to a *Daily Telegraph* correspondent afterwards, there was 'no such country as Malaya'.[84]

The most vocal Malaysian criticism was reserved for the final press briefing when Malaysia's spokesman, Zain Azrai, bluntly questioned the 'seriousness and extent' of Australia's commitment.[85] Both Freeth and Fairhall, at their joint press conference on 20 June, sought to repair the damage caused by Gorton's remarks. Refusing to be drawn into explaining Gorton's speech, Freeth managed to reassert that Australia had not necessarily excluded a commitment in the event of aggression towards East Malaysia. But he also emphasised that Australia reserved the right of independent decision at all times.[86]

Despite open disagreement between Malaysia and Australia, some positive achievements did result from the conference. Malaysia–Singapore co-operation was reflected in Malaysia's readiness to maintain and operate the armament depot in Singapore for the use of partner countries and in the training of Singapore naval personnel by the RMN.[87] Departing from its previous reticence, Malaysia (forced by external concerns and internal instability) now informed the other partners of a planned increase of its armed forces by four infantry and five Police Field Force battalions.

Another Malaysian decision which the conference welcomed was the purchase, through British finance, of two British mobile radar systems, one of which was to be based at Butterworth. The Malaysian system would link up with radar facilities in Singapore and form an important component of the integrated air defence system (IADS). Other contributions to the system were: Australian air deployments, including a second squadron of Mirages; Singapore's purchase of the 56 British Bloodhound missiles;[88] the emerging SAF; the impending transfer of Australian Sabres to Malaysia and arrangements by Britain and Australia to train Malaysian and Singapore personnel.[89]

The issue of political control over the IADS remained unresolved. Although Australia was contributing the Air Defence Commander, it insisted that he be the servant of the Malaysian and Singapore Governments. On the other hand, RAAF units in the area after 1971 would remain under full Australian control and would be assigned to the Commander only on conditions determined by Canberra. This Australian insistence would be operationally almost impracticable once a quick-reaction air defence system came into existence. Indeed, Gorton's distinction between East and West Malaysia could hardly be built into such a system. Understandably, Fairhall only spoke of joint exercises and training in reference to those occasions when the Mirages would be assigned to the Air Defence Commander; rules of engagement and conditions of use still needed to be worked out.[90] The Malaysian and Singapore representatives, after private consultations, returned to the conference the following day proposing that the IADS command should come under multilateral political control.

The British, pleasantly surprised that the Australians, rather than themselves, had borne the brunt of criticisms, were content to remain in the background. Having ruled out any bargaining over their planned withdrawal or participation in post-1971 joint command structures, the British expressed interest in keeping instructors and a Gurkha demonstration platoon at the Jungle Warfare School (JWS), through which two British battalions and eight smaller detachments would pass annually for two months' training each. Britain would even bear most of the expenses. Four ships of the RN would also visit the area for four months annually and RAF aircraft would stage regularly in the area.[91] However, despite Britain's express interest in the JWS, subsequent efforts to convert it into a multi-national centre failed.

Even while functional arrangements were being built up in the area, political trust was being eroded. At Canberra, Healey had ruled out any 'automatic military commitments', while Gorton was emphatic in not laying down 'firm conditions and spelt-out circumstances' for the future use of forces against external aggression in the area.[92] Malaysia's confidence was hardly restored by Gorton's reiteration on Melbourne television in early July that his reference to 'Malaya' was 'quite deliberate'.[93] During late July and early August, Dato Stephens continued to speak of doubts and 'disenchantment' with the Australian position. These statements culminated in the Tunku's remark that, 'as far as Malaysia is concerned, the five-power defence arrangement is useless now'.[94] Razak, possibly hoping to distract attention from the Tunku's deprecatory references, said that Malaysia would prefer 'a clear and unequivocal statement that they (Australia and New Zealand) would come to our aid in the case of aggression'.[95] But he merely added to the growing signs of Malaysian distrust. His suggestion was coolly received by the external partners. Holyoake clearly rejected any five-power treaties of the AMDA variety. Singapore, too, officially dissociated itself from the new Malaysian demand.

Australia did not succeed in soothing Malaysian feelings. Freeth's reaffirmation, that the use of Australian forces outside the peninsula was not necessarily excluded in all circumstances,[96] was, to Razak, a repetition of an old assurance. Controversy over Australian forces in the area was kept alive by the ensuing Australian election campaign. The Labour Party, under Gough Whitlam, had pledged to withdraw all ground forces, though not air and naval units, from the Malaysia–Singapore area. Razak himself spoke of the possible upset to the five-power defence arrangements if Whitlam's policy were carried out. The Liberal–Country coalition was returned to power with a vastly reduced majority in the 25 October elections. Changes in the Defence and External Affairs portfolios followed: Malcolm Fraser assumed Defence from Fairhall, who retired from politics, and William McMahon became External Affairs Minister in place of Freeth, who was not elected. On 4 November officials of the five powers convened in Kuala Lumpur to work out details of a new defence system.

Further bilateral Malaysia–Singapore discussions preceded the meeting at Kuala Lumpur, first when Lim Kim San and E. W. Barker visited Kuala Lumpur in September and later when officials of both countries met in Singapore shortly before the multilateral meeting of 4 November. The Kuala Lumpur meeting, besides reviewing plans for the forthcoming combined five-power exercise and matters of naval co-operation, dealt mainly with problems related to the IADS. Some of these problems had been spelled out by Razak on his return from Canberra: 'If there is to be an attack who is to give the command? Time is the essence. Someone will have to press the button. How are the air forces to be assigned in the time of emergency?'[97] The Australian offer of a commander for the IADS had still left several issues unresolved.[98] In a way, the whole debate hinged on the questionable strength of the external powers' sense of commitment.

Although the final communiqué recorded considerable progress in knitting together the IADS and in naval co-operation, the basis whereby political sanction would be given to the use of the forces available had to be devised. Even the single co-ordinator of the IADS (which came nearest to embodying an automatic commitment) must still receive his directives from a forum representing the various Governments. While proposals were being referred back to the five Governments, political events were influencing attitudes which in turn set the trend towards the final shaping of the arrangements which replaced AMDA.

The prospect of some kind of British reinvolvement was revived by the Conservative leader, Edward Heath, who, in early January 1970, again visited Malaysia and Singapore. Heath offered to adapt British forces still remaining under the last phases of the 1971 withdrawal to a balanced five-power force. But Britain would just be an equal partner. Without specifying the cost or size of force, Heath described his offer as 'a modest insurance premium' for continuing stability and prosperity.[99] He echoed Lee Kuan Yew's claims of the psychological benefits of an actual physical presence as opposed to a general capability. In effect, the difference between Tory and Labour policies was one of approach rather than of substance.

While debate in Britain continued over the cost and the technical problems of modifying the withdrawal plans, the selection of a permanent site for the external forces in Singapore was being held up. The matter was discussed in early February between Lim Kim San and the Australian Army Minister, Andrew Peacock, but a final decision was deferred because of the British elections. Australia, however, was hardly impressed by Heath's promises. In a major policy statement on 10 March 1970, Malcolm Fraser pointed out that withdrawal of British power from the region was irreversible. Accordingly, Australia had been moving from a supporting role to one of partnership, but with the local powers accepting a greater responsibility for their own defence. But he also emphasised that 'Governments nowadays do not sign blank cheques saying automatically that if something happens their troops will march.'[100]

The British Labour Government, for its part, was adhering to its withdrawal programme. Its February 1970 Defence White Paper effectively heralded the end of Britain's major military role outside Europe. As planned, withdrawal would be completed by the end of 1971.[101] For Britain, the time too had come to consider the replacement of AMDA. The Tunku himself had publicly stated that Malaysia was ready to 'renegotiate'. In April 1970 Healey disclosed that Britain had proposed a new five-power political framework and hoped that formal talks could begin soon. His reiteration that there would be no automatic British commitment suggested that some loose consultative framework was contemplated.

Widely expressed public reservations in both Australia and Britain put into a realistic perspective the massive five-power military exercise (which began on 5 April with the deployment of overseas forces to Malaysia and Singapore) then under way. These reservations provided a counterpoint to the political objective of this expensive demonstration of Britain's general capability after 1971. Increasingly, too, the virtue of self-reliance was being brought home to the Malaysians.

The changing political context in which the five-power exercise was held tended to diminish its significance in Malaysian eyes despite the impressive combined effort, which involved altogether 27,000 men, 500 transport vehicles, 10 armoured cars, 104 aircraft,

120 helicopters and 50 ships. The cost to Britain alone was £2.5 million excluding food, equipment and pay. Undeniably, several useful lessons in co-operation and co-ordination were learnt from the exercise, code-named 'Bersatu Padu' ('Complete Unity'). Yet the loss of political will among the external powers undermined the value of the exercise. On the practical level, the six weeks' acclimatisation required of overseas troops and the need for advance establishment of a Brigade headquarters put in doubt the efficacy of long-range emergency reinforcement. There was reported Malaysian cynicism towards what had become more of an exercise in public relations.[102]

The exercise also revealed the sensitive nature of a Singapore military presence on Malaysian soil. 'Bersatu Padu' provided the only occasion when Singapore armed forces in battalion strength crossed into Malaysia for large-scale manoeuvres. But Singapore's newly acquired French AMX tanks were conspicuously absent – a ban on them had reportedly been imposed by Kuala Lumpur in response to fears, quite openly expressed in the Malay press, about Singapore's intentions.[103] Such suspicion was reinforced by the psychological impact of Singapore's rapid military expansion under the guidance of Israeli advisers. There was also a tendency to question not only Singapore's need for jungle warfare training (Lee had openly stated that Singapore had no insurgency problem) but also the acquisition of sophisticated military aircraft. Certainly a basic difference in approach existed: Malaysia's primary concern was with insurgency while Singapore's was with the concept of island defence. Thus, in its relations with the external powers as well as in matters of defence co-operation with Singapore, a mood of increasing realism and self-assertiveness was beginning to pervade Kuala Lumpur. The final stage in the reorganisation of the defence of Malaysia–Singapore must be viewed against this evolving attitude.

Following the return to power of the Tories at the June elections, intra-alliance consultations were renewed when Lord Carrington, the new British Defence Minister, visited the four allies between 25 July and 3 August 1970. In Canberra, reference was made to 'political arrangements of some kind to reflect equality between all five commonwealth partners'.[104] Lord Carrington arrived in the Malaysia–Singapore area with a strong impression of the existence of local enthusiasm for the five-power concept.[105] Certainly, Singapore had reflected this enthusiasm. What Lord Carrington encountered in Kuala Lumpur, however, was an independent, assertive attitude much more inclined to question the basis of multilateral arrangements than had been expected. While the retention of some British forces in the area was, according to Lord Carrington, warmly received in Kuala Lumpur, there were differences of opinion over both the question of force integration and the form of political arrangements to allow for the external military presence.

It seemed that Malaysia's emphasis on AMDA's continuity did not so much reflect its attachment to AMDA *per se*, but was, rather, a counterpoise to excessive multilateralism which could shift the focus away from Malaysia's central or exclusive needs. Multilateralism, as it had emerged in the earlier argument over the IADS, was pertinent where it might pin down an Australian and New Zealand commitment to Malaysia. Razak subsequently dispelled any idea of a collective defence pact. The 'agreement' envisaged was not a formal treaty.[106] Malaysia now accepted that a loose arrangement was the key to bringing Australia and New Zealand into a system which could not be exclusively Anglo-Malaysian. It conceded to multilateralism at the loose, consultative level, but multilateralism was never fully achieved at the military level.

Detailed British defence contributions were decided after Lord Carrington's consultations. The essential difference between the Conservative and Labour contributions was the continuation of a garrison presence in the Singapore area as opposed to a training presence. According to the Supplementary Defence White Paper of 28 October 1970, British units would have access to the JWS facilities in rotation with Australian and New Zealand units, and visits by air and naval units would go on as they would have done under Labour. In addition, five frigates or destroyers would be stationed East of Suez and an infantry battalion would be retained for the Malaysia–Singapore area.[107] These forces, it was announced subsequently, would be based in Singapore.

However, Britain did not offer any RAF strike aircraft, in spite of Singapore's specific request. Britain's air deployments would be confined to a detachment of Nimrod long-range maritime reconnaissance aircraft and some Whirlwind helicopters. In effect, Butterworth now became the main air strike base in the Malaysia–Singapore area. Singapore, however, remained the naval headquarters with the newly established Maritime Joint Operations Centre serving to co-ordinate naval defence. The additional cost of these contributions (i.e. over and above the costs of the preceding Labour Government's proposed policy) would be just over £10 million. AMDA would be replaced by a political commitment of a consultative nature undertaken equally by all the five powers.[108]

The levelling-down of the British commitment and the levelling-up of the Australian and New Zealand contributions led to a 'more equal' partnership within the five-power framework. It also meant that the previous 'consumers' of alliance security had come increasingly into their own as politically separate, but functionally related, centres of the new defence system.

A Malaysian assertiveness in both foreign policy and defence had become more apparent since Tun Razak had assumed the Prime Ministership on 22 September 1970. In a major foreign policy speech, Razak advocated the neutralisation of Southeast Asia guaranteed by the great powers. He held forth the promise of a new dialogue with Peking and at the same time stressed the importance of self-sufficiency in defence. Disillusionment with the revised Commonwealth defence arrangements, the retirement of the more British-orientated Tunku, the emergence of the more pragmatic trio of Razak, Tun Ismail (as Deputy Prime Minister) and Tan Sri Ghazali Shafie, the realisation of the changed Asian environment caused by both British and American withdrawal and the fact that the Philippine claim had become less strident of late[109] had all contributed towards Malaysia's psychological decolonisation. Malaysia's long-term commitment to neutralisation was not considered incompatible with its medium-term contribution to five-power defence.

Singapore, too, was adjusting to the changed circumstances, albeit in a different way. It tended to view regional stability as a function of the involvement of the great powers (they would balance one another) in the region, rather than as a function of their exclusion. In Singapore's conception of a balance-of-power system, the five-power arrangements were quite relevant since they institutionalised a certain sphere of Commonwealth interest. The three external powers could also provide a counterweight to Malaysia. Thus, although Malaysia–Singapore interests were not wholly congruent, they nevertheless found a meeting ground in five-power defence.

In preparation for the ministerial conference promised for the early part of 1971, officials of the five powers met in Singapore on 7 and 8 January 1971 to work out proposals that would incorporate a revised British presence in the Malaysia–Singapore area. The Malaysians now showed a greater willingness to exercise a veto power in negotiations and a tendency to examine all proposals critically. They succeeded in obtaining complete control over the JWS, contrary to earlier hopes that the school would be operated multilaterally. This effectively ruled out any corporate rights in the use of the facility and could have been motivated by Malaysia's avowal of non-alignment, which called for some demonstration of full control over national defence. But Malaysia was also sensitive to Singapore's use of the facility. Indeed, Singapore troops, which had used the JWS when it was under British control, have not trained in Malaysia since the facility passed into Malaysian hands.[110]

However, the structure of the five-nation system had become more definable. The meeting agreed to establish an air defence council responsible for the functioning of the IADS, the only part of the military arrangements that would be truly five-sided. In naval and ground operations, the five powers would effectively function as three: Malaysia, Singapore and the combined ANZUK (i.e. Australia, New Zealand and the United Kingdom) forces. The external forces would have a single command, but only the air component would also be subject to a five-power command. The hitherto unresolved issue of the IADS commander was settled with Australia agreeing to provide a serving officer (Air Vice-Marshal R. T. Susans) for the part. Recommendations on the political consultative framework which was necessary to cover the five-power defence arrangements when AMDA lapsed were contained in a document worked out at the conference and made ready for further ministerial discussions due to open later in London. Informal political consultations were further facilitated by the occasion of the Commonwealth Prime Ministers' Conference held in Singapore in mid-January.

The final British contributions to the area, announced in the Defence White Paper issued on 17 February 1971, represented only a minor increase over the October 1970 proposals (Cmnd. 4521). In addition to the previously announced deployments, Britain would contribute a sixth frigate or destroyer and one submarine to be assigned to the Australian squadron in the Far East, which in turn would provide one submarine in the Singapore area.[111] The groundwork for the phasing out of AMDA was thus almost completed by the time Ministers of the five powers convened in London in April 1971 to sanction officially the consultative framework.

Ministers representing the five powers at the London conference which opened on 15 April were Tun Razak, Dr Goh Keng Swee, Sir Keith Holyoake, Lord Carrington (Conference Chairman), Lord Balniel, British Defence Minister, and John Gorton, who attended as Australian Defence Minister having resigned the Prime Ministership during a Cabinet crisis the previous month. William McMahon was now Prime Minister, his post of Foreign Affairs Minister being taken by Leslie Bury. Nevertheless, Gorton's new portfolio gave him an important influence in the final stages of negotiation. The political 'instrument' which was to provide the framework for the five-power arrangements was simply contained in the final communiqué of the London conference, issued on 18 April. Paragraph 5 of the communiqué stated:

> The Ministers also declared, in relation to the external defence of Malaysia and Singapore, that in the event of any form of armed attack externally organised or supported or the threat of such attack against Malaysia or Singapore, their Governments would immediately consult together for the purpose of deciding what measures should be taken jointly or separately in relation to such attack or threat.[112]

It can be seen that the only acceptable political commitment was a commitment to consult, undertaken equally by each of the powers. AMDA itself would terminate on 1 November 1971.

The phrasing of paragraph 5 had been the subject of lengthy exchanges between Australia, Malaysia and Singapore. Gorton's approach was influenced by his February 1969 declaration defining the use of Australian forces in the area after 1971. He was quite determined to incorporate his earlier specifications against 'externally inspired insurgency' in the five-power agreement. And although paragraph 5 of the communiqué did not mention 'insurgency', Gorton later stated that the defence arrangements were 'also directed against a kind of armed attack which is not civil disorder in the normal sense, but the provision of infiltration forces from abroad, and the arming and controlling of them'.[113]

There was, in fact, no definitive interpretation of paragraph 5. Lord Carrington even conceded that consultations could be called for in a case where rioting was inspired from outside. Razak, for his part, chose to focus on the 'threat of aggression or aggression supported or organised from outside'.[114] In effect, each partner could decide in the light of its own interests what should be regarded as an external threat to Malaysia and Singapore. Because of the consultative nature of the commitment, Gorton no longer found it necessary to distinguish between East and West Malaysia.

In air defence, quick reaction was crucial and integration, as opposed to close co-operation, was necessary. The London conference thus approved the establishment of an Air Defence Council (comprising one senior representative from each power) to be responsible for the functioning of the IADS and to provide direction to the Air Defence Commander on matters of the organisation, development and operational readiness of the system. Apart from the sphere of air defence, there was no fully integrated five-power command structure. The London conference decided on a Joint Consultative Council at senior official level (i.e. High Commissioner level for the external powers) sitting alternately in Malaysia and Singapore under Malaysian and Singapore chairmanship respectively. While this body could provide an initial forum for consultation in an emergency and could summon military or specialist advice, it was essentially a consultative body. The regularised meetings at official level had no parallel at ministerial level – ministerial meetings were to be convened on an *ad hoc* basis. Any partner could call for a review of these arrangements by giving due notice.[115]

Although failure to turn the JWS into a five-power facility was disappointing to Britain, Lord Carrington obtained assurances from Razak that Britain would be given as much access to the facility as possible. One unresolved issue was the rental for facilities in Singapore occupied by antipodean forces. This subject sparked off sharp exchanges between Gorton and Singapore and threatened to delay the implementation of the five-power arrangement. Australia's position (supported by New Zealand) was that it should not be treated differently from Britain which was not paying rent in Singapore. A settlement, however, was reached by the time AMDA was terminated. On 1 November (Gorton having been dismissed from the post in August) the new Australian Defence Minister, David Fairbairn, announced the settlement: no charge would be made on fixed military facilities. But rental at less than market value would be paid for married quarters, recreational and educational facilities.[116] New Zealand agreed to similar terms.

On the same day as the Fairbairn announcement, Letters of Exchange were initialled separately between the three external powers and the two host powers. The documents exchanged between Malaysia and the external powers formally terminated AMDA. But, borrowing much from the AMDA annexes, the new documents set out the rights and status of the external forces either stationed in or visiting Malaysia and the assistance that they were to render.

Broadly similar (but not identical) documents to cover the ANZUK presence in Singapore were signed between the external powers and Singapore. On 1 November, too, the regrouped ANZUK force, now concentrated in the former naval base and in the Sembawang/Nee Soon complex in the north-west of Singapore, was formally phased-in under the command of an Australian officer, Rear-Admiral David Wells.

The process of destructuring AMDA could be deemed accomplished with the issuing of the five-power communiqué on 16 April 1971. The statement of intent embodied in the operative paragraph of the April communiqué replaced the formal AMDA structure. The five partners in the new system were equal in role as well as in status. But Malaysia and Singapore themselves took primary responsibility for their own external defence.

Yet the transition, from a system embracing an open-ended defence guarantee by the protector power to one in which every partner had the right to define, in the light of its own national interest, precisely what constituted a threat, did not involve an actual renegotiation of AMDA. In this sense it is inaccurate to speak of the transformation of AMDA. What had essentially been transformed was a set of alliance relationships, by means of which transformation an evolving process of national identification had accompanied the transition of Malaysia and Singapore from their over-dependence on Britain to their *de facto* partnership with the external powers. The final stages of that transformation were charted by the series of five-power ministerial and official-level conferences out of which had evolved, by a gradual *ad hoc* process, the various functional arrangements which finally fitted into a completely new military system for Malaysia–Singapore defence.

The loose consultative Five-Power Arrangement represented the highest possible common denominator for defence collaboration in the vastly changed circumstances which stemmed from Britain's withdrawal (albeit subsequently modified by the Tories). At the same time, it had become increasingly difficult to find a precise military *raison d'être* for the new arrangements, which were essentially transitional and intended to assist Malaysia and Singapore to adjust to a new equilibrium in the region. AMDA's demise marked the opening of a phase in which defence became even more subordinated to the political relationships of the five powers.

10. CONCLUSIONS

As a framework for defence collaboration in the Malaysia–Singapore region, AMDA was bracketed between two distinct phases of intra-alliance relations. At the beginning was the loose, informal, ANZAM arrangement which reflected a period of Commonwealth defence collaboration in the Malayan area when Malaya itself was essentially an object of international relations. ANZAM was eventually subsumed within AMDA, which aided Malaya's transition into nationhood. AMDA in turn was superseded by a loose consultative arrangement which resembled ANZAM. AMDA, whose cycle was completed in 1971, thus represented a transitional phase in intra-alliance relations.

While intra-alliance relations cannot be wholly understood by reference to AMDA alone, the rise and demise of the treaty were influenced by the process of redefinition of interests among the defence partners. The dismantling of AMDA was the culmination of the treaty's failure to accommodate their increasingly divergent interests. The significant turning points in the course of alliance transformation (from the formation of AMDA to its extension, to its *de facto* amendment, to the stages of its destructuring) were determined more by intra-alliance developments than by influences stemming from changes in the external environment of the alliance.

AMDA was a unique alliance system. While sharing with other unequal burden treaties the characteristic of a great power acting as anchor for the alliance, AMDA also embraced two associate powers which were 'consumers' as well as sub-providers of alliance security. But the British anchor role itself was qualified by an inherent paradox in that the formalisation of the British commitment to defend Malaya was part of a wider process of British disengagement from the region. Underlying this was a parallel process of gradual decline in British power and capability. The trend was already emerging as early as October 1948 when Britain made it clear that the Dominions must shoulder a greatly increased share in Empire defence in view of Britain's economic and manpower difficulties. It was apparent during the Suez crisis and even the Tunku had to admit, during his London visit in December 1956 to negotiate the financial and defence package, that he had 'come at the wrong time, Britain herself is broke'.[1]

Yet the implications of Britain's post-imperial sense of responsibility (i.e. the creation of stable conditions for the survival of the newly independent nation) were never seriously questioned at the time when AMDA was negotiated. The treaty, as the Tunku observed, was not even discussed in the British Parliament.[2] Ready assumption by Britain of its anchor role delayed, in a sense, Malaya's psychological decolonisation, although the 'special relationship' with Britain did serve a Malayan interest in that Malaya was able to devote more resources to socio-economic advancement. In the intra-alliance context, this 'special relationship' instilled in Malaya, and later in Malaysia, a certain 'consumer attitude'. Malaysia's understandable reluctance to spend heavily on defence ran parallel with an equally strong reluctance to come to terms with Britain's withdrawal of its supporting role. The Commonwealth attachment in matters of Malayan defence had also distorted Malaysian expectations with regard to the associate powers, whose *de facto* roles, as well as *de jure* status, within the alliance were fundamentally different from Britain's. Yet the fact that the status of Australian–New Zealand forces based *in* Malaya could only be fully appreciated by reference to AMDA did contribute to an easy (and even, at times, convenient) confusion in the host country between the antipodean and British roles.

The attendant distortion of Malaysian expectations was apparent during the period of external challenge to AMDA. This was evinced by the Tunku's speech at Malacca on 10 March 1963, the embarrassment it caused to Canberra and its hasty retraction. The same distortion provided an undercurrent to much of the open diplomacy and public pressuring of Australia and, to a lesser extent, New Zealand during the first phase of Confrontation, in spite of the obvious comfort, and even political advantage, which such open intra-alliance differences could give to Sukarno. It was again evident during the revival of the Philippines' claim to Sabah, when the future of Britain's protective role had become even less certain. AMDA's failure to provide an adequate framework of reference for defence collaboration was reflected in the destructuring of the formal alliance. The limited liability arrangement that followed had the effect of removing the distortion within AMDA and placed intra-alliance relations on a more equal basis in both a *de facto* and a *de jure* sense.

Intra-alliance relations had not begun with the coming into force of AMDA. Among the external powers, defence collaboration in the Malayan area antedated the treaty by several years and had culminated in the establishment of the CSR in 1955. The advent of Malayan independence necessitated the formalisation of the status and role of foreign forces already in Malaya. Although the land component of the CSR was based *in* Malaya, its main function was perceived by the external powers in wider strategic terms. Indeed, its use in counter-insurgency operations within Malaya was spelled out in a document quite distinct from AMDA. From Kuala Lumpur's perspective, defence against external attack and internal insurgency were the main priorities although, with the ending of the Emergency, the second objective became increasingly a local concern.

The regional, external defence and counter-insurgency roles of the CSR, while not mutually exclusive, were not entirely complementary either. Their priorities altered according to circumstances. Malaya's antipathy towards SEATO meant that the regional role of the CSR had to be played down in the very defence treaty which assisted Malaya's transition into nationhood. Although Malaya's special defence relationship with the anchor power prolonged the *de facto* inequality in their roles within the alliance, the process of decolonisation did have an inner dynamic which indirectly contributed to the gradual transformation of intra-alliance relations. The peculiar structure of AMDA was a reflection of an emerging national identification. The acceleration of internal political advance in Malaya spilled over into defence issues and resulted in the first major Legislative Council debate on the subject in March 1956, a time when Britain still held responsibility for the key areas of defence, foreign policy and economic policy.

Malayan susceptibilities were accommodated in the provisions which preserved Malayan sovereignty in such issues as land tenure and jurisdiction over foreign troops. More important were the provisions which enabled Kuala Lumpur to reserve its position *vis-à-vis* SEATO. The inequality of roles between the provider and consumer of alliance security made it imperative that AMDA should emphasise the equality of their political relationship. Special emphasis was thus put on the need for consultation on such matters as the deployment or redeployment of overseas forces in addition to the consultative provisions relating to an outbreak of hostilities in the treaty area.

Malayan – or, more accurately, Malay – national pride was also perceived in the subsequent vicissitudes in intra-alliance relations, e.g. in pre- as well as post-separation relations between the Central Government and Singapore, in the Anglo-Malaysian dialogue over defence and economic issues following separation and in Malaysian–Australian relations during Confrontation; and especially during the revival of the Philippines' threat, when Gorton's indelicate exclusion of Sabah's defence, coupled with an abrasiveness of style, touched an increasingly sensitive nerve. With the weighing of the British anchor and, later, the retirement of the Tunku from Malaysian politics and the emergence of an increasingly non-aligned Malaysian foreign policy, Malaysian assertiveness became more open and was strongly felt in the course of negotiations to redraw the defence framework.

AMDA not only gave recognition to a distinct local interest and to the existence of local susceptibilities, but it also reflected a differentiation of interests among the external powers. The hierarchy of roles superimposed upon the alliance was made formal by the association in 1959 of Australia and New Zealand with that portion of AMDA which provided for the stationing of the CSR. The Australian–New Zealand 'commitment' to Malayan defence could only be obliquely gathered by a broad interpretation of Article III which, apart from stating that the CSR was 'necessary for the fulfilment of Commonwealth and international obligations', also embraced the external defence of the Federation. Yet it was the UK alone among the external powers which was formally committed to Article I. Underlying that was the assumption that the Australian–New Zealand 'commitments' were dependent on British willingness in the first place to play the guarantor role. Notwithstanding the existence of an intrinsic interest in the defence of the Malaya–Singapore area, the Australian and New Zealand contributions were also 'club fees' for great power protection.

Thus, in accommodating the overlapping interests of the allies, AMDA institutionalised an ambiguity. With respect to the alliance as a whole, the ambiguity was sustainable precisely because of the strength of the British commitment and, with respect to the CSR, was made practicable by the loophole of withdrawal to, and redeployment from, Singapore. But the local political context which facilitated that loophole of redeployment soon changed. In this respect, 1959 was a significant year for the subsequent transformation of the alliance. It witnessed the emergence of important political trends in Singapore which led eventually to Malaysia's formation. In the same year, strategic continuity was reaffirmed among the external powers with the formal association of Australia and New Zealand with AMDA, while the impending end to the Emergency merely resulted in an exchange of ambiguities over the role of the CSR. The problem of 'squaring the circle' of political change and strategic continuity became again an important consideration during the extension phase of AMDA.

With the formation of Malaysia, the formula of useful ambiguity was carried over. The extent of intra-alliance compromise was reflected in the successful accommodation of strategic continuity and political change. AMDA itself was not renegotiated but only marginally amended in a joint Anglo–Malayan statement signed in November 1961 and later incorporated in Article VI of the Malaysia Agreement of July 1963. The Tunku himself candidly confirmed that the ambiguity of the phrase 'for the preservation of peace in Southeast Asia' in Article VI enabled the signatories to impute different interpretations to the role of the Singapore bases. Significantly, just when the alliance was being extended, the treaty itself had become (in the Tunku's words) 'not that important'. What were important were the mutual understanding and the existing state of relations among the allies themselves. The quality of that understanding was soon tested.

The extension of AMDA was also an exercise in the transposition of many of the basic assumptions underlying an alliance framework which had existed formally since 1957. It assumed the continuation of Britain's guarantor role. The formal extension of the associate status of Australia and New Zealand carried with it an extension of the three assumed roles of the CSR. If ambiguity had hitherto served the overlapping interests of the allies, it was soon shown to be inadequate in Malaysian eyes. AMDA, it may be recalled, emerged in a period of relative external calm, albeit one of continuing internal challenge. Its extension, however, was completed in a crisis which, although not exactly anticipated by the alliance at the time the treaty was extended, nevertheless fitted into its *causus foederis*.

Malaysia's formation activated three intra-regional challenges to the new political order. Azahari's short-lived revolt was a test both of British mobility and of Malaya's own obligations under Article VII of AMDA. But limited capability and political sensitivity to deeper intervention in Brunei restrained Kuala Lumpur's response. The revolt's short duration also obviated the need on the part of Australia and New Zealand to offer a more substantial demonstration of solidarity with Britain. Strategically, however, the Brunei revolt posed a new threat that was not readily identifiable within the traditional Australian–New Zealand framework of forward defence.

The second intra-regional challenge to Malaysia was posed by the Philippines' claim to Sabah. The issue, however, did not, during the Confrontation period, pose a direct threat to the territorial integrity of Malaya/Malaysia and hence did not become an immediate concern within AMDA. The most serious test of AMDA was presented by Confrontation, to which the Brunei revolt was a prelude. Confrontation tested both the assumptions upon which the extended AMDA rested and the resilience of a treaty which had to accommodate, in the light of increasing demands on their military resources, the divergent interests of the Commonwealth allies.

From the Australian–New Zealand perspective, their strategic priority in forward defence within an essentially SEATO context had to be reordered against the new threat. Their support for Malaysia was based on a number of considerations: the Indonesian threat to the bases in Malaysia and Singapore, the need to render assistance to a traditionally friendly Commonwealth partner, the moral obligation to uphold Malaysia's parliamentary political system, the need to protect their own economic interests and the desirability, as consumers of alliance security themselves, of demonstrating their solidarity with Britain.

Such considerations had to be weighed (particularly in the case of Australia) against the cost of antagonising Jakarta. That both Australia and New Zealand were able, during the first nine months of Confrontation, to combine military restraint with political support for Kuala Lumpur attested to the flexibility which their associateship with AMDA permitted – it was a status which assumed a qualitative distinction between their roles and the British guarantee. The background of Confrontation, against which the extension of AMDA was completed, enhanced the advantage of association in the eyes of Australia and New Zealand. Association

Conclusions   185

with AMDA was seen to preserve Australian–New Zealand options *via-à-vis* their forces in the area. And even as Confrontation escalated, the extended AMDA continued to permit a certain reservation of position by Australia and New Zealand, whose graduated responses contained a deterrent ingredient which differed significantly from Britain's.

The withholding of Australian–New Zealand forces from Borneo in the hope of dissuading Indonesia from further escalation was possible because the firm treaty commitments undertaken by Britain were not explicitly defined for the antipodes. For this reason, too, Malaysia was especially concerned to extract more tangible expressions of support from Canberra and Wellington. Such Malaysian attempts reflected a certain incompatibility between Australia's deterrence against Indonesia and assurance towards Malaysia. Although the climax of Confrontation marked the failure of deterrence, Australia did not suffer undue disadvantage from pursuing friendship with Indonesia and simultaneously providing military aid to Malaysia.

As anchor power, Britain's responsibilities were quite clearly spelled out. The British deterrent, where attempted, was applied at the tactical level. But Britain's predominant role in Malaysian defence did constrain the British handling of the political aspects of Confrontation lest Jakarta should be given cause to claim British neocolonialist manipulation of Kuala Lumpur. Yet, in the course of Confrontation diplomacy, Britain was concerned lest the Malaysians should concede too much to Indonesia at the expense of Britain's regional interests.

Although Confrontation created a special interest in Britain's policing role, apprehension over the cost of maintaining that role became manifest. Nevertheless, while Confrontation lasted, commitments could not easily be jettisoned. In this sense it could be said that Britain and Australia 'lacked a common sense of time-span. For Australia, Confrontation was a problem that had to be set within an indefinitely extended continuum of relations with Indonesia whereas for Britain it was the last of a series of mishaps that had unduly prolonged her presence in Southeast Asia.'[3] Confrontation also made it difficult for Malaysia to work towards some form of military independence or self-sufficiency.

In the face of its most severe test, AMDA functioned remarkably well, despite the strains within the alliance as a result of early equivocation by Australia and, to a lesser extent, New Zealand. This was made possible partly by the consistent support rendered by Britain and partly by the flexibility and resilience of the treaty framework itself. Even as the treaty framework continued to be upheld, the seeds of transformation in intra-alliance relations were being nurtured by the growing awareness in Britain of the strain on British resources and by the internal contradictions between Kuala Lumpur and Singapore. These contradictions represented a challenge of a different order, but they nevertheless had profound repercussions on alliance cohesion towards the later stages of Confrontation and resulted in a fracturing of the Kuala Lumpur–Singapore axis.

The *raison d'être* for the extension of AMDA did not arise from the existence of an immediate external threat. On the contrary, the formation of Malaysia, which necessitated AMDA's extension, had activated new regional threats to the alliance. By 1964 internal instability within Singapore had been effectively contained, while the continued existence of Singapore within the Federation was seen by the Central Government as a real threat to the political stability of Malaysia. Even the continuation of Confrontation could not prevent the growing rift between Kuala Lumpur and Singapore. And just as political unification in the Malaysian area resulted in the extension of AMDA, so the separation of Singapore in turn adversely affected defence co-operation between Kuala Lumpur and Singapore and between the local and external powers.

The aftermath of separation further tested the assumptions (including the issue of continued external protection and the indivisibility of Malaysia–Singapore defence) of the extended AMDA which Article V and Annex B of the Separation Agreement sought to preserve. The continuing framework of AMDA (crucial to Australian–New Zealand defence contributions in the area) was stretched and strained by forces within the alliance.

First, although the risk of non-consultation with the external powers (over separation) appeared to have been well taken by Kuala Lumpur, there was an atmosphere of growing suspicion among the allies. Kuala Lumpur itself was inclined to believe that Britain was biased towards Singapore. This was reflected in subsequent Anglo-Malaysian friction over defence and economic assistance during early and mid-1966. Malaysian resentment, quite openly expressed, was mixed with a sense of disillusionment with the perceptible decline in British power. This changing attitude, together with increasing Malaysian assertiveness, became more evident with the ending of Confrontation. Desirous of an early *rapprochement* with Indonesia and hoping to counter British influence in East Malaysia, Kuala Lumpur was inclined to hasten the British military out of Borneo. The associate powers, too, were embroiled in the post-separation problems and squabbles by Kuala Lumpur's attempts to use the issue of external protection as a means to pre-empt secessionist moves in East Malaysia. Although these intra-alliance strains and difficulties had no immediate or tangible effects on AMDA itself, they nevertheless fed into a background of changing attitudes and perceptions which affected long-term relationships.

Second, the attempt to preserve the defence status quo after separation was challenged by Singapore's formal emergence as a distinct local polity with *de facto* as well as *de jure* competence in foreign policy and defence. Underlying the post-separation problems of defence co-operation between Kuala Lumpur and Singapore (the Camp Temesek incident, Singapore's withdrawal from the JDC and the perceived threat to Malaysia of a separate peace between Singapore and Indonesia) was the difficulty of psychological and political adjustment to the fact of Singapore's nationhood. The problem of adjustment was complicated by the circumstances of separation, which had the effect of making Kuala Lumpur appear to Singapore as a likely destabilising factor in its own security.

The collective identification of Malaysia–Singapore interests implicit in the preservation of the defence status quo introduced a further distortion into the alliance. Instead of a complete treaty revision, a new circle, with Singapore at its centre, was introduced into AMDA's overlapping interests. And as a formula for the accommodation of divergent interests, ambiguity, too, was increasingly less useful. Yet no progress could be made towards a renegotiation of AMDA. Renegotiation was stalled by the continuing difficulties in defence co-operation between Malaysia and Singapore and the inconclusive review of Britain's East of Suez policy. Indeed, the initiative for a review of AMDA came from the anchor power rather than from the host powers.

In terms of the further transformation of intra-alliance relations, the most significant development was the British decision to abandon its guarantor role. The Labour Government had initiated a defence review in 1964 with the promise to give 'value for money' in its overseas spending. However, Confrontation had delayed an extension of the defence review from the means of policy to its objectives. Indeed, Confrontation reinforced Britain's policing role East of Suez. The continuing external threat to the alliance prevented any major redefinition of British interests *vis-à-vis* AMDA, although Britain was tempted by the opportunity afforded by separation to reconsider its protective role. Thus, for the greater part of 1966, the main result of bilateral intra-alliance consultations initiated by Britain at the beginning of the year had been no more than to start the allies off in their contemplation of future British policy in the region.

With the ending of Confrontation in August 1966 and the British withdrawal from Borneo, the further defence review got under way. Britain also announced its aversion to future Confrontation-type military involvements. Yet the 'British habit' of 'business as usual' (that is, until an established policy had definitely become untenable)[4] was discernible in the pace and result of intra-alliance consultations and in the progressive back-tracking on earlier promises, so that a general understanding not to announce a withdrawal date was overtaken, within a year of the 1966 Defence White Paper, by a firm policy to withdraw completely from East of Suez by the mid-1970s. Within six months of the later announcement, the mounting economic crisis (culminating in the devaluation of sterling in November 1967) was to force the decision to advance the withdrawal date to 1971.

One feature of the intra-alliance discussions on the future British role had been the quality of bilateralism within an ostensibly multilateral framework. The Tunku's suggestion of a five-power conference in July 1967 was not taken up until the following year, when accelerated withdrawal had become an established fact. Bilateral consultations suited Britain in so far as it was spared a confrontation with a 'united front' from the other allies prior to its taking its momentous decisions. But bilateralism also reflected both the failure of the other partners (especially Malaysia and Singapore) to come together with a common strategy *vis-à-vis* Britain and an underlying recognition of the unproductiveness of concerted pressure over the withdrawal issue. The Australian–New Zealand approach had been to do nothing which could give Britain an opportunity to 'get off the hook'. Intra-alliance pressure on Britain had appeared effective (in 1966) precisely when Britain itself was still determined to retain the East of Suez role. When that determination was lacking (as in late

1967), pressure from the other allies was ineffectual. And having failed to obtain a concerted approach towards Britain, Lee Kuan Yew's lone mission of appeal to London had both the appearance and the effect of serving an essentially Singapore interest. The resulting nine months' delay to a complete British withdrawal was significant in terms of the subsequent Tory amendments to Labour policy, but only marginal to the long-term British posture in the region.

For the alliance, the culminating point in its transformation was the July 1967 decision of the anchor power to withdraw completely from East of Suez. It meant the removal of the most important assumption of AMDA. And with that assumption gone, the rationale for Australian–New Zealand association also collapsed. The five-power conferences that followed were essentially a means to enable the other partners to come to terms with this fact of life. In this respect, the first five-power conference was significant in enabling, for the first time, the emergence of a truly multilateral pattern of discussion and relationship, with Britain no longer playing the anchor role, but taking on that of a 'more equal' partner.

Among the other partners, Malaysia, as high contracting party to AMDA, was least ready to make the psychological adjustment to the withdrawal of the British, in spite of, at times, an underlying resentment towards Britain's protective role. This Malaysian ambivalence was later diminished by a growing sense of disillusionment with the whole issue of external defence support. It could almost be said that the renewal of the Philippine threat and the adverse consequences of that on intra-alliance relations had the effect of driving home this Malaysian disillusionment and of exposing the distortive effects of AMDA, which was beginning to prove its inadequacy for Malaysian defence.

The quasi-crisis over Sabah was a parallel development to the attempts at drawing up new provisions for the defence of the Malaysia–Singapore area and had a certain influence on the final 'limited liability' arrangements which emerged. Malaysia itself was inclined to regard this crisis (which developed while AMDA was still a valid framework for defence collaboration) as a test of alliance responsiveness and an indication of the sense of commitment among the external powers to the future defence of the region. In the event, the intense pressure Malaysia put on Canberra represented a final attempt to make ambiguity (as enshrined in Australia's association with AMDA) serve a Malaysian interest. It did not.

While British reaction to the quasi-crisis indicated a continued adherence to its role as protector, it was evident that there could be no more blank cheques for Malaysia–Singapore defence after British withdrawal. To this fundamental shift in the British posture, Australia and (to a lesser extent) New Zealand responded with cautiousness and equivocation which were later compounded by an outbreak of internal instability in Malaysia. Clearly, their future 'commitments' in the area (reflecting a corresponding levelling-up of role and status) would come under even closer national control. In the case of Singapore, its emergence as a separate entity from Kuala Lumpur underlined the fact that the doctrine of indivisibility in Malaysia–Singapore defence could not easily be translated beyond the functional level of co-operation in air defence. This was compounded by Malaysian sensitivity towards any suggestion of a Singapore military presence in Malaysia, quite apart from the fact that their defence priorities were different. The stretching of AMDA's foundations was such that renegotiation was impossible. The treaty was simply abandoned. The destructuring of AMDA's hierarchy and its replacement by a loose consultative framework placed intra-alliance relations on a basis of greater equality and made room for a freer interplay of national interests (and their differentiation) among the five powers.

Decolonisation in Malaya and the emergence of nationalist tendencies; the addition of new political entities to the Federation and the subsequent challenges and intra-alliance strains; the rise of a new local centre in a relationship of conflict and co-operation with Kuala Lumpur; the diminishing capacity of the anchor power and its adverse consequences; these all contributed to the changing fortunes of AMDA. On the other hand, developments in the international environment of the alliance (such as the changing balance of power in the international system, or attempts at promoting a new regional order in Southeast Asia) were not directly related to the major turning points in intra-alliance relationships, although the singular structure of AMDA at its inception reflected an interplay between systemic and sub-systemic influences. The changing tides of the Vietnam War and the subsequent American disengagement had some indirect effects (especially on Australian and New Zealand policies), but any direct effects were essentially confined to the later stages of drawing up the new defence framework. Finally, a correlation could not be established between change within the AMDA system and changes (if any) in its inter-alliance (i.e. the AMDA–SEATO–ANZUS) environment. The major determinants in the rise and demise of AMDA had been mainly sub-systemic.

POSTSCRIPT ON FIVE-POWER ARRANGEMENTS

Following the coming into effect of the Five-Power Defence Arrangements in November 1971, the forces of the external powers were reconstituted as follows:

Australia
2 squadrons of about 40 Mirage fighter aircraft based at Butterworth, Malaysia (HQ of the IADS)
6–8 Mirages, drawn from the above 40, based at Tengah (Singapore)
1 infantry battalion in Singapore
1 destroyer or frigate and 1 submarine in rotation with the UK

New Zealand
1 infantry battalion in Singapore
1 frigate
Transport aircraft and a contribution of HQ and logistical personnel to the IADS
Occasional deployment of air units

Britain
1 infantry battalion in Singapore
Up to 6 frigates
Up to 4 Nimrod maritime reconnaissance aircraft
1 squadron of Whirlwind helicopters
Combat units, ships and aircraft on visits
1 submarine in rotation with Australia

The combined Australian, New Zealand and United Kingdom (ANZUK) force totalled 7,000 men, of whom about 3,300 were Australians, 4,150 New Zealanders and 2,550 British. These forces were the direct responsibility of the ANZUK Commander, who was answerable to the Chiefs of Staff of the three external powers in accordance with the directives approved by their governments.

Within a year of the establishment of these forces, a change of government in Australia was to result in a fundamental alteration to the existing well-balanced force structure. In late 1972 the ALP under Gough Whitlam won office after years in the political wilderness. With the ALP's traditional aversion to overseas commitment of Australian ground forces, the Labour Government moved rapidly towards withdrawing the Australian battalion from Singapore, although it saw a continuing role for its air and naval deployments in the area. By February 1974 all Australian ground forces were withdrawn from Singapore, while their supporting units were in the process of being phased out.

The Labour Government in New Zealand, on the other hand (which came to power under the late Norman Kirk shortly before the ALP victory), did not follow the Australian example. However, the brigade structure could not be sustained and hence the remaining British and New Zealand forces were reorganised under their respective national commands.

The next phase in the restructuring of the external presence was initiated by a British Labour Government, which announced in December 1974 its decision to withdraw all remaining forces in the Malaysia–Singapore area. The last British ground forces left Singapore on 31 March 1976, while Britain's naval presence in Singapore was terminated in September 1975. Like Australia and New Zealand, Britain remains 'committed' to the five-power political framework, which in effect embodies no more than a commitment to consult. Except for the occasional visits by naval units, Britain has hardly a 'presence' to speak of in the area, although a battalion of Gurkhas will remain in Brunei, at least, until 1983.

The most tangible manifestation of the Commonwealth presence is the two squadrons of Australian Mirages in Butterworth which, together with their supporting personnel, constitute the 'teeth' of the IADS. Joint air exercises involving the IADS and five-power naval exercises have been held regularly. The New Zealand battalion in Singapore is the only Commonwealth land force left, although both Labour and National parties had previously expressed a desire to withdraw these forces. In May 1975 the New Zealand Labour Government of Bill Rowling announced its intention to withdraw the battalion in two years' time. The National Party, which came to power later in the year, was less specific about the timetable of withdrawal, although the then Defence Minister, Alan McCready, did state, in connection with the Defence White Paper of November 1978, that he was contemplating withdrawal from Singapore within three years. That Defence White Paper, published shortly before the Vietnamese invasion of Kampuchea, favoured a closer-to-home posture in the Pacific and underlined the transitoriness of the five-power arrangements.

Since that New Zealand statement, the invasion of Kampuchea and new concern over Soviet designs aroused by the Soviet invasion of Afghanistan have revived antipodean, but especially Australian, interest in five-power defence. Although the other partners were receptive to Malcolm Fraser's initiative (put forward when they met on the occasion provided by the Commonwealth Heads of Government Meeting in New Delhi in September 1980) to revitalise five-power exercises reminiscent of 'Bersatu Padu' in 1970, the extent of their collaboration is expected to be limited.

It is unlikely that Britain will be able to make more than a token or coincidental contribution to the exercise. Rather, the symbolic aspect of any such joint venture will be more important than its actual efficacy. Malaysia itself has come to terms with this reality and indeed is playing down the significance of such an exercise which – it is worthy of note – will be held in Australia. Malaysia's growing concern with external defence, reflected in its own series of large-scale military exercises and the purchase of American jet fighters, has led to an emphasis on greater self-reliance and national resilience.

Of significance, however, is the bilateral co-operation that has developed (e.g. between Singapore and the antipodes in matters of military training) within an ostensibly multilateral framework. Renewed Australian interest in five-power defence will not however lead to any replacement of the ageing Mirage jets which are being phased out from Butterworth beginning with the redeployment of one squadron to Darwin in July 1983. It remains true that, conditions being such that an overt threat to the Malaysia–Singapore area is not clearly identifiable, future external redeployments may depend more on domestic political and economic changes within the external powers than on any general conditions of regional instability.

NOTES

1 Introduction

1 P. Darby, 'East of Suez Reassessed' in J. Baylis (ed.), *British Defence Policy in a Changing World* (London, Croom Helm, 1977), p. 52.
2 B. Gordon, *New Zealand Becomes a Pacific Power* (University of Chicago Press, 1960), pp. 134–5.
3 A. A. Cruikshank, 'Changing Perspectives of New Zealand's Foreign Policy', *Pacific Affairs*, vol. 40 (1 and 2) (Spring and Summer 1967), p. 98. See also D. E. McHenry and R. N. Rosecrance, 'The "Exclusion" of the UK from the ANZUS Pact', *International Organisation* (Summer 1958), pp. 320–9.
4 K. Booth, 'Alliances' in J. Baylis (et al.), *Contemporary Strategy: Theories and Policies* (London, Croom Helm, 1975), p. 9.
5 R. E. Osgood, *Alliances and American Foreign Policy* (Baltimore, Johns Hopkins Press, 1968), pp. 18–19.

2 Pre-treaty defence relations

1 *CPD (H/R)*, vol. 208, 31-5-50, p. 3463.
2 *CPD (H/R)*, vol. 196, 29-4-48, p. 1251.
3 T. B. Millar, *Australia's Defence Policies, 1945–65* (Canberra, Australian National University, Working Paper No. 7, 1967), p. 10.
4 A. Watt, *The Evolution of Australian Foreign Policy: 1938–65* (Cambridge University Press, 1967), p. 166.
5 Watt, *The Evolution of Australian Foreign Policy*, p. 165.
6 T. B. Millar, *Australia's Defence* (Melbourne University Press, 1965), pp. 71–3.
7 *CPD (H/R)*, vol. 198, 2-9-48, p. 66.
8 W. Levi, *Australia's Outlook on Asia* (Sydney, Angus and Robertson, 1958), p. 192.
9 *CPD (H/R)*, vol. 198, 7-9-48, p. 143.
10 Millar, *Australia's Defence Policies, 1945–65*, p. 10.
11 *NZPD*, vol. 386, 18-8-49, p. 7381.
12 *British Malaya* (July 1948), p. 34.
13 *CPD (H/R)*, vol. 206, 9-3-50, pp. 623–5.
14 *The Times*, 6-1-50.
15 P. Spender, *Exercises in Diplomacy* (Sydney University Press, 1969), p. 13.
16 *HCD*, vol. 473, 29-3-50, col. 41.
17 *ST*, 18-4-50.
18 *HCD*, vol. 474, 20-4-50, cols. 290–2.
19 *SMH*, 22-4-50.
20 *DT*, 21-4-50.
21 Millar, *Australia's Defence*, p. 70.
22 *The Times*, 1-6-50.
23 *ST*, 28-6-50.
24 *NZPD*, vol. 305, 24-6-55, p. 21.
25 T. R. Reese, *Australia, New Zea-*

land and the United States: A Survey of International Relations, 1941–68 (London, Oxford University Press, 1969), p. 146.
26 DT, 30-6-52.
27 ST, 11-8-52.
28 P. J. Boyce, 'Twenty-one Years of Australian Diplomacy in Malaya', JSEAH, vol. 4 (2) (September 1963), p. 80.
29 Millar, Australia's Defence Policies, 1945–65, p. 31.
30 ST, 11-6-53.
31 Interview with former Secretary of External Affairs, New Zealand.
32 Interview with former Australian official.
33 Economist, 28-5-55, p. 773.
34 CN, vol. 25 (8), p. 568.
35 N. Harper, 'Australia and Regional Pacts: 1950–7', Australian Outlook, vol. 12 (1) (March 1958), p. 15.
36 Percy Spender had spoken of the possible fall of Laos and Cambodia following a communist victory in Vietnam. This would outflank Malaya which, with Burma and Indonesia, would become the next object of 'communist imperialism'. (CPD(H/R), vol. 206, 9-3-50, p. 632.)
37 CSM, 29-11-54.
38 T. B. Millar (ed.), Australian Foreign Minister: The Diaries of R. G. Casey, 1951–60 (London, Collins, 1972), p. 199. (Hereafter referred to as Casey's Diaries.)
39 Australia had difficulty demonstrating this since it had only a limited capability to commit forces abroad. (Casey's Diaries, p. 210.)
40 H. S. Albinski, 'Australia's Search for Regional Security in Southeast Asia', unpublished Ph.D. thesis, University of Minnesota, 1949, f. 437.
41 CPD(H/R), vol. 6, 1955, p. 52.
42 NZGNB, 28-2-55.
43 Ibid.
44 NZPD, vol. 205, 24-3-55, pp. 22–3.
45 NZGNB, 31-3-55.
46 CPD(H/R), vol. 6, 20-4-55, pp. 52–3.
47 Casey's Diaries, p. 206 and pp. 214–15.
48 Millar, Australia's Defence Policies, 1945–65, p. 32.
49 EAR, vol. v (4) (April 1955), p. 9.
50 CPD(H/R), vol. 6, 20-4-55, p. 9.
51 The prevailing idea, which Casey himself thought incorrect, was that the Chinese Communists would make a frontal attack on Malaya via Thailand. (Casey's Diaries, p. 212.)
52 The Scotsman, 5-4-55.
53 During consultations in Kuala Lumpur in February 1955, Casey was made aware of the undesirability of garrisonning Australian troops in Malaya while British troops fought in the jungle. (Casey's Diaries, p. 208.)
54 ST, 5-7-55.
55 Manchester Guardian, 6-7-55.
56 The Times, 20-10-55.
57 NZPD, 31-3-55, vol. 305, p. 147.
58 Quoted in Millar, Australia's Defence Policies: 1945–65, p. 33.
59 NZPD, vol. 305, 24-3-55, p. 25.
60 A. Watt, Australian Diplomat: Memoirs of Sir Alan Watt (Sydney, Angus and Robertson, 1972), p. 229.
61 CPD(H/R), vol. 6, 7-6-55, p. 1425.
62 SLAD, vol. 1, 29-6-55, col. 330.
63 Alliance Platform for the Federal Elections (Kuala Lumpur,

Notes to pp. 21–31   197

Alliance National Council, 1955), p. 24.
64 Boyce, 'Twenty-one Years of Australian Diplomacy in Malaya', pp. 80–2.
65 *Casey's Diaries*, p. 224
66 *ST*, 15-9-55.
67 The amnesty was withdrawn on 8 February 1956.
68 Levi, *Australia's Outlook on Asia*, p. 194.
69 PAP Resolution, 27-6-55. (See *ST*, 26-6-55.)

3 Decolonisation and the institution of the defence agreement

1 Federation of Malaya, Legislative Council Paper No. 6 of 1956, Kuala Lumpur, Government Printer, 1956. (Hereafter referred to as *The 1956 Constitutional Conference Report*.)
2 *Alliance Platform for the Federal Elections* (Kuala Lumpur, Alliance National Council, 1955), p. 24.
3 *The Times*, 19-1-56.
4 *MLCD*, 14-3-56, col. 891.
5 *The 1956 Constitutional Conference Report*, para. 14.
6 *Ibid.*, para. 10.
7 See *Arrangements for the Employment of Overseas Commonwealth Forces in Emergency Operations in the Federation of Malaya after Independence*, Cmnd. 264 (London, HMSO, September 1957). AMDA was published as Cmnd. 263.
8 Cmnd. 264, para. 3(c).
9 *Ibid.*, para. 3(i). This right of appeal could be observed down to battalion level. See R. Clutterbuck, *The Long, Long War – the Emergency in Malaya 1948–60* (London, Cassell, 1967), p. 146.
10 *The 1956 Constitutional Conference Report*, para. 15.
11 *The Times*, 13-8-56.
12 Cmnd. 264, para. 3(f).
13 *ST*, 22-2-56.
14 Cmnd. 264, para. 26.
15 *The Times*, 20-3-56.
16 *CPD(H/R)*, vol. 9, 11-4-56, p. 1187.
17 *MLCD*, 14-3-56, col. 893.
18 Lord Avon, *Full Circle* (London, Cassell, 1960), p. 374.
19 *The 1956 Constitutional Conference Report*, para. 36.
20 *ST*, 12-1-57. The British offer, chiefly in grants, was worth less than M$300 million over a 5-year period.
21 *ST*, 5-1-57.
22 *MLCD*, 20-10-57, col. 3271.
23 *Statement on Defence 1956*, Cmnd. 9691 (London, HMSO, 1956), pp. 4–5.
24 *Defence: Outline of Future Policy*, Cmnd. 124 (London, HMSO, reprinted 1958), p. 2.
25 L. Martin, *British Defence Policy: The Long Recessional* (Institute for Strategic Studies, Adelphi Papers No. 61, November 1969), p. 2.
26 *Manchester Guardian*, 14-3-57.
27 *ST*, 15-3-57.
28 *Casey's Diaries*, p. 266.
29 *Ibid.*, p. 268.
30 *Review of Defence Policy, 1957* (New Zealand Department of External Affairs Publication No. 181), p. 7.
31 N. Mansergh (ed.), *Documents and Speeches on Commonwealth Affairs 1952–62* (London, Oxford University Press, 1963), p. 569.
32 *NZPD*, vol. 313, 23-7-57, p. 1074.
33 *CPD(H/R)*, vol. 16, 19-9-57, pp. 795–6.
34 *CPD(H/R)*, vol. 14, 4-4-57, p. 573.
35 *HCD*, vol. 568, 18-4-57, col. 224.

36 *FT*, 24-8-57.
37 *ST*, 11-1-57.
38 These factors are fully discussed in J. B. Dalton, 'The Development of Malayan External Policy 1957–63', unpublished D. Phil. thesis, Oxford, 1967, ff. 73–6.
39 See G. Modelski, *SEATO: Six Studies* (Melbourne, Cheshire, 1962), p. 43, f.n. 9.
40 Lennox-Boyd. See *HCD*, vol. 573, 12-7-57, col. 662.
41 *MLCD*, 3-10-57, col. 3350.
42 *MLCD*, 11-12-58, col. 6029.
43 J. D. B. Miller, *The Commonwealth in the World* (London, Duckworth, 1958), p. 225.
44 *MLCD*, 3-10-57, col. 3362.
45 *NZGNB*, 11-10-57.
46 *ST*, 21-8-57. General Sir Richard Hull revealed in April 1959 that Britain had established an operational research unit in Malaya to conduct 'theoretical tests' on the possible effects of using nuclear weapons in heavy jungle. (*Manchester Guardian*, 2-4-59.)
47 Razak later cited Article IX of AMDA as the consultative undertaking that covered future requests for the storage of nuclear weapons in Malaya. (*MLCD*, 22-10-58, cols. 5038–9.)
48 *DT*, 24-8-57.
49 Military links with Britain affected Malaya's 'Afro-Asian' image besides allowing Sukarno to make the charge of neo-colonialism.
50 *Dewan Ra'ayat Reports*, vol. 5, 23-8-63, col. 1727.
51 *MLCD*, 2-10-57, col. 3274.
52 See Dalton, 'The Development of Malayan External Policy 1957–63', ff. 68–9.
53 *MLCD*, 2-10-57, col. 3272.

54 AMDA, Annex 4, Cmnd. 263.
55 *Casey's Diaries*, p. 270.
56 *HCD*, vol. 548, 15-2-56, col. 2367.

4 The extension of AMDA

1 Singapore's inclusion in the Malayan Union would upset the entrepôt status of Singapore and the numerical advantage enjoyed by the Malays.
2 C. J. Bartlett, *The Long Retreat* (London, Macmillan, 1972), p. 162.
3 *Statement on Defence 1962*, Cmnd. 1639 (London, HMSO, 1962), p. 4.
4 Modelski (ed.), *SEATO: Six Studies*, p. 107.
5 *SLAD*, vol. 1, 5-4-56, col. 1862.
6 *Ibid.*, col. 1858.
7 *Ibid.*, 4-4-56, col. 1781.
8 *Ibid.*, 4-4-56, col. 1800.
9 Government of Singapore, *Report on the Singapore all-Party Mission to London, April/May 1956*, Cmnd. 31 (Singapore, 1956), Annexure A, p. 18.
10 *Singapore Constitutional Conference, May 1956*, Cmnd. 9777 (London, HMSO, 1956), p. 30 and Appendix 7, p. 30.
11 P. Darby, *British Defence Policy East of Suez, 1947–68* (Oxford University Press, 1973), p. 87.
12 Quoted by Marshall. *SLAD*, vol. 1, 6-6-56, cols. 1978–9.
13 *CPD(H/R)*, vol. 10, 16-5-56, p. 2085.
14 *CPD(H/R)*, vol. 11, 7-6-56, p. 2893.
15 *ST*, 28-5-56.
16 *Report of the Singapore Constitutional Conference held in London in March and April 1957*, Cmnd. 147 (London, HMSO, 1957), para. 27.
17 *SLAD*, vol. 2, 2-11-56, col. 865.

Financial constraints precluded the establishment of a new base in Malaya.
18 *SLAD*, vol. 4, 17-12-57, col. 3091.
19 Under this, Singapore would be self-governing with a fully elected Legislative Assembly and a Cabinet led by the Prime Minister.
20 *ST*, 17-9-57.
21 Darby, *British Defence Policy East of Suez*, p. 88.
22 *Casey's Diaries*, p. 274.
23 H. Macmillan, *Riding the Storm: 1956–69* (London, Macmillan, 1971), p. 409.
24 *Ibid.*, pp. 404–5.
25 *CN*, vol. 29 (2), p. 116.
26 *Report on Defence*, Cmnd. 363 (London, HMSO, February 1958), p. 8.
27 *HCD*, vol. 582, 18-2-58, col. 1031.
28 *Casey's Diaries*, p. 291.
29 G. Clark, *In Fear of China* (Melbourne, Landsdowne Press, 1967), p. 192.
30 T. Bellows, *The People's Action Party of Singapore* (New Haven, Yale University, 1970), p. 35, f.n. 14. Lord Boyd, while visiting Singapore in January 1980, said that the British, even while Lim Yew Hock was in office, had anticipated a PAP victory before long and had made sure that 'confidential relations were established with the inevitable successor'. (*Sun. T (S)*, 20-1-80.)
31 *ST*, 19-5-59.
32 *The Times*, 6-6-59.
33 *Dawn*, 21-7-59.
34 *The Times*, 6-10-59.
35 Britain promised £500,000 annually towards the recurrent cost of the local military forces and half of the recurrent cost of the Singapore Division of the Malayan Royal Naval Volunteer Reserve.
36 *SLAD*, vol. 11, 14-10-59, col. 662.
37 *Colony of North Borneo. Annual Report 1958* (North Borneo, Government Printers, 1959), p. 1.
38 *Colony of North Borneo. Annual Report 1961* (North Borneo, Government Printers, 1961), p. 12.
39 *ST*, 12-3-59.
40 *ST*, 14-3-59.
41 *ST*, 5-3-58.
42 *Casey's Diaries*, p. 292.
43 Interview, former New Zealand High Commissioner to Malaysia.
44 *Documents Concerning New Zealand Forces Serving in Malaysia* (Wellington, Department of External Affairs, Publication No. 283, 1963), p. 25.
45 *ST*, 10-11-59.
46 *ST*, 18-11-59.
47 He meant Indonesia, which he visited *en route* to Malaya. (*ST*, 9-12-59.)
48 *Casey's Diaries*, p. 273.
49 *Dewan Ra'ayat Reports*, vol. 3, 16-10-61, col. 1591. M. N. Sopiee, *From Malayan Union to Singapore Separation* (Kuala Lumpur, Pernerbit Universiti Malaya, 1974), pp. 137–42.
50 *Dewan Ra'ayat Reports*, vol. 3, 16-10-61, col. 1594.
51 *OFNS*, no. 17415, 11-10-61, p. 2.
52 *HCD*, vol. 659, 17-5-62, cols. 1535–6.
53 *Dewan Ra'ayat Reports*, vol. 3, 16-10-61, cols. 1611–12.
54 *ST*, 3-10-61.
55 *FT*, 25-9-61.
56 H. Macmillan, *At the End of the Day, 1961–3* (London, Macmillan, 1973), p. 240.
57 *Dewan Ra'ayat Reports*, vol. 3, 16-

10-61, col. 1612.
58 Macmillan, *At the End of the Day*, p. 248.
59 London did not deny this, but explained that complicated issues were involved. (*ST*, 4-10-61.)
60 *Sun. T*, 1-10-61.
61 *Ibid.*
62 *Memorandum setting out Heads of Agreement for a Merger between the Federation of Malaya and Singapore* (Singapore Legislative Assembly, Cmnd. 33 of 1961).
63 *ST*, 17-11-61.
64 *ST*, 24-10-61.
65 In private communications with Britain, Menzies had reflected similar anxieties. (Macmillan, *At the End of the Day*, pp. 250–1.)
66 'Review of Defence Policy, 1961', *NZAJHR*, vol. 1, A.19, pp. 4 and 6.
67 *ST*, 18-11-61.
68 *ST*, 21-11-61.
69 *Federation of Malaysia: Joint Statement by the Governments of the United Kingdom and the Federation of Malaya*, Cmnd. 1563 (London, HMSO, November 1961).
70 *Ibid.*
71 *ST*, 24-11-61.
72 *HCD*, vol. 650, 28-11-61, col. 244.
73 *ST*, 1-12-61.
74 *HCD*, vol. 650, 28-11-61, col. 244.
75 *Dewan Ra'ayat Reports*, vol. 3, 10-1-62, col. 2530.
76 *ST*, 6-12-61.
77 *ST*, 2-12-61.

5 The external testing of AMDA

1 *ST*, 8-9-62. The relative strengths of the three services in September 1962 were: army: 12,000; navy: 1,000; and air force: 500.
2 *ST*, 10-8-62.
3 *Statement on Defence, 1962*, Cmnd. 1639 (London, HMSO, 1962), para. 3(b).
4 *Ibid.*, p. 8.
5 *CN*, vol. 33 (8), p. 81.
6 *CPD(H/R)*, vol. 34, 27-3-62, p. 941.
7 *ST*, 27-3-62.
8 *HCD*, vol. 681, 19-7-63, col. 933.
9 *Ibid.* This tension revolved partly around the PAP's communal challenge to the ruling Alliance Party in Malaya and partly around PAP–MCA rivalry.
10 R. S. Milne and K. J. Ratnam, *Malaysia: New States in a New Nation – Political Development in Sarawak and Sabah* (London, Frank Cass, 1974), p. 21.
11 *CPD(H/R)*, vol. 53, 29-9-66, p. 1503.
12 *HCD*, vol. 635, 27-2-61, col. 1234.
13 Healey. See *HCD*, vol. 640, 17-5-61, col. 1408.
14 *HCD*, vol. 648, 1-11-61, cols. 296–7.
15 Darby, *British Defence Policy East of Suez*, p. 164.
16 *ST*, 13-5-63.
17 *HCD*, vol. 669, 10-12-62, col. 31. See J. A. C. Mackie, *Konfrontasi: The Indonesia–Malaysia Dispute 1963–6* (Kuala Lumpur, Oxford University Press, 1975), pp. 112–22.
18 *HCD*, vol. 669, 20-12-62, col. 1455.
19 *ST*, 13-12-62.
20 *HCD*, vol. 669, 10-12-62, col. 33.
21 *Ibid.*
22 *HCD*, vol. 670, 23-1-63, cols. 64–5.
23 *Malaysia: Select Documents on International Affairs* (Australia, Department of External Affairs, No. 1, 1963), pp. 105–6.

24 *HCD*, vol. 673, 4-3-63, col. 46.
25 Darby, *British Defence Policy East of Suez*, p. 234.
26 *Malaysia: Select Documents on International Affairs*, p. 106.
27 *ST*, 15-12-62.
28 P. J. Boyce, *Malaysia and Singapore in International Diplomacy: Documents and Commentaries* (Sydney University Press, 1968), pp. 69–70.
29 J. M. van der Kroef, 'Indonesia, Malaya and the North Borneo Crisis', *Asian Survey*, vol. 3 (4) (April 1963), p. 173.
30 For an analysis of Confrontation as a function of domestic Indonesian pressures see Mackie, *Konfrontasi: The Indonesia–Malaysia Dispute 1963–6*, pp. 326–33.
31 *ST*, 25-1-63.
32 *ST*, 12-2-63.
33 By the following year, defence and internal security accounted for 16% of Government spending. In late 1964 about M$100 million had been redirected from the 1961–4 Five-Year Plan to the supplemental defence budget for 1963–4.
34 M. Sopiee, 'Defence Co-operation in Malaysia', *Commonwealth Journal*, vol. 7 (6) (December 1964), p. 258.
35 *ST*, 2-4-63.
36 *ST*, 22-8-63.
37 *SMH*, 27-3-63.
38 *SMH*, 28-2-63.
39 Watt, *The Evolution of Australian Foreign Policy*, p. 165.
40 For a discussion of the Tange mission see R. Catley, 'Australia, Malaysia and the Problem of Confrontation', unpublished Ph.D. thesis, Canberra, Australian National University, 1967, f. 117.

41 Reese, *Australia, New Zealand and the United States: A Survey of International Relations, 1941–68*, pp. 208–15.
42 See Barwick's speech to the AIIA on 23 March 1963 reproduced in *CN*, vol. 34 (5), pp. 23–35.
43 *CN*, vol. 34 (3), p. 36.
44 *CPD(H/R)*, vol. 40, 30-10-63, p. 2460.
45 *ST*, 14-3-63.
46 *SMH*, 8-3-63.
47 See T. B. Millar, *Australian Defence Policy 1951–63: Major International Aspects* (Canberra, Australian National University, Working Paper No. 4, 1964), pp. 58–61.
48 T. B. Millar, 'Australia's Defence Needs' in J. Wilkes (ed.), *Australia's Defence and Foreign Policy* (Sydney, Angus and Robertson, 1964), p. 71.
49 The ANZUS Communiqué of 6 June 1963 merely hoped that Indonesian–Malayan–Philippine discussions would promote renewed friendship and regional stability.
50 *SMH*, 6-3-63.
51 *Ibid*.
52 *ST*, 12-3-63.
53 *Ibid*.
54 *Press conference given by Sir Garfield Barwick in Sydney* (Department of External Affairs, Press Release, 15 March 1963), p. 3.
55 P. J. Boyce, 'Canberra's Malaysia Policy', *Australian Outlook* (August 1963), p. 156. For Barwick's statement see *CPD(H/R)*, vol. 38, 28-3-63, pp. 196–200.
56 *CPD(H/R)*, vol. 38, 26-3-63, p. 4.
57 *CPD(H/R)*, vol. 38, 27-3-63, p. 131.

58 Millar, *Australian Defence Policy, 1951–63*, p. 54.
59 *CPD(H/R)*, vol. 38, 22-5-63, p. 1671.
60 Ibid., p. 1669.
61 *ST*, 20-3-63.
62 *ST*, 2-5-63.
63 *NZAJHR*, vol. 2, H.19 (1963), p. 3.
64 *ST*, 25-2-63.
65 Prior to Confrontation, the Indonesian trade accounted for only 2.5–3% of the GDP of Malaya compared to 8.5–10.5% of Singapore's GDP.
66 *ST*, 13-2-63 and 25-2-63.
67 *ST*, 23-2-63.
68 *ST*, 18-5-63.
69 P. J. Boyce, 'Policy Without Authority: Singapore's External Affairs Power', *JSEAH*, vol. 6 (2) (September 1965), p. 87.
70 *ST*, 4-5-63.
71 *Malaysia Agreement concluded between the United Kingdom of Great Britain and Northern Ireland, the Federation of Malaya, North Borneo, Sarawak and Singapore*, Cmnd. 2094 (London, HMSO, July 1963).
72 *CN*, vol. 34, p. 58.
73 *The Age*, 29-6-63.
74 *CN*, vol. 34, p. 58.
75 *NZPD*, vol. 335, 30-7-63, p. 902.
76 *ST*, 2-8-63.
77 *Malaya–Philippines Relations: 31 Aug. 1957 to 15 Sept. 1962* (Malaysia, Department of Information, Life Printers (n.d.)), Appendix VIII, p. 29.
78 *Sun. T(M)*, 11-8-63.
79 *ST*, 15-8-63.
80 Colonial Office dismay with Kuala Lumpur was openly expressed. See *Recent Developments in Anglo-Indonesian Relations* (London, Foreign Office, September 1963), p. 5.
81 These issues concerned Common Market arrangements, Singapore's retention of special powers to suppress gangsterism and reciprocal rights to restrict the entry of 'undesirables'.
82 *The Times*, 9-9-63. The British press widely reported that Sandys warned Lee against the proclamation. Having failed to dissuade Lee, Sandys decided not to sanction it and quietly left for a cruise off the east coast of Malaya.

6 Towards a closing of ranks

1 *ST*, 19-9-63.
2 *ST*, 26-10-63.
3 *The Times*, 21-9-63.
4 *Sun. T(M)*, 22-9-63.
5 *ST*, 20-9-63.
6 A Gallup poll conducted among 1,900 Australians showed that 2 out of 3 believed that Australia should fight for the defence of Malaysia if the latter were attacked by Indonesia. (*ST*, 16-9-63.)
7 For texts of the Australian and New Zealand Letters see *CN*, vol. 34, p. 47, and *Documents concerning New Zealand Forces Serving in Malaysia* (Wellington, Department of External Affairs, Publication No. 283, 1963), p. 31.
8 *EAR*, vol. XIII (9) (September 1963), p. 21.
9 *CPD(H/R)*, vol. 40, 25-9-63, p. 1339.
10 *ST*, 28-9-63.
11 *ST*, 26-9-63.
12 J. D. B. Miller, 'Problems of Australian Foreign Policy: July–December 1963', *AJPH*, vol. IX (c) (April 1964), p. 12.
13 Holyoake's statement simply confined itself to the eventuality

of 'an armed attack on Malaysia'.
14 *CPD(H/R)*, vol. 40, 15-10-63, p. 1794.
15 *ST*, 19-11-63.
16 *ST*, 7-12-63.
17 *ST*, 14-12-63.
18 *The Age*, 24-12-63.
19 *Dewan Ra'ayat Reports*, vol. 5, no. 37, 3-1-64, col. 3955.
20 *DT*, 6-1-64.
21 *CPD(H/R)*, vol. 41, 3-3-64, p. 192.
22 *ST*, 11-1-64.
23 *CN*, vol. 35 (1), p. 62.
24 Article V of ANZUS Treaty. Barwick refused to be drawn into saying whether such American assurance had been given.
25 Menzies himself claimed that the subsequent activities instituted under his 25 September 1963 statement were 'clearly in "the Pacific area"' and hence covered by ANZUS. (R. G. Menzies, *Afternoon Light – Some Memories of Men and Events* (London, Cassell, 1967), p. 264.
26 Miller, 'Problems of Australian Foreign Policy: July–December 1963', p. 15.
27 *CPD(H/R)*, vol. 42, 21-4-64, p. 1279. For an analysis of US policy towards Confrontation see F. Bunnell, *The Kennedy Initiatives in Indonesia, 1962–3*, unpublished Ph.D. thesis, Cornell University, 1969, ff. 286–300.
28 *CPD(H/R)*, vol. 42, 21-4-64, pp. 1279–80.
29 T. Pocock, *Fighting General: The Public and Private Campaigns of General Sir Walter Walker* (London, Collins, 1973), p. 178.
30 Following his US visit in July 1964, the Tunku admitted that President Johnson did indicate that 'it would not be right for him to step in now while the British are able . . . to help us'. (*Malaysia Newsletter*, no. 28/64, 28 August 1964.)
31 *EAR*, vol. XIV (4) (April 1964), pp. 23–4.
32 *ST*, 30-1-64.
33 *ST*, 13-4-64.
34 *CPD(H/R)*, vol. 41, 11-3-64, pp. 477–80.
35 *CPD(H/R)*, vol. 41, 11-3-64, p. 444.
36 *ST*, 12-4-64.
37 *CPD(H/R)*, vol. 41, 16-4-64, pp. 1192–3.
38 *ST*, 12-6-64.
39 Barwick's remark was hotly debated in Parliament on 21 April 1964. The Opposition accused him of trying to suggest that Australia would receive automatic US support. Documents obtained by the *Bulletin* (23-9-80, p. 24) under the US Freedom of Information Act show that some oblique assurance of American protection was given by Averell Harriman to Australia's Defence Minister, Shane Paltridge. However, Paltridge did not become Defence Minister until after Barwick's surprise resignation, three days after the parliamentary uproar.
40 *AJPH*, vol. X (3) (December 1964), p. 286.
41 *ST*, 19-4-64. Holyoake later withdrew the invitation.
42 Pocock, *Fighting General*, p. 178.
43 *Statement on Defence 1964*, Cmnd. 2270 (London, HMSO, February 1964).
44 Darby, *British Defence Policy East of Suez*, p. 241.
45 *HCD*, vol. 693, 22-4-64, col. 1291.
46 *Ibid.*, col. 171.
47 *Sunday Telegraph*, 28-6-64. In

fact, Malaysian plans for military expansion were announced only the previous month. (*The Times*, 20-5-64.)
48 *FEER*, 3-9-64, p. 422.
49 *FEER*, 8-10-64, p. 62.
50 *EAR*, vol. XIV (6) (June 1964), p. 28.
51 These official figures were published in *ST*, 28-10-64.
52 *ST*, 18-8-64.
53 *NZPD*, vol. 16, 8-9-64, p. 1939.
54 *Guardian*, 19-8-64.
55 *CN*, vol. 35 (8), p. 36.
56 *CPD(H/R)*, vol. 44, 30-10-64, p. 2357.
57 *ST*, 1-7-64.
58 Pocock, *Fighting General*, p. 195.
59 Mackie, *Konfrontasi: The Indonesia–Malaysia Dispute 1963–6*, p. 262. The naval force was later diverted to the Lombok Straight.
60 Mackie, *Konfrontasi: The Indonesia–Malaysia Dispute 1963–6*, p. 262.
61 *The Times*, 14-9-64.
62 *ST*, 15-7-64.
63 These secret operations, codenamed 'Claret', are discussed in Pocock, *Fighting General*, pp. 194–207.
64 This approach was favoured by Admiral Begg, the British Commander-in-Chief, Far East. (Pocock, *Fighting General*, p. 195.)
65 *The Times*, 9-11-64.
66 *Guardian*, 29-9-64.
67 *CPD(H/R)*, vol. 44, 30-9-64, p. 1628.
68 *DT*, 24-11-64.
69 *ST*, 4-12-64.
70 Pocock, *Fighting General*, p. 194.
71 *ST*, 22-1-65.
72 *ST*, 23-1-65.
73 *The Times*, 22-1-65.
74 On 4 January, following Indonesia's withdrawal from the UN, Malaysia requested the AMDA partners to review the latest position and to send reinforcements if necessary. (*ST*, 5-1-65.)
75 *ST*, 27-1-65.
76 H. Wilson, *The Labour Government 1964–70 – A Personal Record* (London, Weidenfeld and Nicolson, 1971), p. 42.
77 *FEER*, 7-1-65, p. 12.
78 *ST*, 5-2-65.
79 *CPD(H/R)*, vol. 45, 25-3-63, p. 331.
80 See *EAR*, vol. XV (2) (February 1965), pp. 19–20.
81 *The Times*, 12-2-65.
82 *NYT*, 4-2-65.
83 *CN*, vol. 36 (3), p. 126. Until November 1964, Australia continued to train Indonesian army officers. Under reciprocal arrangements, an Australian army officer was also attending the Indonesian staff college at Bandung. (*CPD(H/R)*, vol. 44, 12-11-64, p. 2963.)

7 The fractured axis

1 *Dewan Ra'ayat Reports*, vol. 5, 11-12-63, col. 1967.
2 *Petir*, March 1965, p. 5.
3 An analysis of the vexing problems between the Central Government and Singapore is beyond the purview of this book. See Sopiee, *From Malayan Union to Singapore Separation*, chapter 7, in which Sopiee exhaustively charts seven stages in the decline of Malaysia–Singapore relations.
4 Wilson, *The Labour Government 1964–70*, pp. 130–1.
5 Sopiee, *From Malayan Union to Singapore Separation*, p. 223.
6 G. Liska, *Nations in Alliance* (Baltimore, Johns Hopkins Press,

1962), p. 86.
7 G. Williams and B. Reed, *Denis Healey and the Policies of Power* (London, Sidgwick and Jackson, 1971); p. 206.
8 *ST*, 10-8-65.
9 *EAR*, vol. XV (9) (September 1965), p. 17.
10 A. Josey, *Lee Kuan Yew* (Singapore, Asia Pacific Press, 1971), p. 418.
11 Lee asked, rhetorically, whether Australia and New Zealand could afford to be associated with the defence of any form of Malaysia other than a united 'Malaysian Malaysia'. (*ST*, 23-5-65.)
12 The Australian representative in Singapore was W. B. Prichett. An Australian MP, Don Chipp, wondered whether the two Australian representatives had not become too closely involved with the disputing personalities to the extent that the objectivity of their reports was lessened. (*CPD(H/R)*, vol. 47, 19-8-65, p. 297.)
13 *ST*, 1-9-65.
14 Josey, *Lee Kuan Yew*, p. 414.
15 *CN*, vol. 36 (8), p. 504.
16 *Ibid*.
17 'An Agreement relating to the Separation of Singapore from Malaysia as an Independent and Sovereign State', *State of Singapore Government Gazette*, vol. VII (66) (9 August 1965), pp. 2188–91. (Hereafter referred to as the 'Separation Agreement'.)
18 'Separation Agreement', pp. 2198–9.
19 Wilson, *The Labour Government 1964–70*, p. 131.
20 *ST*, 12-8-65.
21 *The Times*, 16-8-65.
22 *CPD(H/R)*, vol. 47, 18-8-65, pp. 186–7.
23 *CPD(H/R)*, vol. 47, 24-8-65, p. 323.
24 *Guardian*, 25-8-65.
25 Before separation, the National Defence Council (under the Tunku's chairmanship and comprising eight Malaysian ministers and one minister each from Singapore, Sabah and Sarawak) was responsible for the defence of Malaysia. It was advised by the British Commander-in-Chief, Far East. After separation, the same structure, function and membership were preserved. The NDC was simply renamed the Combined Defence Council. (Singapore Defence Ministry Statement, *ST*, 1-4-66.)
26 *ST*, 19-8-65.
27 *Guardian*, 14-8-65.
28 *ST*, 10-8-65.
29 *Daily Express*, 13-8-65.
30 *Sun. T(M)*, 15-8-65.
31 *ST*, 29-9-65. In fact, as Suharto revealed in June 1966, the Indonesians had also secretly contacted the Malaysians.
32 *FEER*, 16-9-65, p. 526.
33 *ST*, 12-8-65.
34 *Daily Express*, 12-8-65.
35 *Guardian*, 13-8-65.
36 *FEER*, 16-9-65, pp. 526–7.
37 *The Times*, 1-9-65.
38 *ST*, 1-9-65.
39 *ST*, 2-9-65.
40 *NYT*, 16-9-65.
41 *The Age*, 3-9-65.
42 *HCD*, vol. 718, 28-10-65, cols. 350–1.
43 *CN*, vol. 36 (10), p. 692.
44 *The Times*, 19-8-65.
45 *ST*, 1-2-66.
46 *SPD*, vol. 25 (1), 25-2-66, cols. 16–22.
47 *ST*, 18-2-66.
48 *ST*, 19-2-66.

49 *ST*, 21-2-66.
50 *SPD*, vol. 25 (1), 23-2-66, cols. 19–20.
51 *ST*, 1-4-66.
52 *The Times*, 3-12-65.
53 *Ibid.*
54 *Daily Express*, 26-4-66.
55 *ST*, 13-4-66.
56 *ST*, 12-4-66.
57 *ST*, 26-4-66.
58 Published in *ST*, 26-4-66. The letter set out the Singapore Cabinet's views on current relations with Kuala Lumpur and hoped that both would strive for mutual co-operation. With regard to Indonesia, neither letter nor cable added anything new to what Singapore had already stated publicly.
59 *HCD*, vol. 727, 26-4-66, col. 566.
60 *ST*, 13-5-66.
61 *ST*, 18-6-66.
62 *HCD*, vol. 730, 28-6-66, cols. 1588–9.
63 *ST*, 28-6-66.
64 Within a week of the Bangkok Accord's ratification, Malaysia adopted a new gold parity for its currency and terminated Commonwealth preference on a number of goods.
65 *Sun. T(M)*, 5-6-66.
66 *ST*, 7-6-66.
67 *The Times*, 8-6-66.
68 *The Times, Guardian* and *DT*, 8-6-66.
69 Williams and Reed, *Denis Healey and the Policies of Power*, p. 221.
70 *DT*, 6-7-66.
71 *Sun. T*, 26-6-66.
72 *ST*, 6-7-66.
73 Williams and Reed, *Denis Healey and the Policies of Power*, p. 221.
74 *Ibid.*
75 *ST*, 17-8-66.
76 *Bulletin*, 10-2-68, p. 31.
77 *ST*, 25-8-66.

8 Britain weighs anchor

1 Gross military expenditure overseas, including defence aid, had been running at about £350 million a year, or nearly half of the established 1964 deficit on current and capital accounts. (*HCD*, vol. 104, 16-12-64, col. 420.)
2 Darby, *British Defence Policy East of Suez*, pp. 286–7.
3 *HCD*, vol. 704, 16-12-64, cols. 423–6.
4 Wilson, *The Labour Government 1964–70*, p. 243.
5 *Statement on Defence, February 1965*, Cmnd. 2592 (London, HMSO, 1965), pp. 8–9.
6 *HCD*, vol. 707, 3-3-65, col. 1338.
7 Darby, *British Defence Policy East of Suez*, pp. 296–7.
8 R. Crossman, *The Diaries of a Cabinet Minister* (3 vols., London, Hamilton and Cape, 1975–7), vol. 1, p. 456. (Hereafter referred to as *The Crossman Diaries*.)
9 Wilson, *The Labour Government 1964–70*, p. 212.
10 *HCD*, vol. 707, 3-3-65, col. 1338.
11 Cmnd. 2592, p. 9.
12 *DT*, 29-1-66.
13 *FT*, 31-3-66.
14 *EAR*, vol. XVI (1) (January 1966), p. 27.
15 *The Times*, 2-2-66.
16 *The Observer*, 6-2-66.
17 C. Mayhew, *Britain's Role Tomorrow* (London, Hutchinson, 1967), p. 89.
18 *CT*, 3-2-66.
19 *CPD(H/R)*, vol. 50, 8-3-66, p. 24.
20 Andrew Wilson, *OFNS*, no. 22656, 18-5-66.
21 *The Defence Review, February 1966: Statement on the Defence Estimates, 1966, Part I*, Cmnd. 2901 (Lon-

22 *HCD*, vol. 730, 22-6-66, col. 72.
23 Darby, *British Defence Policy East of Suez*, p. 298, f.n. 57.
24 *The Crossman Diaries*, vol. 1, p. 456.
25 *ST*, 14-2-66.
26 *ST*, 19-2-66.
27 Cmnd. 2901, p. 8.
28 Cmnd. 2901, p. 7, para. 19.
29 *The Times*, 26-5-66.
30 *The Times*, 28-5-66.
31 *Sun. T*, 29-5-66. A verbatim record of the meeting given by Woodrow Wyatt (*Daily Mirror*, 2-6-66) claimed that only Healey and Michael Stewart spoke in support of the Government's East of Suez policy.
32 *The Times*, 3-6-66.
33 See *HCD*, vol. 729, 14-6-66, cols. 1239–42.
34 News Release issued by the Labour Party Press Publicity Department, 15 June 1966.
35 See also P. Gordon-Walker, *The Cabinet* (London, Jonathan Cape, 1970), pp. 124–5.
36 *ST*, 28-6-66.
37 Darby, *British Defence Policy East of Suez*, p. 312.
38 *HCD*, vol. 732, 20-7-66, col. 632.
39 Williams and Reed, *Denis Healey and the Policies of Power*, p. 221.
40 Wilson, *The Labour Government 1964–70*, p. 297.
41 *HCD*, vol. 734, 19-10-66, col. 208.
42 Wilson, *The Labour Government 1964–70*, p. 297.
43 *The Crossman Diaries*, vol. 2, pp. 85–6.
44 *The Times*, 12-1-66.
45 *FT*, 12-10-66.
46 Wilson, *The Labour Government 1964–70*, p. 297.
47 *Statement on Defence 1967*, Cmnd. 3203 (London, HMSO, 1967), p. 7, para. 26.
48 *HCD*, vol. 742, 28-2-67, cols. 395–6.
49 Cmnd. 3203, p. 2, para. 4.
50 *EAR*, vol. XVII (2) (February 1967), p. 25.
51 *HCD*, vol. 743, 21-3-67, col. 1434.
52 *HCD*, vol. 742, 27-2-67, cols. 103–4.
53 *CN*, vol. 38 (4), p. 165.
54 Holyoake thanked Razak for being 'good enough' to say that. (*EAR*, vol. XVII (4) (April 1967), p. 16.)
55 *The Crossman Diaries*, vol. 2, p. 308.
56 *ST*, 3-6-67.
57 *Daily Express*, 19-4-67.
58 *ST*, 27-4-67.
59 *The Times*, 29-4-67.
60 Darby, *British Defence Policy East of Suez*, p. 319.
61 *Commonwealth*, vol. X (4), pp. 155–9.
62 *Sun. T(M)*, 18-6-67.
63 *ST*, 28-6-67.
64 *The Crossman Diaries*, vol. 2, p. 397.
65 *ST*, 29-6-67.
66 By early 1968, there were only 9,500 British troops in the peninsula, employing fewer than 5,000 people.
67 *ST*, 5-7-67.
68 *The Times*, 8-7-67.
69 *The Age*, 22-8-67.
70 *Supplementary Statement on Defence Policy 1967*, Cmnd. 3357 (London, HMSO, July 1967), p. 5, para. 6.
71 *HCD*, vol. 751, 27-7-67, col. 1103.
72 *CN*, vol. 38 (7), p. 296.
73 *EAR*, vol. XVII (7) (July 1967), p. 25.
74 *CPD(H/R)*, vol. 56, 17-8-67, p. 207.

75 *The Times*, 10-11-67.
76 *ST*, 11-11-67.
77 *The Age*, 11-11-67.
78 Darby, *British Defence Policy East of Suez*, p. 322.
79 *The Age*, 11-1-68.
80 *ST*, 9-1-68.
81 *FEER*, 15-2-68, p. 266.
82 *ST*, 9-1-68.
83 *ST*, 13-1-68.
84 *ST*, 10-1-68.
85 *ST*, 11-1-68.
86 *EAR*, vol. XVII (1) (January 1968), p. 18.
87 *Guardian*, 17-1-68.
88 *ST*, 18-1-57.
89 *The Times*, 15-1-68.
90 *Ibid*. Singapore stood to inherit the centre of a sophisticated radar system based at Bukit Gumbak since 1962. Working with another autonomous radar centre in Penang and an RAF aircraft movements information section at Paya Lebar, the system covered both Singapore and Malaysia. (*ST*, 26-1-68.)
91 *The Times*, 18-1-68.
92 Interview, former British High Commissioner in Singapore.
93 *HCD*, vol. 756, 16-1-68, cols. 1580–5.
94 *The Age*, 11-1-68.
95 Darby, *British Defence Policy East of Suez*, p. 326.
96 Gordon-Walker, *The Cabinet*, pp. 130–1.
97 Darby, *British Defence Policy East of Suez*, p. 309.
98 *HCD*, vol. 756, 16-1-68, col. 1581.

9 From AMDA to the five-power defence system

1. V. Singh, 'Malaysia, Singapore and Indonesia', *India Quarterly*, vol. XXV (4) (October–December 1969), p. 329.
2 See *SPD*, vol. 26, no. 16, 24-1-68, col. 1105.
3 *ST*, 1-2-68.
4 *HCD*, vol. 758, 15-2-68, col. 1572.
5 K. Holyoake, 'Report of the Department of External Affairs', *NZAJHR*, vol. 1, app. 1, p. 452.
6 *CN*, vol. 39 (2), p. 65.
7 J. M. van der Kroef, 'The Gorton Manner: Australia, Southeast Asia and the US', *Pacific Affairs*, vol. 42 (3) (Fall 1969), p. 316.
8 *CPD(H/R)*, vol. 58, 26-3-68, p. 542.
9 Holyoake, 'Report of the Department of External Affairs', 31-3-68, p. 32.
10 *ST*, 7-2-68.
11 *Bulletin*, 7-9-68, p. 18.
12 van der Kroef, 'The Gorton Manner', p. 317.
13 *ST*, 11-3-68.
14 Apart from the army, Singapore would acquire two interceptor aircraft squadrons, anti-aircraft units and coastal patrol boats. (*ST*, 27-3-68.)
15 J. M. van der Kroef, 'Malaysia–Singapore: Neutrality or Regional Defence?', *World Review*, vol. 8, no. 1 (March 1969), p. 5.
16 *Sun. T(M)*, 7-3-68.
17 *Bulletin*, 10-2-68, p. 38.
18 *The Age*, 20-4-68.
19 M. Leifer, 'The Philippines and Sabah Irredenta', *The World Today* (October 1968), pp. 424–6.
20 At least 79% of the total aid offered would be tied to the procurement of British goods and services. (*HCD*, vol. 769, 25-7-68, col. 177.)
21 *Sun. T(M)*, 12-5-68.

22 *ST*, 4-6-68.
23 Interest-free loans repayable within seven years made up the rest. The terms for Malaysia were similar. (*FEER*, 13-6-68, p. 556.)
24 *The Age*, 18-5-68.
25 *The Times*, 11-6-68.
26 Final communiqué, Five-Power Conference, *CN*, vol. 39 (6), p. 250, para. 10.
27 *ST*, 11-6-68.
28 *FEER*, 11-7-68, pp. 116–17.
29 The air defence system was the only practical expression of an automatic five-power commitment. The actual British role was not decided until the Conservatives returned to power.
30 The Australian Prime Minister, William McMahon, caused considerable diplomatic embarrassment when he mentioned this publicly in October 1972.
31 *CN*, vol. 39 (6), p. 250, paras. 6, 8, 9.
32 *FEER*, 11-7-68, p. 117.
33 *CN*, vol. 39 (6), p. 250, para. 8.
34 See *CPD(H/R)*, vol. 58, 2-5-68, pp. 1073–6 especially.
35 Although Gorton was visiting Singapore and Malaysia, he did not attend the conference.
36 *ST*, 14-6-68.
37 *CPD(H/R)*, col. 58, 2-5-68, p. 1075.
38 J. M. van der Kroef, 'Australia's New Search for Collective Security', *Orbis*, vol. XIII (2) (Summer 1969), p. 512.
39 *CPD(H/R)*, vol. 62, 27-2-69, p. 282.
40 Van der Kroef, 'Australia's New Search for Collective Security', p. 532.
41 *ST*, 11-6-68.
42 *CN*, vol. 39 (6), para. 13.
43 *ST*, 1-8-68.
44 *ST*, 19-9-68.
45 *The Times*, 20-9-68.
46 *CN*, vol. 39 (9), pp. 385–6.
47 *Bulletin*, 5-10-68, p. 20.
48 *ST*, 21-9-68.
49 *Sun. T(M)*, 22-9-68.
50 *ST*, 15-10-68.
51 *ST*, 8-1-69.
52 Interview with one of the authors of the report.
53 *CPD(H/R)*, vol. 61, 19-11-68, p. 2983.
54 *EAR*, vol. XVIII (11) (November 1968), p. 29.
55 *NZPD*, vol. 358, 2-11-68, p. 3218.
56 *EAR*, vol. XVIII (12) (December 1968), pp. 33–4.
57 *ST*, 4-1-69.
58 *EAR*, vol. XIV (1) (January 1969), p. 38.
59 *ST*, 28-1-69.
60 Interview with former New Zealand Defence Minister.
61 *CT*, 31-1-69.
62 *CT*, 4-2-69.
63 *CT*, 29-1-69.
64 *ST*, 4-2-69.
65 Malaysia's election budget saw an increase in defence spending of just 2.2% more than was spent in 1968.
66 *ST*, 5-2-69.
67 *ST*, 1-5-69.
68 *The Australian*, 21-2-69.
69 *ST*, 5-2-69.
70 *ST*, 28-2-69.
71 *CN*, vol. 40 (2), pp. 41–6.
72 B. Brown, 'The Expendable Nation? New Zealand's International Relations in the 60s', *Pacific Viewpoint*, vol. 10 (1) (May 1969), p. 106.
73 *CN*, vol. 40 (2), p. 43.
74 *CN*, vol. 42 (2), p. 45.
75 *Ibid.*, p. 47.

76 *Ibid.*, p. 45.
77 *Ibid.*, p. 43.
78 *CPD(H/R)* vol. 63, 15-5-69, p. 1831.
79 M. Leifer, 'Retreat and Reappraisal in Southeast Asia' in M. Leifer (ed.), *Constraints and Adjustments in British Foreign Policy* (London, Allen and Unwin, 1972), p. 97.
80 *SMH*, 19-6-69.
81 Gorton delivered the opening speech but the Australian delegation was led jointly by Fairhall and Freeth.
82 *CN*, vol. 40 (6), p. 302.
83 The revelations were made by Zain Azrai, the Principal Secretary to the Malaysian Foreign Minister. (*Bulletin*, 28-6-69, p. 31.)
84 *DT*, 20-6-69.
85 *CT*, 24-6-69. Holyoake managed to avoid controversy at Canberra. He later affirmed that when he used the term 'Malaysia' he meant just that. (*CT*, 23-6-69.)
86 *CN*, vol. 40 (6), pp. 305–11.
87 Final communiqué, Canberra conference. *CN*, vol. 40 (6), p. 305.
88 Similar missiles at Butterworth were offered for sale to Malaysia but were rejected. (*ST*, 5-4-69.)
89 *CN*, vol. 40 (6), p. 305.
90 *Ibid.*, p. 309.
91 *OFNS*, no. 26674, 30-6-69.
92 *CN*, vol. 40 (6), p. 302.
93 *AFR*, 7-7-69.
94 *The Australian*, 2-8-69.
95 *The Age*, 9-8-69.
96 *CPD(H/R)*, vol. 64, 14-8-69, p. 315.
97 *Sun. T(M)*, 2-11-69.
98 For example, the legal status of the RAAF at Butterworth after FEAF's disbandment and the rental to be paid to Malaysia – an issue not settled until June 1970.
99 *ST*, 9-1-70. The value of British investments in Malaysia and Singapore was estimated to be in excess of £800 million. (Sir Ian Orr-Ewing, 'What Tory Defence Plans Would Cost', *The Times*, 9-2-70.)
100 *CPD(H/R)*, vol. 66, 10-3-70, p. 235.
101 *Statement on the Defence Estimates 1970*, Cmnd. 4290 (London, HMSO, February 1970), p. 3.
102 *ST*, 10-4-70; *Daily Mail* and *Guardian*, 13-4-70.
103 I. Buchanan, *Singapore in Southeast Asia: An Economic and Political Appraisal* (London, Bell, 1972), pp. 324–5, f.n. 2. See also Dick Wilson, *The Future Role of Singapore* (London, Oxford University Press, 1972), p. 39.
104 *FEER*, 6-8-70, p. 5.
105 Interview, former British official in Singapore.
106 *ST*, 4-8-70.
107 *Supplementary Statement on Defence Policy 1970*, Cmnd. 4521 (London, HMSO, October 1970), p. 5.
108 *Ibid.*, p. 4, para 8.
109 Malaysian–Philippine relations were normalised in mid-December 1969.
110 In July 1971 the Australian Foreign Minister, Leslie Bury, admitted that he knew of Malaysian displeasure at Singapore's access to training facilities in Australia. (*ST*, 10-7-71.) Official documents published in Australia in 1980 showed that the Defence Department felt in March 1972

that Singapore was angling for 'a special defence relationship with Australia'. Hence Canberra had to be cautious not to favour Singapore over Malaysia. (Extracts in *ST*, 15-11-80.)
111 *Statement on the Defence Estimates, 1971*, Cmnd. 4592 (London, HMSO, February 1971), para. 20, pp. 5–6.
112 Communiqué issued at the conclusion of the five-power Ministerial Meeting, London, 15–16 April 1971 (*HCD*, vol. 815, 19-4-31, col. 348). Hereafter referred to as London Communiqué.
113 *ST*, 19-4-71.
114 *ST*, 17-4-71.
115 London Communiqué, para. 7.
116 Press Release, Canberra, Defence PR No. 477/71, p. 3. The annual cost to Australia was about A$1.25 million.

10 Conclusions

1 *ST*, 5-1-57.
2 *MLCD*, 2-10-57, col. 3276.
3 B. D. Beddie, 'Australian Policy Towards Indonesia', *Australian Outlook*, vol. 22 (2) (August 1968), p. 137.
4 F. S. Northedge, 'Britain as a Second-Rank Power', *International Affairs*, vol. 46 (1) (January 1970), p. 40.

SELECT BIBLIOGRAPHY

Ariff, M. O. *The Philippines' Claim to Sabah: Its Historical, Legal and Political Implications*, Singapore, O.U.P., 1970.

Bartlett, C. J. *The Long Retreat: A Short History of British Defence Policy 1945–70*, London, Macmillan, 1972.

Bayliss, John (ed). *British Defence Policy in a Changing World*, London, Croom Helm, 1977.

Beer, Francis A. (ed). *Alliances: Latent War Communities in the Contemporary World*, New York, Holt, Rinehart & Winston, 1970.

Bellows, Thomas J. *The People's Action Party of Singapore: Emergence of a Dominant Party System*, New Haven, Conn., Yale University Southeast Asia Series No. 14, 1970.

Boyce, Peter. *Malaysia and Singapore in International Diplomacy: Documents and Commentaries*, Sydney University Press, 1968.

Casey, R. G. (Lord Casey). *Friends and Neighbours*, Melbourne, Cheshire, 1954.

Chan Heng Chee. *Singapore: The Politics of Survival 1965–7*, Singapore, O.U.P., 1971.

Chandran, Jeshurun. *The Growth of the Malaysian Armed Forces, 1963–73: Some Foreign Press Reactions*, Singapore, Institute of Southeast Asian Studies, Occasional Paper No. 35, 1975.

Malaysian Defence Policy: A Study in Parliamentary Attitudes 1963–73, Kuala Lumpur, Pernerbit Universiti Malaya, 1980.

Chin Kin Wah. *The Five Power Defence Arrangements and AMDA: Some Observations of an Evolving Partnership*, Singapore, Institute of Southeast Asian Studies, Occasional Paper No. 23, 1974.

Clutterbuck, Richard. *The Long, Long War: The Emergency in Malaya, 1948–60*, London, Cassell, 1967.

Riot and Revolution in Singapore and Malaya, 1945–63, London, Faber & Faber, 1973.

Fletcher, Nancy McH. *The Separation of Singapore from Malaysia*, Ithaca, N.Y., Cornell University, Southeast Asia Programme, Data Paper No. 73, 1969.

Gelber, H. G. (ed.). *Problems of Australian Defence*, Melbourne, O.U.P., 1970.

George, T. J. S. *Lee Kuan Yew's Singapore,* London, Andre Deutsch, 1973.

Grant, Bruce. *The Crisis of Loyalty: A Study of Australian Foreign Policy*, Sydney, Angus & Robertson, 1972.

Hawkins, David. *The Defence of Malaysia and Singapore: from AMDA to ANZUK*, London, Royal United Services Institute for Defence Studies, 1972.

James, Harold & Shiel-Small, Denis. *The Undeclared War: the story of the Indonesian Confrontation, 1962–66*, London, Cooper, 1971.
Josey, Alex. *Lee Kuan Yew* (new ed), Singapore, Times Books, 1980.
Lee Kuan Yew and the Commonwealth, Singapore, Moore, 1969.
Leifer, Michael (ed). *Constraints and Adjustments in British Foreign Policy*, London, Allen & Unwin, 1972.
The Philippine Claim to Sabah, Hull Monographs on Southeast Asia No. 1, Zug, Switzerland, Inter Documentation Co., 1968.
Mackie, J. A. C. *Konfrontasi: the Indonesia-Malaysia Dispute, 1963–6*, London, O.U.P., 1975.
McIntyre, W. D. *Britain, New Zealand and the Security of Southeast Asia in the 1970s*, Wellington, NZIIA, 1969.
Martin, L. W. *British Defence Policy: the Long Recessional*, Adelphi Papers No. 61, London, ISS, 1969.
Mayhew, Christopher. *Britain's Role Tomorrow*, London, Hutchinson, 1967.
Means, G. P. *Malaysian Politics* (2nd ed), London, Hodder & Stoughton, 1976.
Millar, T. B. *Australia in Peace and War: External Relations, 1788–1977*, N.Y., St. Martin's Press, 1978.
(ed) *Australian–New Zealand Defence Cooperation*, Canberra, Australian National University Press, 1968.
(ed) *Australian Foreign Minister: the Diaries of R. G. Casey, 1951–60*, London, Collins, 1972.
Australia's Defence (2nd ed), Melbourne University Press, 1969.
Northedge, F. S. *Descent from Power: British Foreign Policy, 1945–73*, London, Allen & Unwin, 1974.
Pocock, Tom. *Fighting General: the Public and Private Campaigns of General Sir Walter Walker*, London, Collins, 1973.
Reese, T. R. *Australia, New Zealand and the United States: a Survey of International Relations, 1941–68*, London, O.U.P., 1969.
Robinson, Alan. *Australia and New Zealand: the Search for New Security Policies*, Wellington, NZIIA, 1970.
Rose, Saul. *Britain and Southeast Asia*, London, Chatto & Windus, 1962.
Short, Anthony. *The Communist Insurrection in Malaysia, 1948–60*, London, Frederick Muller, 1975.
Sopiee, M. N. *From Malayan Union to Singapore Separation: Political Unification in the Malaysia Region, 1945–65* Kuala Lumpur, Pernerbit Universiti Malaya, 1974.
Spender, Sir Percy. *Exercises in Diplomacy: the ANZUS Treaty and the Colombo Plan*, Sydney University Press, 1969.
Starke, J. G. *The ANZUS Treaty Alliance*, Melbourne University Press, 1965.
Tilman, R. O. *Malaysian Foreign Policy*, Strategic Studies Department Report RAC-R-63-2, Research Analysis Corporation, Virginia, 1969.
Walker, Partrick Gordon. *The Cabinet*, London, Jonathan Cape, 1970.
Watt, Sir Alan. *Australian Diplomat: Memoirs of Sir Alan Watt*, Sydney, Angus & Robertson, 1972.
The Evolution of Australian Foreign Policy, 1938–65, Cambridge University Press, 1967.

Williams, Geoffrey & Reed, Bruce. *Denis Healey and the Policies of Power*, London, Sidgwick & Jackson, 1971.
Wilson, Dick. *The Future Role of Singapore*, London, O.U.P., 1972.
Wilson, Harold. *The Labour Government, 1964–70: a personal record*, London, Weidenfeld & Nicolson and Michael Joseph, 1971.
Wu, Yuan Li. *The Strategic Importance of Singapore: A Study in Balance of Power*, American Enterprise Institute for Policy Research, Washington, D.C., 1973.

INDEX

Abdul Rahman, *see* Tunku Abdul Rahman
Alliance (Government): MCP, amnesty offer to, 21, 23; peace talks with, 21; SEATO, views on, 22, 31, 34
Alliance Party: 1955 elections, 21, 23; foreign troops, views on, 20–1
AMDA, 1–2, 46, 60
  ANZUS and SEATO, overlap with, 3–4
  Articles I, 32, 74, 184; II, 32; III, 32, 35, 55, 182; VII, 32, 64, 68, 184; VIII, 32–3, 38, 51, 52; IX, 33, 138, 198(n47)
  causus foederis, 100
  demise of, 5, 171, 174, 176, 178
  extension of, 37
  jurisdiction over foreign troops, 35
  negotiations of, 27, 28–9, 31, 32–6, 52, 57
  nuclear weapons, stationing of, 33, 198(n47)
  Sabah, defence of, 162
ANZAM, 3, 8–12, 22, 47; proposed integrated command, 30
ANZUK force, 175, 178
ANZUS treaty, 2, 13; AMDA, overlap with, 3–4, 89; Britain, 'exclusion' of, 3; Malaysia area, applicability to, 72, 89, 91, 99
ASEAN, 7, 148
Australia
  AMDA, association with, 36, 38, 48–9, 81–2, 182
  British withdrawal, 128
  Brunei revolt, responses to, 64–5
  Confrontation: cautious policy towards, 72–5; deterrence, attempts at, 88–9; first contact with Indonesian troops, 95; graduated response to, 90–100
  CSR, views on, 25
  forward defence, 47, 57, 139; reassessment of, 145, 160
  Malaysia, defence of, *see* Barwick: Malaysia, defence of; Gorton: Malaysia and Singapore, defence of; Hasluck: Malaysia, defence of; Menzies: Malaysia, defence of
  Malaysia plan, reactions to, 54
  Sabah, defence of, 110, 158. *See also* Gorton: Sabah, defence of
  separation of Singapore from Malaysia, 104–7
  Singapore, withdrawal of ground forces from, 192–3; Singapore base, alternative to, 129–30, 133
  Terendak Camp, withdrawal from, 160–1
  troops in Malaya, 16, 17–19, 33
Australian Labour Party: military aid to Malaya, 13, 19, 27
Azahari, A. M., 63, 69

Baling talks, 21, 23
Barisan Sosialis, 64
Barwick, Sir Garfield, 59
  ANZUS applicability to Malaysia, 203(n24, n39). *See also* ANZUS treaty: applicability to Malaysia area
  Brunei revolt, 64–5
  Confrontation, graduated response to, 91
  ECAFE meeting in Manila, 71
  Malaysia, defence of, 73–4, 84, 90
  resignation, 93
  Sukarno, meeting with, 83
'Bersatu Padu' exercises, 171–2
Bevin, Ernest, 11
Borneo, *see* North Borneo
Bottomley, Arthur, 60, 121
Bowden, Herbert, 134, 135

215

Britain
  AMDA, anchor role in, 125
  bases in Malaya, 24
  Borneo, withdrawal from, 122–4, 134
  Brunei revolt, 65
  Confrontation: financial costs to, 92–3; manpower strains, 86–7, 98; responses to, 68, 77, 79, 95–6
  devaluation of sterling, 139–40
  East of Suez, withdrawal from, 135–7, 138–41; policing role, 29, 60–1, 125–6
  Malaysia Federation, 53, 59–60, 61–2; negotiations with Malaya, 55
  Sabah, defence of, 157
  SEATO, 18–19, 31, 37, 39
British Defence White Papers: (1957), 29, 30, 43; (1958), 43; (1962), 59, 61; (1964), 92; (1965), 126, 127; (1966), 127, 129, 143; (1967), 135, 138–9; (1970), 171, 173–4; (1971), 175
British Labour Party, 44; East of Suez role, 60; Malaysia, defence of, 98
British Strategic Reserve, 65, 67
Brown, George (later Lord George-Brown), 61, 115, 134, 136
Brunei revolt, 59, 62, 63; Indonesian aid to, 66, 69. *See also*, Barwick: Brunei revolt; Britain: Brunei revolt; Holyoake: Brunei revolt; Malaya: Brunei revolt
Bury Leslie, 210(n110)
Butterworth air base, 34, 47, 154, 155, 173

Calcutta (Communist) Youth Conference, 10
Callaghan, James, 44
Calwell, Arthur, 9
Camp Temasek, controversy over, 116
Carrington, Lord, 30, 172–3
Casey, Richard (later Lord Casey): AMDA, 36; Malaya, defence of, 14, 30; Malaya's association with SEATO, views on, 27, 30–1, 47–8, 50; Singapore's constitutional talks, 41, 42; Singapore's internal security, 44
Chifley, Ben, 9
Churchill, Sir Winston, 14
Cobbold, Lord, 62
cold war, 10, 17, 19
Combined Defence Council: Singapore's withdrawal from, 117

Commonwealth Prime Minister's Conference: (1946), 8; (1948), 12; (1953), 14; (1955), 14, 16; (1964), 95–6; (1965), 103; (1969), 161; (1971), 175
Commonwealth Strategic Reserve (CSR), 3, 4, 14, 22, 24, 30, 31, 32, 34, 37, 39, 50, 138–9, 145; counter insurgency role, 25–6, 46, 181; General Hull's revelations, 69; Malaysia, defence of, 38, 46, 181; SEATO role, 25, 46, 48–9, 51, 55
Confrontation: causes, 66; escalation, 82, 93–4, 95; Indonesian military activities, 67, 68, 78, 82, 85–6, 92, 93–4, 97; termination, 120
Corregidor incident, 149–50
Critchley, T. K., 70, 105
Crossman, H. R. S., 61, 127, 134

Doidge, Sir Frederick, 11
domino theory, 3, 15
Downer, Sir Alexander, 131

Eden, Sir Anthony (Lord Avon), 28
Emergency Operations Council (EOC), 25
Evatt, Dr H. V., 18
Eyre, Dean, 54, 75, 88

Fairbairn, (Sir) David, 177
Fairhall, (Sir) Allen, 154, 156, 157
Far East Air Forces (FEAF), 38
Far East Land Forces (FARELF), 19, 38, 46
Fu'ad, Tun Mohd, *see* Stephens, Tun Mohd Fu'ad
Fiji, 13, 39
Five-power Conference: (June 1968), 150–6, 189; (June 1969), 166–70; (Nov. 1969), 170; (Jan. 1971), 175–5; (April 1971), 175–8
Five-power defence arrangements, 5, 176–8
Francis, Josiah, 11
Fraser, Malcolm, 171
Freeth, Gordon, 167

Ghazali bin Shafie, (later Tan Sri) Muhammad, 166, 174
Goh Keng Swee, Dr, 111, 117, 144–5, 147, 159, 176

Gordon-Walker, Patrick (later Lord Gordon-Walker), 12, 60, 65, 143
Gorton (Sir) John, 141, 154–5, 159–60; Malaysia and Singapore, defence of, 176; forward defence posture, 146–7; Sabah, defence of, 161, 162, 164, 167; Terendak Camp, withdrawal from, 160–1
Griffiths, James, 36
Gurkhas, 64
Gurney, Sir Henry, 13

Harding, Field Marshal Sir John, 14
Hasluck, (Sir) Paul, 139, 145–6; British withdrawal, reactions to, 136, 139; Malaysia: defence of, 90–1; defence treaty with, views on, 115; Sabah, defence of, 110, 153, 158, 161; Singapore's separation from Malaysia, 107, 109–10
Head, Lord, 95, 104–5, 109
Healey, Denis, 60, 64, 65, 152; Borneo, withdrawal from, 122–4, 134; East of Suez policy, 128–9, 131, 133–4, 135, 136–7
Heath, Edward, 160, 170–1
Holland, Sir Sidney, 11, 41; dispatch of troops to Malaya, 17
Holt, Harold: British withdrawal, reactions to, 128, 129, 131, 132, 133, 135, 137, 139
Holyoake, Sir Keith, 154, 159–60; AMDA, see New Zealand: AMDA, associate status within; British withdrawal, reactions to, 139, 141; Brunei revolt, 64–5; Confrontation, retaliatory measures, 96; CSR, concern over, 139; Malaysia, defence of, 79, 82, 92; Malaysia–Singapore differences, views on, 106–7; Sabah, defence of, 110, 164–5; Sukarno, meeting with, 91–2; Terendak Camp, withdrawal from, 159–60, 163
Home, Sir Alec Douglas (Lord Home), 30, 42
Hong Kong, 32, 39
Hull, General (later Field Marshal) Sir Richard, 9, 44, 68, 69

Indochina, 8, 15
Indonesia: see Confrontation: Indonesian military activities

Indonesian Communist Party (PKI): abortive coup, 116; opposition to Malaysia, 59
Integrated Air Defence System (IADS), 168, 170, 177
Internal Security Council (ISC), 37, 41–2
Ismail, Tun (Dr), 148, 174

Joint Defence Council (JDC), 82, 108, 111
Jungle Warfare School: Canungra, 15; Kota Tinggi, 152, 169, 175, 177

Kennedy, Robert, 88
'Kogam', 119, 120
Korean war, 12
Kota Tinggi: see Jungle Warfare School

Lansdowne, Lord, 62
Laos crisis, 34, 51
Lee Kuan Yew, 39, 43, 61, 64, 160, 161; British bases, views on, 40, 44, 52, 53, 113, 114; British withdrawal, 137, 141–2; Confrontation, reactions to, 76, 82, 90; Indonesia, normalisation of relations with, 112, 119, 120; separation from Malaysia, 103, 106–7; unilateral declaration of independence, 80
Lennox-Boyd, Alan (later Lord Boyd), 23, 29, 36, 40
Lim Chin Siong, 45
Lim Kim San, 147, 158–9
Lim Yew Hock, 41–2, 43
Lloyd, Selwyn, 40, 50

Macapagal, President: Manila conference, 78; Maphilindo, 78; Sabah, claim to, 62; Tokyo conference, 92
McBride, Sir Philip, 15
MacDonald, Malcolm, 10, 16
MacDonald, T. L., 17, 48
McIntosh, A. D., 41
McMahon, (Sir) William, 153, 176, 209(n30)
Macmillan, (Sir) Harold, 40, 43, 51, 53
Malaya: British bases, 50; Brunei revolt, 64, 65; constitutional conference (1956), 23–6; Emergency, 9, 10, 13, 46, 48; External Defence Committee, 27; merger with

Malaya *cont.*
  Singapore, 52, 53; SEATO:
    aversion to, 47, 54; indirect links
    with, 52, 56; Singapore, internal
    security of, 41
Malaysia
  British influence, resentment of, 121–2
  British withdrawal, 135–6, 137, 138,
    139, 140, 148, 150–1, 152
  Confrontation: fears of separate peace,
    112, 118, 119; military build-up, 98
  defence treaties with antipodes, views
    on, 85, 139
  federation: *raison d'être* for, 37, 102;
    proposed, 50–1, 52
  race riots (1969), 165–6
  Sabah, reactions to revived Philippine
    claim to, 149–50, 156–7, 162–3
Malaysia–Singapore
  defence: air, 144, 147; hiatus in, 121;
    indivisibility of, 144, 153, 156, 166,
    167, 108, 110–11
  separation: decision on, 104; defence
    adjustments resulting from, 107–12,
    116; intra-alliance strains, 104–7
Malik, Adam, 118, 120, 149
Manila Pact, 16
Maphilindo, 78, 120
Marshall, David, 20, 39, 40, 41
Mayhew, Christopher, 61, 131
Menzies, Sir Robert, 8, 11, 12, 30, 49, 54,
  82, 99
  ANZUS applicability to Malaysia
    area, 88–9
  Malaya, dispatch of troops to, 14–16,
    18–19, 49
  Malaysia, defence of, 72, 84–5
  SEATO, 15, 17–19
  Singapore's separation from Malaysia,
    104–7
Mulley, Frederick, 97

Nash, Sir Walter, 43, 47, 48
Nehru, Jawaharlal, 11
New Zealand
  AMDA, associate status within, 33,
    48–9, 75, 165; association with, 36,
    38, 48–9, 81–2, 182
  Britain-centred attitudes, 3, 17, 19–20
  British withdrawal, reactions to, 128,
    133, 139, 141, 145, 146, 154
  Brunei revolt, 64–5

  Confrontation, policy towards, 75–6,
    79, 103. *See also*, Holyoake:
    Confrontation, retaliatory measures
  forward defence, 47, 57
  Malaya, commitments in, 33
  Sabah, defence of, 158–9, 163–4
  SEATO, views on association with,
    30–1, 48, 54
Ningkan, Datuk Stephen Kalong, 95
North Borneo, 32, 46–7, 59, 62, 63;
  Philippine claim to, 59, 62–3,
  149–50, 156

Ong Eng Guan, 43, 50

Pacific Pact, 11
Pan-Malayan Islamic Party (PMIP), 47
Parliamentary Labour Party (British):
  East of Suez controversy, 130–3
Party Negara (Malaya), 21
Party Ra'ayat (Brunei), 63
People's Action Party (PAP), 38, 43;
  British bases, 44; Malaya, merger
  with, 44, 45, 50

Rajaratnam, S., 112, 113–14
Razak, Dato (later Tun) Abdul, 33, 61,
  67, 86–7, 98, 162, 174; British bases
  in Singapore, 55, 56; CSR, use of in
  SEATO operations, 32

Sandys, Duncan (later Lord), 32, 42, 55,
  64, 83; AMDA and regional defence,
  views on, 56; Defence White Paper
  (1957), 29, 30, 43; nuclear weapons
  in Malaya, 33, 198(n47); Singapore's
  unilateral declaration of independence,
  80
Sarawak, 37, 59, 62, 63
SEATO, 3, 15, 17, 22, 39, 44, 47, 63
Selkirk, Lord, 53, 60, 64, 70
Shackleton, Lord, 122, 123
Singapore
  bases, 51, 55, 59, 61, 65; British
    attitudes to, 51, 53, 55; and Malayan
    defence, 52; SEATO role, 52, 53, 55,
    56
  British presence, economic dependence
    on, 40, 52
  British withdrawal, economic aid, 151
  Confrontation, responses to, 76–7,
    82–3, 87, 90

Index 219

constitutional conference (1956), 37, 40
defence, *see* Malaysia–Singapore, defence
Internal Security Council (ISC), 45, 51
Malaysia, separation from, *see* Malaysia–Singapore: separation
Maphilindo, views on, 80
Preservation of Public Security Ordinance, 45–6
Rendel constitution, 20
riots, 41, 94, 103, 165
Sabah, defence of, 158
strategic importance to Britain, 37, 38–9, 41, 43
Spender, Sir Percy, 10–11
Stephens, Tun Mohd Fu'ad, 60, 110, 158, 169
Stewart, Michael, 114, 118, 119, 128, 131
Subandrio, Dr, 66, 118
Suharto, President, 117–18
Sukarno, President, 59, 78, 79; Manila conference, 79; Tokyo conference, 92

Tan Siew Sin, Tun, 121
Tange, Sir Arthur, 70, 72
Templar, General (later Field Marshal) Sir Gerald, 13, 14
Tengah airfield, 45, 154
Tentera Nasional Kalimantan Utara (TNKU), 63, 69
Terendak Camp, 50, 124, 155, 160–1
Thomson, David, 146, 147
Thomson, George, 140, 143, 154
Thorneycroft, Peter (later Lord), 92–3
Toh Chin Chye, Dr, 45, 90
Tory, Sir Geoffroy, 31
Tunku Abdul Rahman, 21, 36, 52, 53
  AMDA, abrogation of, 140, 145, 152, 155

British bases in Singapore, views on, 54, 115
British withdrawal, accelerated, 140
Commonwealth military presence, 21, 24, 26, 27, 34, 48–9, 54
Five-power Conference proposed, 138, 145
Malaysia Federation, negotiations with Britain, 53, 54. *See also* Britain: Malaysia Federation, negotiations with Malaya
Manila conference, 79–80
SEATO, views on, 32, 47
Singapore: merger with, 50–1, 52; separation, decision on, 104
Tokyo conference, 92

United Malays National organisation (UMNO), 14, 21, 34–5
United States of America, 11; ANZUS, 13; British withdrawal, views on, 127–8; Confrontation, non-involved cordiality, 72; Malaysia defence, 17, 79, 89

Walker, General Sir Walter, 65, 89, 92, 97
Watkinson, Sir Harold (later Lord), 55, 59
Watt, Sir Alan, 9, 20
Whitlam, E. G., 169, 192–3
Wigg, George (later Lord), 61, 65
Wilson, (Sir) Harold, 98, 103, 134, 145; East of Suez role, 126, 127, 132; Malaysia–Singapore separation, reaction to, 109
Wyatt, Woodrow, 207(31n)

Zain Azrai, 167